Thomas Pennant

A tour in Scotland, MDCCLXIX

Thomas Pennant

A tour in Scotland, MDCCLXIX

ISBN/EAN: 9783743345881

Manufactured in Europe, USA, Canada, Australia, Japa

Cover: Foto ©Andreas Hilbeck / pixelio.de

Manufactured and distributed by brebook publishing software (www.brebook.com)

Thomas Pennant

A tour in Scotland, MDCCLXIX

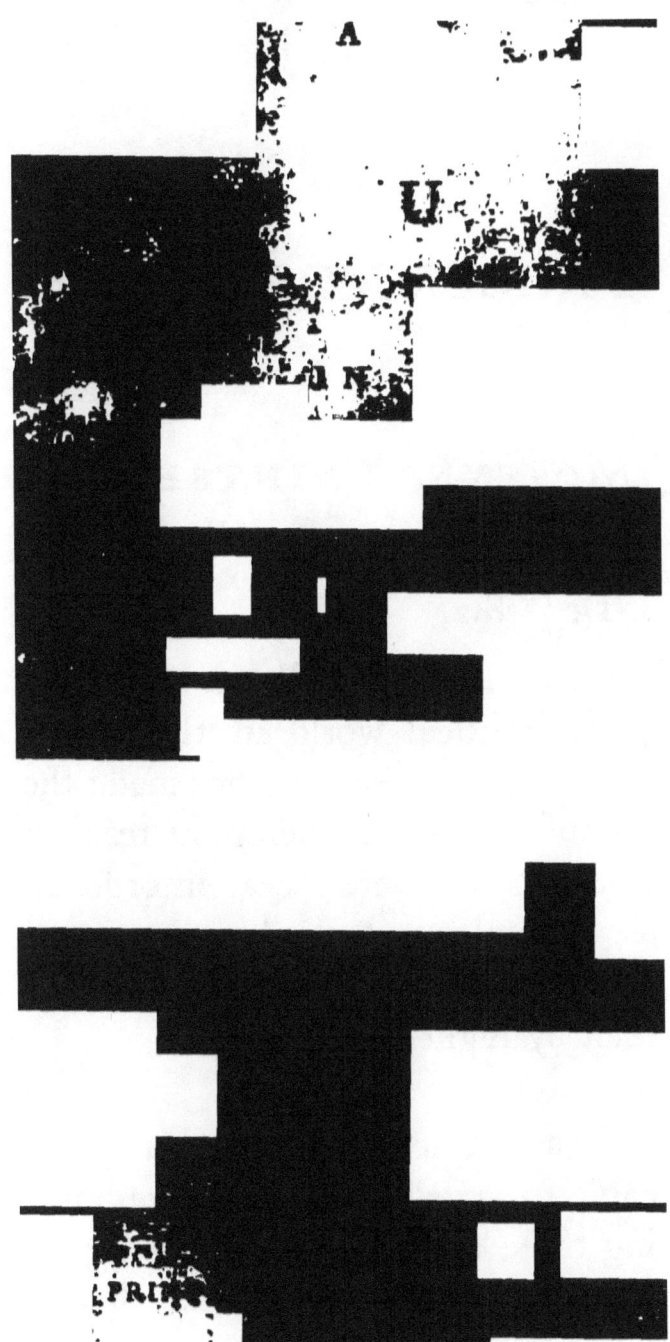

TO

Sir ROGER MOSTYN, Bart.

OF

MOSTYN, FLINTSHIRE.

DEAR SIR,

A Gentleman well known to the political world in the beginning of the present century made the tour of *Europe*, and before he reached *Abbeville* discovered that in order to see a country to best advantage it was infinitely preferable to travel by day than by night.

I cannot help making this applicable to myself, who, after publishing three volumes of the *Zoology* of GREAT BRITAIN, found out that to

DEDICATION.

be able to speak with more precision of the subjects I treated of, it was far more prudent to visit the whole than part of my country: struck therefore with the reflection of having never seen SCOTLAND, I instantly ordered my baggage to be got ready, and in a reasonable time found myself on the banks of the *Tweed*.

As soon as I communicated to you my resolution, with your accustomed friendship you wished to hear from me: I could give but a partial performance of my promise, the attention of a traveller being so much taken up as to leave very little room for the discharge of epistolary duties; and I flatter myself you will find this tardy execution of my engagement more satisfactory than the hasty accounts I could send you on my road: but this is far from being the sole motive of this address.

I have

DEDICATION.

I have irresistable inducements of public and of a private nature: to you I owe a most free enjoyment of the little territories Providence had bestowed on me; for by a liberal and equal cession of fields, and meads and woods, you connected all the divided parts, and gave a full scope to all my improvements. Every view I take from my window reminds me of my debt, and forbids my silence, causing the pleasing glow of gratitude to diffuse itself over the whole frame, instead of forcing up the imbittering sigh of *Oh! si angulus ille!* Now every scene I enjoy receives new charms, for I mingle with the visible beauties, the more pleasing idea of owing them to you, the worthy neighbor and firm friend, who are happy in the calm and domestic paths of life with abilities superior to ostentation, and goodness

DEDICATION.

goodness content with its own reward: with a sound judgement and honest heart you worthily discharge the senatorial trust reposed in you, whose unprejudiced vote aids to still the madness of the People, or aims to check the presumption of the Minister. My happiness in being from your earliest life your neighbor, makes me confident in my observation; your increasing and discerning band of friends discovers and confirms the justice of it: may the reasons that attract and bind us to you ever remain, is the most gratefull wish that can be thought of, by

DEAR SIR,

Your obliged and

affectionate Friend,

Downing,
October 20, 1771.

Thomas Pennant.

PLATES.

PLATES.

I. EIDER Drake and Duck, page 35
II. *Dunkeld* Cathedral, 75
III. Cascade near *Taymouth*, 80
IV. View from the King's Seat near *Blair*, 98
V. *Brae-mar* Castle, with a distant View of *Inver-cauld*, 106
VI. *Inverness*, 137
VII. *Freswick* Castle, 152
VIII. The Gannet darting on its Prey, 155
IX. Castle *Urquhart*, 169
X. Upper Fall of *Fyers*, 170
XI. *Sterling* Castle, 208
XII. *Arthur's* Oven, and two *Lochaber* Axes, 212
XIII. Pillars in *Penrith* Church-Yard, 272
XIV. Roebuck. White Hare 274
XV. Cock of the Wood, 278
XVI. Hen of the Wood. Ptarmigan, 279
XVII. Saury. Greater Weever, 284
XVIII. Thorney Crab. Cordated Crab. The last from the Isle of *Wight*. 286

Opposite Page 1. A View of the gigantic Yew-Tree in *Fortingal* Church-Yard. The middle part is now decayed to the ground; but within memory was united to the height of three feet: Captain *Campbell* of *Glen-Lion* having assured me that when a boy he has often climbed over, or rode on the then connecting part.

ERRATA.

ERRATA.

Page	Line		read	
2	30	thick,	read	deep.
21	5	round,		toad.
31	28	appartments,		apartments.
48	17	Dele In a small square.		
53	27	ædifice,		edifice.
55	30	Belecon,		Peleçon.
81	12	inftratum,		inftratam.
88	30	favourite,		favorite.
		prevail,		prevale.
93	15	fæmines,		fæmineo.
94	9	mojore,		majore.
95	5	Glein Raidr,		Glain Naidr.
109	8	clifts,		cliffs.
129	laft	Ptolomy,		Ptolemy.
146	3	heroe,		hero.
153	20	Cornuna,		Cornana
159	28	Bel-tein,		rural facrifice; for Bel-tein, according to the ingenious Mr. James Mac Pherfon, fignifies the *fire of the rock*; and of courfe is applicable only to the fpecies defcribed, p. 96.
174	9	After other,	add	the defcent.

A TOUR

A TOUR
IN
SCOTLAND.
MDCCLXIX.

ON *Monday* the 26th of JUNE take my depar- CHESTER. ture from CHESTER, a city without parallel for the singular structure of the four principal streets, which are as if excavated out of the earth, and sunk many feet beneath the surface; the carriages drive far beneath the level of the kitchens, on a line with ranges of shops, over which on each side of the streets passengers walk from end to end, in covered galleries, secure from wet or heat. The back courts of all these houses are level with the ground, but to go into any of these four streets it is necessary to descend a flight of several steps.

The *Cathedral* is an antient structure, very ragged on the outside, from the nature of the red friable stone * with which it is built: the tabernacle work in the choir is very neat; but the beauty, and elegant simplicity of a very antique gothic chapter-house, is what merits a visit from every traveller.

The *Hypocaust* near the *Feathers* Inn, is one of the remains of the *Romans***, it being well known that this place was a principal station. Among

* Saxum arenarium friabile rubrum *Da Costa fossils.* I. 139.
** This city was the *Deva* and *Devana* of *Antonine*, and the station of the *Legio vicessima victrix*.

B   many

many antiquities found here, none is more singular than the rude sculpture of the *Dea Armigera Minerva*, with her bird and her altar on the face of a rock in a small field near the *Welch* end of the bridge.

The castle is a decaying pile. The walls of the city, the only complete specimens of antient fortifications, are kept in excellent order, being the principal walk of the inhabitants; the views from the several parts are very fine; the mountains of *Flintshire*, the hills of *Broxton*, and the insulated rock of *Beeston*, form the ruder part of the scenery; a rich flat forms the softer view, and the prospect up the river towards *Boughton*, recalls in some degree the idea of the *Thames* and *Richmond* hill.

Passed thro' *Tarvin*, a small village; in the church-yard is an epitaph in memory of Mr. *John Thomasen*, an excellent penman, but particularly famous for his exact and elegant imitation of the *Greek* character.

Delamere, which *Leland* calls a faire and large forest, with plenty of redde deer and falow, is now a black and dreary waste; it feeds a few rabbets, and a few black *Terns* * skim over the splashes that water some part of it.

Pits.

A few miles from this heath lies *Northwich*, a small town, long famous for its rock salt, and brine pits; some years ago I visited one of the mines; the stratum of salt lies about forty yards thick; that which I saw was hollowed into the form of a temple; I descended thro' a dome, and found the roof supported by rows of pillars, about two

* Br. Zool. II. 430.

yards

yards thick, and several in height; the whole was illuminated with numbers of candles, and made a most magnificent and glittering appearance. Above the salt is a bed of whitish clay*, used in making the *Liverpool* earthen-ware; and in the same place is also dug a good deal of the *Gypsum*, or plaister stone. The fossil salt is generally yellow, and semi-pellucid, sometimes debased with a dull greenish earth, and is often found, but in small quantities, quite clear and color-less.

The road from this place to *Macclesfield* is thro' a flat, rich, but unpleasant country. That town is in a very flourishing state, is possessed of a great manufacture of mohair and twist buttons; has between twenty and thirty silk mills, and a very considerable copper smelting house, and brass work.

After leaving this place the country almost instantly changes and becomes very mountanous and barren, at left on the surface; but the bowels compensate for the external sterility, by yielding sufficient quantity of coal for the use of the neighboring parts of *Cheshire*, and for the burning of lime; vast quantity is made near *Buxton*, and being carried to all parts for the purposes of agriculture, is become a considerable article of commerce.

The celebrated warm bath of BUXTON ** is seated in a bottom, amidst these hills, in a most chearless spot, and would be little frequented, did not *Hygeia* often reside here, and dispense to her

BUXTON.

---

* Argilla cærula-cinerea *Da Costa fossils*. I. 48.
** The *Romans*, who were remarkably fond of warm baths, did not over-look these agreeable waters; they had a bath, inclosed with a brick wall, adjacent to the present St. *Anne's* well, which Dr. *Short*, in his essay on mineral waters, says was razed in 1709.

votaries the chief bleſſings of life, eaſe and health: with joy and gratitude I this moment reflect on the efficacious qualities of the waters; I recollect with rapture the return of ſpirits, the flight of pain, and re-animation of my long, long crippled rheumatic limbs. But how unfortunate is it, that what Providence deſigned for the general good, ſhould be rendered only a partial one, and denied to all, except the opulent; or I may ſay to the (comparatively) few that can get admittance into the houſe where theſe waters are impriſoned. There are other ſprings (*Cambden* ſays nine) very near that in the *Hall*, and in all probability of equal virtue. I was informed that the late Duke of *Devonſhire*, not long before his death, had ordered ſome of theſe to be incloſed and formed into baths. It is to be hoped that his ſucceſſor will not fail adopting ſo uſefull and humane a plan; that he will form it on the moſt enlarged ſyſtem, that they may open not ſolely to thoſe whom miſuſed wealth hath rendered invalids, but to the poor cripple, whom honeſt labor hath made a burden to himſelf and his country; and to the ſoldier and ſailor, who by hard ſervice have loſt the uſe of thoſe very limbs which once were active in our defence. The honor reſulting from ſuch a foundation would be as great, as the ſatisfaction ariſing from a conſciouſneſs of ſo benevolent a work would be unſpeakable; the charms of diſſipation would then loſe their force, and dull and taſteleſs would every human luxury appear to him who had it in his power thus to lay open theſe fountains of health, and to be able to exult in ſuch pathetic and comfortable ſtrains as theſe: *When the ear heard me, then*

then it blessed me, and when the eye saw me it gave witness to me;

Because I delivered the poor that cried, and the fatherless, and him that had none to help him.

The blessing of him that was ready to perish came upon me, and I caused the widow's heart to sing for joy.

I was eyes to the blind, and feet was I to the lame.

After leaving *Buxton*, passed thro' *Middleton* dale, a deep narrow chasm between two vast clifts, which extend on each side near a mile in length: this road is very singular, but the rocks in general are too naked to be beautifull. At the end is the small village of *Stoney Middleton*; here the prospect opens, and at *Barsly Bridge* exhibits a pretty view of a small but fertile vale, watered by the *Derwent*, and terminated by *Chatsworth*, and its plantations. Arrived and lay at

Chesterfield; an ugly town. There is here a great manufacture of worsted stockings, and another of a brown earthen-ware, much of which is sent into *Holland*; the clay is found near the town, over the bass or cherty * stratum, above the coal. The steeple of *Chesterfield* church is a spire, covered with lead, but by a violent wind strangely bent, in which state it remains.

In the road side, about three miles from the town, are several pits of iron stone, about nine or ten feet deep. The stratum lies above the coal, and is two feet thick. I was informed that the adventurers pay ten pounds per annum to the Lord of the Soil, for liberty of raising it; that the la-

JUNE 27

* Or flinty.

borers have six shillings per load for getting it; each load is about twenty strikes or bushels, which yields a tun of metal. Coal, in these parts, is very cheap, a tun and a half being sold for five shillings.

Changed horses at *Workjop* and *Tuxford*; crossed the *Trent* at *Dunham-Ferry*, where it is broad but shallow; the spring tides flow here, and rise about two feet, but the common tides never reach this place. Pass along the *Foss-Dyke*, or the canal opened by *Henry* I. * to form a communication between the *Trent* and the *Witham*; it was opened** the year 1121, and extends from *Lincoln* to *Torkesey*; its length is eleven miles three quarters, the breadth between dike and dike at the top is about sixty feet, at bottom twenty-two; vessels from fifteen to thirty-five tuns navigate this canal, and by its means a considerable trade in coals, timber, corn and wool, is carried on. In former times, the persons who had landed property on either side were obliged to scower it whenever it was choaked up, and accordingly we find presentments were made by juries in several succeeding reigns for that purpose. Reach

LINCOLN, an antient but ill-built city, much fallen away from its former extent. It lies partly on a plain, partly on a very steep hill, on whose summit are the cathedral and the ruins of the castle. The first

---

* *Dugdale* on embanking, 167.
** I make use of this word, as Doctor *Stukely* conjectures this canal to have been originally a *Roman* work; and that another of the same kind (called the *Cardike*) communicated with it, by means of the *Witham*, which began a little below *Washenbry* three miles from *Lincoln*, and was continued thro' the fens as far as *Peterborough*. The gentlemen who favored me with the account of the *Cardike*, referred me to *Stukely*'s *Carausius*, and his life of *Richard* of *Cirencester*, books I have not at present before me.

is a vaſt pile of gothic architecture, has nothing remarkable on the outſide, but within is of matchleſs beauty and magnificence: the ornaments are exceſſively rich, and in the fineſt gothic taſte; the pillars light, the centre lofty, and of a ſurpriſing grandeur. The windows at the N. and S. ends very antient, but very elegant; one repreſents a leaf with its fibres, the other conſiſts of a number of ſmall circles. There are two other antient windows on each ſide the great iſle: the others, as I recollect, are modern. This church was, till of late years, much out of repair, but has juſt been reſtored in a manner that does credit to the Chapter. There is indeed a ſort of arch near the W. end, that ſeems placed there (for the ſame end as *Bayes* tells us he wrote one of his ſcenes) meerly to ſet off the reſt.

The proſpect from this eminence is very extenſive, but very barren of objects, a vaſt flat as far as the eye can reach, conſiſting of plains not the moſt fertile, or of fens* and moors: the laſt are far leſs extenſive than they were, many being drained, and will ſoon become the beſt land in the country. But ſtill much remains to be done; the fens near *Reveſby-Abby*, eight miles beyond *Horncaſtle*, are of vaſt extent; but ſerve for little other purpoſe than the rearing great numbers of geeſe, which are the wealth of the fenmen.

* The fens, naked as they now appear, were once well wooded; oaks have been found buried in them, which were ſixteen yards long, and five in circumference; fir trees from thirty to thirty-five yards long, and a foot or eighteen inches ſquare. Theſe trees had not the mark of the ax, but appeared as if burnt down by fire applied to their lower parts. Acorns and ſmall nuts have alſo been found in great quantities in the ſame places. *Dugdale* on embanking, 141.

During the breeding feafon, thefe birds are lodged in the fame houfes with the inhabitants, and even in their very bed-chambers: in every appartment are three rows of coarfe wicker pens placed one above another; each bird has its feparate lodge divided from the other, which it keeps poffeffion of during the time of fitting. A perfon, called a *Gozzard* *, attends the flock, and twice a day drives the whole to water; then brings them back to their habitations, helping thofe that live in the upper ftories to their nefts, without ever mifplacing a fingle bird.

The geefe are plucked five times in the year; the firft plucking is at *Lady-Day*, for feathers and quils, and the fame is renewed, for feathers only, four times more between that and *Michaelmas*. The old geefe fubmit quietly to the operation, but the young ones are very noify and unruly. I once faw this performed, and obferved that goflins of fix weeks old were not fpared; for their tails were plucked, as I was told, to habituate them early to what they were to come to. If the feafon proves cold, numbers of geefe die by this barbarous cuftom **.

Vaft numbers are drove annually to *London*, to fupply the markets; among them, all the fuperannuated geefe and ganders (called here *Cagmags*) which ferve to fatigue the jaws of the good Citizens, who are fo unfortunate as to meet with them.

---

* i. e. Goofe-herd.
** It was alfo practifed by the antients. *Candidorum alterum vectigal: Velluntur quibufdam locis bis anno.* Plinii lib. x. c. 22.

Fen birds.

The fen called the *West Fen*, is the place where the Ruffs and Reeves resort to in the greatest numbers *; and many other sorts of water fowl, which do not require the shelter of reeds or rushes, migrate here to breed; for this fen is very bare, having been imperfectly drained by narrow canals, which intersect it for great numbers of miles. These the inhabitants navigate in most diminutive shallow boats; they are, in fact, the roads of the country.

The *East Fen* is quite in a state of nature, and gives a specimen of the country before the introduction of drainage: it is a vast tract of morass, intermixed with numbers of lakes, from half a mile to two or three miles in circuit, communicating with each other by narrow reedy straits: they are very shallow, none are above four or five feet in depth; but abound with fish, such as Pike, Pearch, Ruff, Bream, Tench, Rud, Dace, Roach, Burbolt, Sticklebacks and Eels. The fen is covered with reeds, the harvest of the neighboring inhabitants, who mow them annually; for they prove a much better thatch than straw, and not only cottages but many very good houses are covered with them. Stares, which during winter resort in myriads to roost in the reeds, are very destructive, by breaking them down by the vast numbers that perch on them. The people are therefore very diligent in their attempts to drive them away, and are at great expence in powder to free themselves from these troublesome guests. I have seen a stock of reeds harvested and stacked worth two or three

* Br. Zool. II. 363. Suppl. tab. xv. p. 22.

hundred

hundred pounds, which was the property of a single farmer.

The birds which inhabit the different fens are very numerous: I never met with a finer field for the Zoologist to range in. Besides the common Wild-duck, of which an account is given in another place *, wild Geese, Garganies, Pochards, Shovelers and Teals, breed here. I have seen on the *East Fen* a small flock of the tufted Ducks; but they seemed to make it only a baiting place. The Pewit Gulls and black Terns abound; the last in vast flocks almost deafen one with their clamors: a few of the great Terns, or Tickets, are seen among them. I saw several of the great crested Grebes on the *East Fen*, called there *Gaunts*, and met with one of their floating nests with eggs in it. The lesser crested Grebe, the black and dusky Grebe, and the little Grebe, are also inhabitants of the fens; together with Coots, Water-hens, spotted Water-hens, Water-rails, Ruffs, Redshanks, Lapwings or Wipes, Red-breasted Godwits and Whimbrels. The Godwits breed near *Washenbrough*; the Whimbrels only appear for about a fortnight in *May* near *Spalding*, and then quit the country. Opposite to *Fossdyke Wash*, during summer, are great numbers of *Avosettas*, called there *Yelpers*, from their cry: they hover over the sportsman's head like the Lapwing, and fly with their necks and legs extended.

Knots are taken in nets along the shores near *Fossdyke* in great numbers during winter; but they disappear in the spring.

* *Br. Zool.* II. 462. In general, to avoid repetition, the reader is referr'd to the four *Octavo* volumes of *British Zoology*, for a more particular account of animals mentioned in this Tour.

IN SCOTLAND.

The short-eared owl, *Br. Zool.* I. 156. visits the neighborhood of *Washenbrough*, along with the Woodcocks, and probably performs its migrations with those birds, for it is observed to quit the country at the same time: I have also received specimens of them from the *Danish* dominions, one of the retreats of the Woodcock. This owl is not observed in this county to perch on trees, but conceals itself in long old grass; if disturbed, takes a short flight, lights again and keeps staring about, during which time its horns are very visible. The farmers are fond of the arrival of these birds, as they clear the fields of mice, and will even fly in search of prey during day, provided the weather is cloudy and misty.

But the greatest curiosity in these parts is the vast Herony at *Cressi-Hall*, six miles from *Spalding*. The Herons resort there in *February* to repair their nests, settle there in the spring to breed, and quit the place during winter. They are numerous as Rooks, and their nests so crouded together, that myself and the company that was with me counted not fewer than eighty in one tree. I here had opportunity of detecting my own mistake, and that of other Ornithologists, in making two species of Herons; for I found that the crested Heron was only the male of the other: it made a most beautifull appearance with its snowy neck and long crest streaming with the wind. The family who owned this place was of the same name with these birds, which seems to be the principal inducement for preserving them.

Heronry.

In the time of *Michael Drayton*,
*Here stalk'd the stately crane, as though he march'd
in war.*

But at present this bird is quite unknown in our island; but every other species enumerated by that observant Poet still are found in this fenny tract, or its neighborhood.

June 28, Spalding. — Visited *Spalding*, a place very much resembling, in form, neatness, and situation, a *Dutch* town: the river *Welland* passes through one of the streets, a canal is cut through another, and trees are planted on each side. The church is a handsome structure, the steeple a spire. The churches in general, throughout this low tract, are very handsome; all are built of stone, which must have been brought from places very remote along temporary canals; for, in many instances, the quarries lie at least twenty miles distant. But these ædifices were built in zealous ages, when the benedictions or maledictions of the church made the people conquer every difficulty that might obstruct these pious foundations. The abby of *Crowland*, seated in the midst of a shaking fen, is a curious monument of the insuperable zeal of the times it was erected in; as the beautifull tower of *Boston* church, visible from all parts, is a magnificent specimen of a fine gothic taste.

June 29, Swineshead-Abby. — Passed near the site of *Swineshead-Abby*, of which there are not the least remains. In the walls of a farm house, built out of the ruins, you are shewn the figure of a Knight Templar, and told it was the monk who poisoned King *John*, a fact denied by our best historians.

Returned

Returned thro' *Lincoln*, went out of town under the *Newport-Gate*, a curious *Roman* work; paſſed over part of the heath, changed horſes at *Spittle*, and at *Glanford-Bridge*, dined at the ferry-houſe on the banks of the *Humber*, and after a paſſage of about five miles, with a briſk gale, landed at *Hull*, and reached that night *Burton-Conſtable*, the ſeat of Mr. *Conſtable*, in that part of *Yorkſhire* called *Holderneſs*; a dull, flat country, but excellent for producing large cattle, and a good breed of horſes, whoſe prices are near doubled ſince the *French* have grown ſo fond of the *Engliſh* kind.

Made an excurſion to *Hornſea*, a ſmall town on the coaſt, remarkable only for its mere, a piece of water about two miles long, and one broad, famous for its pike and eels; it is divided from the ſea by a very narrow bank, ſo is in much danger of being ſometime or other loſt.

The cliffs on the coaſt of *Holderneſs* are high, and compoſed of clay, which falls down in vaſt fragments. Quantity of amber is waſhed out of it by the tides, which the country people pick up and ſell; it is found ſometimes in large maſſes, but I never ſaw any ſo pure and clear as that from the *Baltic*. It is uſually of a pale yellow color within, and prettily clouded; the outſide covered with a thin coarſe coat.

Amber.

After riding about twenty-two miles thro' a flat grazing country, reached *Burlington-Quay*, a ſmall town cloſe to the ſea. There is a deſign of building a pier, for the protection of ſhipping; at preſent there is only a large wooden quay, which projects into the water, from which the place takes its name

July 2.

name. From hence is a fine view of the white cliffs of *Flamborough*-Head, which extends far to the East, and forms one side of the *Gabrantuicorum finus portuofus* of *Ptolomy*, a name derived from the *British Gyfr*, on account of the number of goats found there, according to the conjecture of *Cambden*.

A mile from hence is the town of *Burlington*. The body of the church is large, but the steeple, by some accident, has been destroyed; near it is a large gateway, with a noble gothic arch, possibly the remains of a priory of black canons, founded by *Walter de Gant*, in the beginning of the reign of *Henry* I.

This coast of the kingdom is very unfavourable to trees, for, except some woods in the neighborhood of *Burton-Constable*, there is a vast nakedness from the *Humber*, as far as the extremity of *Caithness*, with a very few exceptions, which shall be noted in their proper places.

July 3, *Flamborough-Head.*

Went to *Flamborough*-Head. The town is on the North side, consists of about one hundred and fifty small houses, entirely inhabited by fishermen, few of whom, as is said, die in their beds, but meet their fate in the element they are so conversant in. Put myself under the direction of *William Camidge*, Ciceroni of the place, who conducted me to a little creek at that time covered with fish, a fleet of cobles having just put in. Went in one of those little boats to view the *Head*, coasting it for upwards of two miles. The cliffs are of a tremendous height, and amazing grandeur; beneath are several vast caverns, some closed at the end,

others

others are pervious, formed with a natural arch, giving a romantic paffage to the boat, different from that we entered. In fome places the rocks are infulated, are of a pyramidal figure, and foar up to a vaft height; the bafes of moft are folid, but in fome pierced thro', and arched; the color of all thefe rocks is white, from the dung of the innumerable flocks of migratory birds, which quite cover the face of them, filling every little projection, every little hole that will give them leave to reft; multitudes were fwimming about, others fwarmed in the air, and almoft ftunned us with the variety of their croaks and fcreams; I obferved among them corvorants, fhags in fmall flocks, guillemots, a few black guillemots very fhy and wild, auks, puffins, kittiwakes *, and herring gulls. Landed at the fame place, but before our return to *Flamborough*, vifited *Robin Leith*'s hole, a vaft cavern, to which there is a narrow paffage from the land fide; it fuddenly rifes to a great height, the roof is finely arched, and the bottom is for a confiderable way formed in broad fteps, refembling a great but eafy ftair-cafe; the mouth opens to the fea, and gives light to the whole.

Its birds.

Lay at *Hunmandby*, a fmall village above *Filey Bay*, round which are fome plantations that thrive tolerably well, and ought to be an encouragement to gentlemen to attempt covering thefe naked hills.

Filey Brig is a ledge of rocks running far into the fea, and often fatal to fhipping. The bay is fandy, and affords vaft quantities of fine fifh, fuch

---

* Called here *Petrels*. Br. Zool. Suppl. tab. xxiii. p. 26.

as Turbot, Soles, &c. which during summer approach the shore, and are easily taken in a common seine or dragging-net.

JULY 4. Set out for *Scarborough*, passed near the site of *Flixton*, a hospital founded in the time of *Athelstan*, to give shelter to travellers from the *wolves, that they should not be devoured by them* *; so that in those days this bare tract must have been covered with wood, for those ravenous animals ever inhabit large forests. These *hospitia* are not unfrequent among the *Alps*; are either appendages to religious houses, or supported by voluntary subscriptions. On the spot where *Flixton* stood is a farm-house, to this day called the *Spital* House. Reach

SCARBOROUGH, a large town, built in form of a crescent on the sides of a steep hill; at one extremity are the ruins of the castle seated on a cliff of a stupendous height, from whence is a very good view of the town. In the castle-yard is a handsome barrack for one hundred and fifty men, but at present untenanted by soldiery. Beneath, on the south side, is a large stone pier, (another is now building) which shelters the shipping belonging to the town. It is a place absolutely without trade, yet owns above 300 sail of ships, which are hired out for freight: in the late war the Government had never less than 100 of them in pay.

The number of inhabitants belonging to this place are above 10,000, but as great part are sailors, nothing like that number are resident, which makes one church sufficient for those who live on shore. It is large, and seated almost on

* *Cambden Brit*. II. 902.

the

the top of the hill. The range of buildings on the *Cliff* commands a fine view of the caftle, town, and fhore, and of innumerable fhipping that are perpetually paffing backward and forward on their voyages. The fpaw * lies at the foot of one of the hills, S. of the town; this and the great conveniency of sea-bathing, occafion a vaft refort of company during fummer; it is at that time a place of great gayety, for with numbers health is the pretence, but diffipation the end.

The fhore is a fine hard fand, and during low water is the place where the company amufe themfelves with riding. This is alfo the fifh market; for every day the cobles, or little fifhing boats, are drawn on fhore here, and lie in rows, often quite loaden with variety of the beft fifh. There was a fifherman, on the 9th of *May*, 1767, brought in at one time,

20 Cods,

14 Lings,

17 Skates,

8 Holibuts, befides a vaft quantity of leffer fifh; and fold the whole for 3 l. 15 s. It is fuperfluous to repeat what has been before mentioned, of the methods of fifhing, being amply defcribed *Vol*. III. p. 193, of the *Britifh Zoology*; yet it will be far from impertinent to point out the peculiar advantages of thefe feas, and the additional benefit this town might

---

* The waters are impregnated with a purgative falt, *(Glauber's)* a fmall quantity of common falt, and of fteel. There are two wells, the fartheft from the town is more purgative, and its tafte more bitter; the other is more chalybeate, and its tafte more brifk and pungent. D. H.

experience,

experience, by the augmentation of its fisheries. For this account, and for numberless civilities, I think myself much indebted to Mr. *Travis*, surgeon, who communicated to me the following Remarks:

Scarborough is situated at the bottom of a bay, formed by *Whitby* rock on the North, and *Flamborough*-head on the South; the town is seated directly opposite to the centre of the W. end of the *Dogger* bank; which end, (according to *Hammond*'s chart of the North Sea) lies S. and by W. and N. and by E. but by a line drawn from *Tinmouth* castle, would lead about N. W. and S. E. Tho' the *Dogger* bank is therefore but 12 leagues from *Flamborough*-head, yet it is 16 and a half from *Scarborough*, 23 from *Whitby*, and 36 from *Tinmouth* castle. The N. side of the bank stretches off E. N. E. between 30 and 40 leagues, untill it almost joins to the *Long-Bank*, and *Jutt*'s Riff.

It is to be remarked, that the fishermen seldom find any Cod, Ling, or other round fish upon the *Dogger* bank itself, but on the sloping edges and hollows contiguous to it. The top of the bank is covered with a barren shifting sand, which affords them no subsistence; and the water on it, from its shallowness, is continually so agitated and broken, as to allow them no time to rest. The flat fish do not suffer the same inconvenience there; for when disturbed by the motion of the sea, they shelter themselves in the sand, and find variety of suitable food. It is true, the *Dutch* fish upon the *Dogger* bank, but it is also true they take little except Soles, Skates, Thornbacks, Plaise, &c. It is in the hollows

lows between the *Dogger* and the *Well-Bank*, that the Cod are taken, which supply *London* market.

The shore, except at the entrance of *Scarborough* pier, and some few other places, is composed of covered rocks, which abound with Lobsters and Crabs, and many other shell fish, (no Oysters) thence, after a space covered with clean sand, extending in different places from one to five or six miles. The bottom, all the way to the edge of the *Dogger* banks, is a scar; in some places very rugged, rocky, and cavernous; in others smooth, and overgrown with variety of submarine plants, Mosses, Corallines, &c. * some parts again are spread with sand and shells; others, for many leagues in length, with soft mud and ooze, furnished by the discharge of the *Tees* and *Humber*.

Upon an attentive review of the whole, it may be clearly inferred, that the shore along the coast on the one hand, with the edges of the *Dogger* bank on the other, like the sides of a decoy, give a direction towards our fishing grounds to the mighty shoals of Cod, and other fish, which are well known to come annually from the Northern ocean into our seas; and secondly, that the great variety of fishing grounds near *Scarborough*, extending upwards of 16 leagues from the shore, afford secure retreats and plenty of proper food for all the various kinds of fish, and also suitable places for each kind to deposit their spawn in.

The fishery at *Scarborough* only employs 105 men, and brings in about 5250l. per annum, a

---

* I met with on the shores near *Scarborough*, small fragments of the true red coral.

trifle to what it would produce, was there a canal from thence to *Leeds* and *Manchester*; it is probable it would then produce above ten times that sum, employ some thousands of men, give a comfortable and cheap subsistence to our manufacturers, keep the markets moderately reasonable, enable our manufacturing towns to undersell our rivals, and prevent the hands, as is too often the case, raising insurrections, in every year of scarcity, natural or artificial.

On discoursing with some very intelligent fishermen, I was informed of a very singular phœnomenon they annually observe about the spawning of fish*. At the distance of 4 or 5 leagues from shore, during the months of *July* and *August*, it is remarked, that at the depth of 6 or 7 fathom from the surface, the water appears to be saturated with a thick jelly, filled with the *Ova* of fish, which reaches 10 or 12 fathoms deeper; this is known by its adhering to the ropes the cobles anchor with when they are fishing, for they find the first 6 or 7 fathom of rope free from spawn, the next 10 or 12 covered with slimy matter, the remainder again free to the bottom. They suppose this gelatinous stuff to supply the new-born fry with food, and that it is also a protection to the spawn, as being disagreeable to the larger fish to swim in.

There is great variety of fish brought on shore; besides those described as *British* fish, were two species of Rays: the Whip-Ray has also been taken

---

* Mr. *Osbeck* observed the same in S. *Lat.* 35, 36, in his return from *China*. The seamen call it the flowering of the water. *Vol.* II. 72.

here

here, and another species of Weever; but these are subjects more proper to be referred to a *Fauna*, than an Itinerary, for a minute description.

Left *Scarborough*, passed over large moors to *Robin Hood's Bay*. On my round, observed the vast mountains of alum stone, from which that salt is thus extracted: It is first calcined in great heaps, which continue burning by its own phlogiston, after being well set on fire by coals, for six, ten, or fourteen months, according to the size of the heap, some being equal to a small hill. It is then thrown into pits and steeped in water, to extract all the saline particles. The liquor is then run into other pits, where the vitriolic salts are præcipitated, by the addition of a solution of the *sal sodæ*, prepared from kelp; or by the volatile *alkali* of stale urine. The superfluous water being then evaporated duely by boiling in large furnaces, the liquor is set to cool; and lastly, is poured into large casks, to crystallize.

_{JULY 10.}

_{Alum Works.}

The alum works of this county are of some antiquity; they were first discovered by Sir *Thomas Chaloner*, in the reign of Queen *Elizabeth*, who observing the trees tinged with an unusual color, made him suspicious of its being owing to some mineral in the neighborhood. He found out that the strata abounded with an aluminous salt.

At that time, the *English* being strangers to the method of managing it, there is a tradition that Sir *Thomas* was obliged to seduce some workmen from the *Pope*'s alum-works near *Rome*, then the greatest in *Europe*. If one may judge from the curse which his Holiness thundered out against Sir *Thomas* and the fugitives, he certainly was not a little enraged; for he cursed by the very form that *Ernulphus* * has left us, and not varied a tittle from that most comprehensive of imprecations.

The first pits were near *Gisborough*, the seat of the *Chaloners*, who still flourish there, notwithstanding his Holiness's *anathema*. The works were so valuable as to be deemed a royal mine. Sir *Paul Pindar*, who rented them, payed annually to the King 12,500l. to the Earl of *Mulgrave* 1,640l. to Sir *William Pennyman* 600l. kept 800 workmen in pay, and sold his alum at 26l. per tun. But this monopoly was destroyed on the death of *Charles* I. and the right restored to the proprietors.

In these alum rocks are frequently found *cornua ammonis*, and other fossils, lodged in a stony nodule. Jet is sometimes met with in thin flat pieces, externally of the appearance of wood. According to *Solinus*, *Britain* was famous for this fossil **.

Jet.

The sands near *Robin Hood*'s village were covered with fish of several kinds, and with people who met the cobles in order to purchase their cargo: the place seemed as if a great fish fair had been held there; some were carrying off their bargains, others busied in curing the fish; and a little out at sea was a fleet of cobles and five men boats, and others arriving to discharge the capture of the preceding

* Vide *Tristram Shandy*.
** GAGATES *hic plurimus optimusque est lapis: si decorem requiras, nigro gemmeus: si naturam aqua ardet, oleo restinguitur: si potestatem attritu calefactus applicita detinet, atque succinum.* C. xxiv.

tides,

tides *. There are 36 of the first belonging to this little place. The houses here make a grotesque appearance, are scattered over the face of a steep cliff in a very strange manner, and fill every projecting ledge, one above another, in the same manner as the peasants do in the rocky parts of *China*. *Sand's End*, *Runwick*, and *Staithes*, three other fishing-towns on this coast, are (as I am told) built in the same manner.

The country through this day's journey was hilly, the coast high. Reach

WHITBY, called by the *Saxons*, *Streaneshalch*, or bay of the light-house, a large town, oddly situated between two hills, with a narrow channel running through the middle, extending about a mile farther up the vale, where it widens, and forms a bay. The two parts of the town are joined by a good draw-bridge, for the conveniency of letting the shipping pass. From this bridge are often taken the viviparous Blenny, whose back-bone is as green as that of the Sea Needle. The river that forms this harbor is the *Esk*, but its waters are very inconsiderable when the tide is out. Here is a pretty brisk trade in ship-building; but except that, a small manufacture of sail-cloth, and the hiring out of ships as at *Scarborough*, like that town it has scarce any commerce. It is computed there are about 270 ships belonging to this place. Of late, an attempt has been made to have a share in the *Greenland* fishery; four ships were sent out, and had very good success. There are very good dry

---

* From hence the fish are carried in machines to *Derby*, *Lichfield*, *Birmingham*, and *Worcester*: the towns which lie beyond the last are supplied from the West of *England*.

docks

docks towards the end of the harbor; and at the mouth a most beautifull pier. At this place is the first salmon-fishery on the coast.

St. Hilda's Church. On the hill above the S. side of the town is a fine ruin of St. *Hilda*'s church. The site was given to that saint by *Oswy*, king of *Northumberland*, about A. D. 657; possibly in consequence of a vow he made to found half a dozen monasteries, and make his daughter a nun, should heaven favor his arms. St. *Hilda* founded a convent here for men and women, dedicated it to St. *Peter*, and put it under the direction of an abbess. This establishment was ruined by the excursions of the *Danes*; but after the conquest it was rebuilt, and filled with *Benedictines*, by *Walter de Percy*. In less enlightened times it was believed that not a wild goose dared to fly over this holy ground, and if it ventured was sure to fall precipitate and perish in the attempt.

Went about two miles along the shore, then turned up into the country, a black and barren moor; observed on the right a vast artificial mount, or *Tumulus*, called *Freeburgh* Hill, a monument, in all probability, the work of the *Danes*, whose custom it was to fling up such *Tumuli* over the graves of their kings or leaders; or, in memory of the slain in general, upon the spot where they had obtained any great victory. It is possible that this mount owed its rise to the victory gained by *Ivar*, a *Danish* prince, over *Ella*, king of *Bernicia*, who was on his way from the North to succour *Osbert*; for we are told that *Ivar*, after defeating the last, went from *York* to meet *Ella*, and fought and slew him on his march.

At

At the end of this moor, about three miles from *Gisborough*, is a beautifull view over the remaining part of *Yorkshire*, towards *Durham*, *Hartlepool*, and the mouth of the *Tees*, which mæanders through a very rich tract. The country instantly assumes a new face; the road lies between most delightfull hills finely wooded, and the little vales between them very fertile: on some of the hills are the marks of the first alum works, which were discovered by Sir *Thomas Chaloner*.

GISBOROUGH, a small town, pleasantly situated in a vale, surrounded at some distance by hills, and open on the east to the sea, which is about five miles distant. It is certainly a delightfull spot, but I cannot see the reason why *Cambden* compares it to *Puteoli*. Here was once a priory of the canons of the order of St. *Austin*, founded by *Robert de Brus*, 1129, after the dissolution granted by *Edward* VI. to the *Chaloners*: a very beautifull east window of the church is still remaining. The town has at present a good manufacture of sail cloth.

GISBOROUGH.

The country continues very fine quite to the banks of the *Tees*, a considerable river, which divides *Yorkshire* from the bishoprick of *Durham*. After travelling 109 miles in a strait line through the first, enter *Durham*, crossing the river on a very handsome bridge of   arches, the battlements neatly panneled with stone; and reach

STOCKTON, lying on the *Tees* in form of a crescent. A handsome town; the principal street is remarkably fine, being 165 feet broad; and several lesser streets run into it at right angles. In the middle of the great street are neat shambles, a town-house,

house, and large assembly-room. There is besides a large square. About a century ago, according to *Anderson*, it had scarce a house that was not made of clay and thatch; but is now a flourishing place. Its manufacture is sail cloth; and great quantities of corn, and lead, (from the mineral parts of the county) are sent off from hence by commission. As the river does not admit of large vessels so high as the town, those commodities are sent down to be shipped.

The salmon fishery here is neglected, for none are taken beyond what is necessary to supply the country. Smelts come up the river in the winter time. On the west side of the town stood the castle; what remained of it is at present converted into a barn. The country from hence to *Durham* is flat, very fertile, and much inclosed. Towards the west is a fine view of the highlands of the country: those hills are part of that vast ridge which commence in the north and deeply divide this portion of the kingdom; and on that account are called by *Cambden* the *Appennines* of *England*.

DURHAM.

The approach to DURHAM is romantic, through a deep hollow, cloathed on each side with wood. The city is pretty large, but the buildings old. Part are on a plain, part on the side of a hill. The abby, or cathedral, and the castle, where the Bishop lives when he resides here, are on the summit of a cliff, whose foot is washed on two sides by the river *Were*. The walks on the opposite banks are very beautifull, flagged in the middle and paved on the sides, and are well kept. They are cut through

the

the wood, impend over the river, and receive a venerable improvement from the caftle and antient cathedral which foar above.

The laft is very old *; plain without, and fupported within by maffy pillars, deeply engraved with lozenge-like figures, and zigzag furrows: others are plain; and each forms a clufter of pillars. The fkreen to the choir is wood covered with a coarfe carving. The choir neat, but without ornament.

The chapter-houfe feems very antient, and is in the form of a theatre. The cloifters large and handfome. All the monuments are defaced, except that of Bifhop *Hatfield*. The Prebendal houfes are very pleafantly fituated, and have a fine view backwards.

There are two handfome bridges over the *Were* to the walks; and a third covered with houfes, which join the two parts of the town. This river produces Salmon, Trout, Roach, Dace, Minow, Loche, Bulhead, Sticklebacks, Lamprey, the leffer Lamprey, Eels, Smelts and Samlet, which are called here *Rack-riders*, becaufe they appear in winter, or bad weather; *Rack*, in the northern dialect, fignifying the driving of the clouds by tempefts. It is obferved here, that before they go off to fpawn, thofe fifh are covered with a white flime.

There is no inconfiderable manufacture, at *Durham*, of fhalloons, tammies, ftripes and callamancoes. I had heard on my road many complaints of the ecclefiaftical government this county is fubject

---

* Begun in 1093, by Bifhop *William de Carilepho*.

to; but, from the general face of the country, it seems to thrive wonderfully under them.

JULY 12. Saw *Coker*, the seat of Mr. *Car*; a most romantic situation, layed out with great judgment; the walks are very extensive, principally along the sides or at the bottom of deep dells, bounded with vast precipices, finely wooded; and many parts of the rocks are planted with vines, which I was told bore well, but late. The river *Were* winds along the hollows, and forms two very fine reaches at the place where you enter these walks. Its waters are very clear, and its bottom a solid rock. The view towards the ruins of *Finchal*-Abby is remarkably great; and the walk beneath the cliffs has a magnificent solemnity, a fit retreat for its monastic inhabitants. This was once called the Desert, and was the rude scene of the austerities of St. *Godric*, who carried them to the most senseless extravagance *. A sober mind may even at present be affected with horror at the prospect from the summits of the cliffs into a darksome and stupendous chasm, rendered still more

---

* St. *Godric* was born at *Walpole* in *Norfolk*, and being an itinerant merchant got acquainted with St. *Cuthbert* at *Farn Island*. He made three pilgrimages to *Jerusalem*; at length, was warned by a vision to settle in the desert of *Finchal*. He lived a hermetical life there during 63 years, and practised unheard-of austerities: he wore an iron shirt next his skin, day and night, and wore out three: he mingled ashes with the flower he made his bread of; and, least it should then be too good, kept it three or four months before he ventured to eat it. In winter, as well as summer, he passed whole nights, up to his chin in water, at his devotions. Like St. *Antony*, he was often haunted by fiends in various shapes; sometimes in form of beautifull damsels, so was visited with evil concupiscence, which he cured by rolling naked among thorns and briars: his body grew ulcerated; but, to encrease his pain, he poured salt into the wounds. Wrought many miracles, and died 1170. *Britannia sacra*, 304. About ten years after his decease, a *Benedictine* priory of thirteen monks was founded there in his honor, by *Hugh Pudsey*, Bishop of *Durham*.

tremendous

tremendous by the roaring of the waters over its
distant bottom.

Passed through *Chester-le-Street*, a small town,
near which is *Lumly-Castle*, the seat of the Earl of
Scarborough; a place, as I was told, very well
worth seeing; but unfortunately it proved a public
day, and I lost sight of it. The country, from
Durham to *Newcastle*, was very beautifull; the
risings gentle, and prettily wooded, and the views
agreeable; that on the borders remarkably fine,
there being, from an eminence not far from the
capital of *Northumberland*, an extensive view of a
rich country, watered by the coaly *Tyne*. Reach

NEWCASTLE, a large, disagreeable, and dirty NEWCASTLE.
town, divided in two unequal parts by the river,
and both sides very steep. The lower parts are
inhabited by Keelmen and their families, a muti-
nous race; for which reason this town is always
garrisoned.

The great business of the place is the coal trade.
The collieries lie at different distances, from five to
eighteen miles from the river; and the coal is
brought down in waggons along rail roads, and
discharged from covered buildings at the edge of
the water into the keels or boats that are to convey
it on shipboard. These boats are strong, clumsy and
round, will carry about 25 tuns each; sometimes are
navigated with a square sail, but generally are
pushed along with large poles. No ships of large
burthen can come up as high as *Newcastle*, but are
obliged to lie at *Shields*, a few miles down the river,
where stage coaches go thrice every day for the
conveniency of passengers. This country is most
remarkably

remarkably populous; *Newcastle* alone contains near 40,000 inhabitants; and there are at left 400 fail of ships belonging to that town and its port. The effect of the vast commerce of this place is very apparent for many miles round; the country is finely cultivated, and bears a most thriving and opulent aspect.

July 13. Left *Newcastle*; the country in general flat; passed by a large stone column with three dials on the capital, with several scripture texts on the sides, called here *Pigg*'s Folly, from the founder.

A few miles further is *Stannington* Bridge, a pleasant village. *Morpeth*, a small town with a neat town-house, and a tower for the bell near it. The castle was on a small eminence, but the remains are now very inconsiderable. Some attempt was made a few years ago to introduce the *Manchester* manufacture, but without success. There is a remarkable story of this place, that the inhabitants reduced their own town to ashes, on the approach of King *John*, A. D. 1215, out of pure hatred to their monarch, in order that he might not find any shelter there.

This place gave birth to *William Turner*, as Dr. *Fuller* expresses it, an excellent *Latinist, Grœcian, Oratour,* and *Poet*; he might have added polemic divine, champion and sufferer in the protestant cause, physician and naturalist. His botanic writings are among the first we had, and certainly the best of them; and his criticisms on the birds of *Aristotle* and *Pliny*, are very judicious. He was the first who flung any light on those subjects in our island;

ifland; therefore clames from a naturalift this tribute to his memory *.

Felton, a pleafant village on the *Coquet*, which, fome few miles lower, difcharges itfelf into the fea, oppofite to a fmall ifle of the fame name, remarkable for the multitudes of water-fowl which refort there to breed.

At *Alnwick*, a fmall town, the traveller is difappointed with the fituation and environs of the caftle, the refidence of the *Percies*, the antient Earls of *Northumberland*. You look in vain for any marks of the grandeur of the feudal age; for trophies won by a family eminent in our annals for military prowefs and deeds of chivalry; for halls hung with helms and haberks, or with the fpoils of the chace; for extenfive forefts, and venerable oaks. You look in vain for the *helmet* on the tower, the antient fignal of hofpitality to the traveller, or for the grey-headed porter to conduct him to the hall of entertainment. The numerous train, whofe countenances gave welcome to him on his way, are now no more; and inftead of the difinterefted ufher of the old times, he is attended by a *valet* eager to receive the fees of admittance.

Alnwick Caftle.

There is vaft grandeur in the appearance of the outfide of the caftle; the towers magnificent, but injured by the numbers of rude ftatues crouded on the battlements. The appartments are large, and lately finifhed in the gothic ftyle with a moft incompatible elegance. The gardens are equally inconfiftent, trim to the higheft degree, and more adapted

---

* He was born in the reign of *Henry* VIII. died in 1568.

to a *villa* near *London*, than the antient seat of a great Baron. In a word, nothing, except the numbers of unindustrious poor that swarm at the gate, excites any one idea of its former circumstances.

A stage further is *Belford*, the seat of *Abraham Dixon*, Esq; a modern house; the front has a most beautifull simplicity in it. The grounds improved as far as the art of husbandry can reach; the plantations large and flourishing: a new and neat town, instead of the former wretched cottages; and an industrious race, instead of an idle poor, at present fill the estate.

Bamborough Castle.

On an eminence on the sea coast, about four miles from *Belford*, is the very antient castle of *Bamborough*, built by *Ida*, first king of the *Northumbrians*, A. D. 548. But, according to the conjecture of an antiquarian I met with there, on the site of a *Roman* fortress. It was also his opinion, that the square tower was actually the work of the *Romans*. It had been of great strength; the hill it is founded on excessively steep on all sides, and accessible only by flights of steps on the south east. The ruins are still considerable; the remains of a great hall are very singular; it had been warmed by two fire-places of a vast size, and from the top of every window ran a flue, like that of a chimney, which reached the summits of the battlements. Many of the ruins are now filled with sand, caught up by the winds that rage here with great impetuosity, and carried to very distant places.

This castle, and the manour belonging to it, was once the property of the *Forsters*; but purchased
by

by Lord *Crew*, Bifhop of *Durham*, and with other confiderable eftates, left vefted in Truftees, to be applied to unconfined charitable ufes. Three of thefe Truftees are a majority: one of them makes this place his refidence, and bleffes the coaft by his judicious and humane application of the Prelate's generous bequeft. He has repaired and rendered habitable the great fquare tower: the part referved for himfelf and family is a large hall and a few fmaller apartments; but the reft of the fpacious edifice is allotted for purpofes which make the heart to glow with joy when thought of. The upper part is an ample grainary; from whence corn is difpenced to the poor without diftinction, even in the deareft time, at the rate of four fhillings a bufhel; and the diftreffed, for many miles round, often experience the conveniency of this benefaction.

Bifhop *Crew's* Charity.

Other apartments are fitted up for the reception of fhipwrecked failors; and bedding is provided for about thirty, fhould fuch a number happen to be caft on fhore at the fame time. A conftant patrole is kept every ftormy night along this tempeftuous coaft, for above eight miles, the length of the manour, by which means numbers of lives have been preferved. Many poor wretches are often found on the fhore in a ftate of infenfibility; but by timely relief, are foon brought to themfelves.

It often happens, that fhips ftrike in fuch a manner on the rocks as to be capable of relief, in cafe numbers of people could be fuddenly affembled: for that purpofe a cannon * is fixed on the top of

* Once belonging to a *Dutch* frigate of 40 guns; which, with all the crew, was loft oppofite to the caftle, about fixty years ago.

the tower, which is fired once, if the accident happens in such a quarter; twice, if in another, and thrice, if in such a place. By these signals the country people are directed to the spot they are to fly to; and by this means, frequently preserve not only the crew, but even the vessel; for machines of different kinds are always in readiness to heave ships out of their perillous situation.

In a word, all the schemes of this worthy Trustee have a humane and useful tendency: he seemed as if selected from his brethren for the same purposes as *Spenser* tells us the first of his seven *Beadsmen* in the house of *holinesse* was.

> The first of them, that eldest was and best,
>   Of all the house had charge and governement,
> As guardian and steward of the rest:
>   His office was to give entertainement
> And lodging unto all that came and went:
>   Not unto such as could him feast againe,
> And doubly quite for that he on them spent;
>   But such as want of harbour did constraine;
> Those, for GOD's sake, his dewty was to entertaine.

Farn Isles. Opposite to *Bamborough* lie the *Farn* islands, which form two groupes of little isles and rocks to the number of seventeen, but at low water the points of others appear above the surface; they all are distinguished by particular names. The nearest isle to the shore is that called the *House Island*, which lies exactly one mile 68 chains from the coast: the most distant is about seven or eight miles. They are rented for 16 l. *per annum*: their produce is kelp, some few feathers, and a few seals, which the tenant watches and shoots for the sake of the oil and skins. Some of them yeild a little

little grafs, and ferve to feed a cow or two, which the people are defperate enough to tranfport over in their little boats.

Vifited thefe iflands in a coble, a fafe but feem- JULY 15. ingly hazardous fpecies of boat, long, narrow and flat-bottomed, which is capable of going thro' a high fea, dancing like a cork on the fummits of the waves.

Touched at the rock called the *Meg*, whitened with the dung of corvorants which almoft covered it; their nefts were large, made of tang, and moft excefsively fætid.

Rowed next to the *Pinnacles*, an ifland in the fartheft groupe; fo called from fome vaft columnar rocks at the fouth end, even at their fides, and flat at their tops, and entirely covered with guillemots and fhags: the fowlers pafs from one to the other of thefe columns by means of a narrow board, which they place from top to top, forming a narrow bridge, over fuch a horrid gap, that the very fight of it ftrikes one with horror.

Landed at a fmall ifland, where we found the female *Eider* ducks * at that time fitting: the lower Eider Ducks. part of their nefts was made of fea plants; the upper part was formed of the down which they pull off their own breafts, in which the eggs were furrounded and warmly bedded: in fome were three, in others five eggs, of a large fize and pale olive color, as fmooth and glofsy as if varnifhed over. The nefts are built on the beach, among the loofe pebbles, not far from the water. The

---

* Vide *Br. Zool.* II. 454. I have been informed that they alfo breed on *Inch-Colm*, in the *Firth of Forth*.

Ducks

Ducks fit very close, nor will they rise till you almost tread on them. The Drakes separate themselves from the females during the breeding season. We robbed a few of their nests of the down, and after carefully separating it from the tang, found that the down of one nest weighed only three quarters of an ounce, but was so elastic as to fill the crown of the largest hat. The people of this country call these St. *Cuthbert*'s ducks, from the saint of the islands.

Besides these birds, I observed the following:

    Puffins, called here *Tom Noddies*,
    Auks, here *Skouts*,
    Guillemots,
    Black Guillemot,
    Little Auks,
    Shiel-ducks,
    Shags,
    Corvorants,
    Black and white Gulls,
    Brown and white Gulls,
    Herring Gulls, which I was told fed sometimes on eggs of other birds,
    Common Gull, here *Annets*,
    Kittiwakes, or Tarrocks,
    Pewit Gulls,
    Great Terns,
    Sea Pies,
    Sea Larks, here *Brokets*,
    Jackdaws, which breed in rabbet-holes,
    Rock Pigeons,
    Rock Larks.

The Terns were so numerous, that in some places it was difficult to tread without crushing some of the eggs.

The last isle I visited was the *House island*, the sequestered spot where St. *Cuthbert* passed the two last years of his life. Here was afterwards established a priory of *Benedictines* for six or eight Monks subordinate to *Durham*. A square tower, the remains of a church, and some other buildings, are to be seen there still; and a stone coffin, which, it is pretended, was that of St. *Cuthbert*. At the north end of the isle is a deep chasm, from the top to the bottom of the rock, communicating to the sea; through which, in tempestuous weather, the water is forced with vast violence and noise, and forms a fine *jet d'eau* of sixty-six feet high: it is called by the inhabitants of the opposite coast the *Churn*.

Reached shore through a most turbulent rippling, occasioned by the fierce current of the tides between the islands and the coast.

Pursued my journey northward. Saw at a distance the *Cheviot* hills; on which, I was informed, the green Plovers breed; and that, during winter, flocks innumerable of the great Bramblings, or Snow-flakes, appear; the most southern place of their migration, in large companies.

July 1

The country almost woodless, there being but one wood of any consequence between *Belford* and *Berwick*. Saw on the left an antient tower, which shewed the character of the times when it was unhappily necessary, on these borders, for every house to be a fortress.

On the right, had a view of the sea, and, not remote from the land, of *Lindesfarn*, or *Holy* Island, once an episcopal seat, afterwards translated to *Durham*. On it are the ruins of a castle and a church. In some parts are abundance of *Entrochi*, which are called by the country people St. *Cuthbert*'s beads.

After a few miles riding, have a full view of *Berwick*, and the river *Tweed* winding westward for a considerable way up the country; but its banks were without any particular charms*, being almost woodless. The river is broad; and has over it a bridge of sixteen very handsome arches, especially two next the town.

BERWICK is fortified in the modern way; but is much contracted in its extent to what it was formerly, the old castle and works now lying at some distance beyond the present ramparts. The barracks are large, consist of a center and two wings. The church was built by *Cromwel*, and, according to the spirit of the builder, without a steeple. Even in *Northumberland*, (towards the borders) the steeples grew less and less, and as if it were forewarned the traveller that he was speedily to take leave of episcopacy. The town-house has a large and handsome modern tower to it: the streets in general are narrow and bad, except that in which the town-house stands.

Abundance of wool is exported from this town: eggs in vast abundance collected through all the

---

* I was informed that the beautifull banks of the *Tweed* verify the old song at the passage at *Colstream*.

country,

country, almoſt as far as *Carliſle*: they are packed in boxes, with the thick end downwards, and are ſent to *London* for the uſe of ſugar refiners. I was told that as many are exported as bring in annually the ſum of fourteen thouſand pounds.

The ſalmon fiſheries here are very conſiderable, and likewiſe bring in vaſt ſums: they lie on each ſide the river; and are all private property, except what belongs to the Dean and Chapter of *Durham*, which, in rent and tythe of fiſh, brings in 450 l. *per ann.* for all the other fiſheries are liable to tythe. The common rents of thoſe are 50 l. a year, for which the tenants have as much ſhore as ſerves to launch out and draw their nets on ſhore: the limits of each are ſtaked; and I obſerved that the fiſhers never failed going as near as poſſible to their neighbor's limits. One man goes off in a ſmall flat-bottomed boat, ſquare at one end, and taking as large a circuit as his net admits, brings it on ſhore at the extremity of his boundary, where others aſſiſt in landing it. The beſt fiſhery is on the ſouth ſide *: very fine ſalmon trout are often taken here, which come up to ſpawn from the ſea, and return in the ſame manner as the ſalmon do. The chief import is timber from *Norway* and the *Baltic*.

Salmon fiſhery.

Almoſt immediately on leaving *Berwick*, enter

---

* For a fuller account of this fiſhery, vide *Britiſh Zoology*, III. 241. to it may be alſo added, that in the middle of the river, not a mile weſt of the town, is a large ſtone, on which a man is placed, to obſerve what is called the *reck* of the ſalmon coming up.

A TOUR

SCOTLAND,

in the shire of *Merch*, or *Mers**. A little way from *Berwick*, on the west, is *Halydon* hill, famous for the overthrow of the *Scots* under the regent *Douglas*, by *Edward* III. on the attempt of the former to raise the siege of that town. A cruel action blasted the laurels of the conqueror: *Seton*, the governor, stipulated to surrender in fifteen days, if not relieved in that time, and gave his son as hostage for performance. The time elapsed; *Seton* refused to execute the agreement, and with a *Roman* unfeelingness beheld the unhappy youth hung before the walls.

The entrance into *Scotland* has a very unpromising look; for it wanted, for some miles, the cultivation of the parts more distant from *England*: but the borders were necessarily neglected; for, till the accession of *James* VI. and even long after, the national enmity was kept up, and the borderers of both countries discouraged from improvement, by the barbarous inroads of each nation. This inattention to agriculture continued till lately; but on reaching the small village of *Eytown*, the scene was greatly altered; the wretched cottages, or rather hovels of the country, were vanishing; good comfortable houses arise in their stead; the lands are inclosing, and yield very good barley, oats, and clover; the banks are planting: I speak in the present tense; for there is still a mixture of the

---

* *Boethius* says, that in his time bustards were found in this county; but they are now extirpated: the historian calls them *Gustardes*. *Desc. Scot.* xiii.

old

old negligence left amidst the recent improvements, which look like the works of a new colony in a wretched impoverished country.

Soon after the country relapses; no arable land is seen; but for four or five miles succeeds the black joyless heathy moor of *Coldingham*: happily, this is the whole specimen that remains of the many miles, which, not many years ago, were in the same dreary unprofitable state. Near this was the convent of that name immortalized by the heroism of its Nuns; who, to preserve themselves inviolate from the *Danes*, cut off their lips and noses; and thus rendering themselves objects of horror, were, with their abbess *Ebba**, burnt in the monastery by the disappointed savages.

Coldingham.

At the end of the moor came at once in sight of the *Firth*** of *Forth*; a most extensive prospect of that great arm of the sea, of the rich country of *East Lothian*, the *Bass Isle*; and at a distance, the isle of *May*, the coast of the county of *Fife*, and the country as far as *Montrose*.

After going down a long descent dine at *Old Cambus*, at a mean house, in a poor village; where I believe the Lord of the soil is often execrated by the weary traveller, for not enabling the tenant to furnish more comfortable accommodations, in so considerable a thoroughfare.

---

* A. D. 870.

** *Bodotria* of *Tacitus*, who describes the two Firths of *Clyde* and *Forth*, and the intervening Isthmus, with much propriety, speaking of the fourth summer *Agricola* had passed in *Britain*, and how conconvenient he found this narrow tract for shutting out the enemy by his fortresses, says, *Nam* Glota (Firth of *Clyde*) *et* Bodotria, *diversi maris æstu per immensum revecti, angusto terrarum spatio dirimuntur:* Vit. Agr.

The

. The country becomes now extremely fine; bounded at a distance, on one side, by hills; on the other, by the sea: the intervening space is as rich a tract of corn land as I ever saw; for *East Lothian* is the *Northamptonshire* of *North Britain:* the land is in many places manured with sea tang; but I was informed, that the barley produced from it is much lighter than barley from other manure.

On the side of the hills on the left is Sir *John Hall*'s, of *Dunglas*; a fine situation, with beautifull plantations. Pass by *Broxmouth*, a large house of the *Duke* of *Roxborough*, in a low spot, with great woods surrounding it. Reach

DUNBAR.

DUNBAR: the chief street broad and handsome; the houses built of stone; as is the case with most of the towns in *Scotland*. There are some ships sent annually from this place to *Greenland*, and the exports of corn are pretty considerable. The harbour is safe, but small; its entrance narrow, and bounded by two rocks. Between the harbour and the castle is a very surprising stratum of stone, in some respects resembling that of *Giant's Causeway* in *Ireland:* it consists of great columns of a red grit stone, either triangular, quadrangular, pentangular, or hexangular; their diameter from one to two feet, their length at low water thirty, dipping or inclining a little to the south.

Columnar rocks.

They are jointed, but not so regularly, or so plainly, as those that form the *Giant's Causeway*. The surface of several that had been torn off appear as a pavement of numbers of convex ends, probably answering to the concave bottoms of other joints once incumbent on them. The space between the columns

columns was filled with thin septa of red and white sparry matter; and veins of the same pervaded the columns transversely. This range of columns faces the north, with a point to the east, and extends in front about two hundred yards. The breadth is inconsiderable: the rest of the rock degenerates into shapeless masses of the same sort of stone, irregularly divided by thick septa. This rock is called by the people of *Dunbar*, the *Isle*.

Opposite are the ruins of the castle, seated on a rock above the sea; underneath one part is a vast cavern, composed of a black and red stone, which gives it a most infernal appearance; a fit representation of the pit of *Acheron*, and wanted only to be peopled with witches to make the scene complete: it appears to have been the dungeon, there being a formed passage from above, where the poor prisoners might have been let down, according to the barbarous custom of war in early days. There are in some parts, where the rock did not close, the remains of walls; for the openings are only natural fissures; but the founders of the castle taking advantage of this cavity, adding a little art to it, rendered it a most complete and secure prison.

On the other side are two natural arches, through which the tide flowed; under one was a fragment of wall, where there seems to have been a portal for the admission of men or provisions from sea: thro' which, it is probable that *Alexander Ramsay*, in a stormy night, reinforced the garrison, in spite of the fleet which lay before the place, when closely besieged by the *English*, in 1337, and galantly defended

fended for nineteen weeks by that heroine *black Agnes*, Countess of *March* *.

Through one of these arches was a most picturesque view of the *Bass Isle*, with the sun setting in full splendor; through the other of the *May* island, gilt by its beams.

Over the ruins of a window were the three legs, or arms of the Isle of *Man*, a lion rampant, and a St. *Andrew*'s cross.

JULY 18. Rode within sight of *Tantallon* castle, now a wretched ruin; once the seat of the powerfull *Archibald Douglas*, Earl of *Angus*, which for some time resisted all the efforts of *James* V. to subdue it.

Bass Isle. A little further, about a mile from the shore, lies the *Bass* Island, or rather rock, of a most stupendous height; on the south side the top appears of a conic shape, but the other over-hangs the sea in a most tremendous manner. The castle, which was once the state prison of *Scotland*, is now neglected: it lies close to the edge of the precipice, facing the little village of *Castleton*; where I toke boat, in order to visit this singular spot; but the weather proved unfavorable, the wind blew so fresh, and the waves ran so high, that it was impossible to attempt landing; for even in calmer weather it cannot be done without hazard, there being a steep rock to ascend, and commonly a great swell, which often removes the boat while you are scaling the precipice; so, in case of a false

---

* *Buchanan, lib.* ix. c. 25. The *English* were obliged to desist from their enterprize.

step,

step, there is the chance of falling into a water almost unfathomable.

Various sorts of water fowl repair annually to this rock to breed; but none in greater numbers than the *Gannets*, or *Soland* geese, multitudes of which were then sitting on their nests near the sloping part of the isle, and others flying over our boat: it is not permitted to shoot at them, the place being farmed principally on account of the profit arising from the sale of the young of these birds, and of the *Kittiwake*, a species of gull, so called from its cry. The first are sold at *Edinburgh** for twenty-pence apiece, and served up roasted a little before dinner. This is the only kind of provision whose price has not been advanced; for we learn from Mr. *Ray*, that it was equally dear above a century ago**. It is unnecessary to say more of this singular bird, as it has been very fully treated of in the second volume of the *British Zoology*.

Gannets.

With much difficulty landed at *North Berwick*, three miles distant from *Castleton*, the place we intended to return to. The first is a small town, pleasantly seated near a high conic hill, partly planted with trees: it is seen at a great distance, and is called the *Law of Berwick*; a name given to several other high hills in this part of the island.

---

* SOLAN GOOSE.
There is to be sold, by JOHN WATSON, Jun. at his Stand at the Poulty, *Edinburgh*, all lawfull days in the week, wind and weather serving, good and fresh *Solan* Geese. Any who have occasion for the same may have them at reasonable rates.
Aug. 5, 1768.   EDINBURGH ADVERTISER.
** *Ray's Itineraries,* 192.

Preston Pans. — Pass through *Abberladie* and *Preston Pans:* the last takes its name from its salt-pans, there being a considerable work of that article; also another of vitriol. Saw at a small distance the field of battle, or rather of carnage, known by the name of the battle of *Preston Pans*, where the Rebels gave a lesson of severity, which was more than retaliated, the following spring, at *Culloden*. Observed, in this day's ride, (I forget the spot) the once princely seat of the Earl of *Wintoun*, now a ruin; judiciously left in that state, as a proper remembrance of the sad fate of those who engage in rebellious politicks. There are great marks of improvement on approaching the capital; the roads good, the country very populous, numbers of manufactures carried on, and the prospect embellished with gentlemen's seats. Reach

EDINBURGH.

EDINBURGH,

A city that possesses a boldness and grandeur of situation beyond any that I had ever seen: it is built on the edges and sides of a vast sloping rock, of a great and precipitous height at the upper extremity, and the sides declining very quick and steep into the plain. The view of the houses at a distance strikes the traveller with wonder; their own loftiness, improved by their almost aerial situation, gives them a look of magnificence not to be found in any other part of *Great Britain*. All these conspicuous buildings form the upper part of the great street, are of stone, and make a handsome appearance: they are generally six or seven stories high in front; but, by reason of the declivity of the hill, much higher backward; one in particular,

called

called *Babel*, has about twelve or thirteen stories. Every house has a common staircase, and every story is the habitation of a separate family. The inconvenience of this particular structure need not be mentioned; notwithstanding the utmost attention, in the article of cleanliness, is in general observed. The common complaint of the streets of *Edinburgh* is now taken away, by the great vigilance of the magistrates *, and their severity against any that offend in any gross degree **. It must be observed, that this unfortunate species of architecture arose from the turbulence of the times in which it was in vogue; every body was desirous of getting as near as possible to the protection of the castle, the houses were crouded together; and I may say, piled one upon another, meerly on the principle of security.

The castle is antient, but strong, placed on the summit of the hill, at the edge of a very deep precipice. Strangers are shewn a very small room, in which *Mary* Queen of *Scots* was delivered of *James* VI.

Castle.

From this fortress is a full view of the city and its environs; a strange prospect of rich country, with vast rocks and mountains intermixed: on the south and east are the meadows, or the publick walks, *Herriot*'s hospital, part of the town over-

---

* The streets are cleaned early every morning. Once the City payed for the cleaning; at present, it is rented for 4 or 500l. per annum.

** In the closes, or allies, the inhabitants are very apt to fling out their filth, &c. without regarding who passes; but the sufferer may call every inhabitant of the house it came from to account, and make them prove the delinquent, who is always punished with a heavy fine.

shadowed

shadowed by the stupendous rocks of *Arthur*'s seat and *Salusbury*'s *Craigs*, the *Pentland* hills at a few miles distance, and at a still greater, those of *Muirfoot*, whose sides are covered with verdant turf.

To the north is a full view of the *Firth* of *Forth*, from *Queen's-Ferry* to its mouth, with its southern banks covered with towns and villages. On the whole, the prospect is singular, various and fine.

Reservoir. The reservoir of water* for supplying the city lies in the Castle-street, and is well worth seeing: the great cistern contains near two hundred and thirty tuns of water, which is conveyed to the several conduits, that are disposed at proper distances in the principal streets; these are conveniences that few towns in *North Britain* are without.

In a small square, on the south side of *High-street*, is the Parlement Close, a small square, in which is the Parlement-House, where the courts of justice are held. Below stairs is the Advocate's library, founded by Sir *George Mackenzie*, and now contains above thirty thousand volumes, and several manuscripts: among the more curious are the four Evangelists, very legible, notwithstanding it is said to be several hundred years old.

Advocate's Library.

St. *Jerome*'s Bible, wrote about the year 1100.

A *Malabar* book, wrote on leaves of plants.

A *Turkish* manuscript, illuminated in some parts like a missal. *Elogium in sultan morad filium filii Soliman Turcici. Script. Constantinopoli. Anno Hegiræ*, 992.

* It is conveyed in pipes from the *Pentland* hills five miles distant.

A Cartulary,

A Cartulary, or records of the monasteries, some very antient.

A very large Bible, bound in four volumes; illustrated with scripture prints, by the first engravers, pasted in, and collected at a vast expence. There are besides great numbers of antiquities, not commonly shewn, except enquired after.

The *Luckenbooth* row, which contains the *Tolbooth*, or city prison, and the weighing-house, which brings in a revenue of 500l. *per annum*, stands in the middle of the High-street, and, with the guard-house, contributes to spoil as fine a street as most in *Europe*, being in some parts eighty feet wide, and finely built.

The exchange is a handsome modern building, in which is the custom-house: the first is of no use, in its proper character; for the merchants always chuse standing in the open street, exposed to all kinds of weather.

The old cathedral is now called the New Church, and is divided into four places of worship; in one the Lords of the Sessions attend: there is also a throne and a canopy for his Majesty, should he visit this capital, and another for the Lord Commissioner. There is no music either in this or any other of the *Scotch* churches, for *Peg* still faints at the sound of an organ.

The same church has a large tower, oddly terminated with a sort of crown.

On the front of a house in the *Nether Bow*, are two fine profile heads of a man and woman, of *Roman* sculpture, supposed to be those of *Severus* and

Roman heads.

and *Julia:* but, as appears from an inscription *
made by the person who put them into the wall,
were mistaken for *Adam* and *Eve.*

Near the *Trone* church are the remains of the
house once inhabited by *Mary Steuart*; now a
tavern.

Holy-Rood House.

At the end of the *Cannongate-Street* stands *Holy-
Rood* palace, originally an abby founded by *David*
I, in 1128. The towers on the N. W. side were
erected by *James* V. together with other buildings,
for a royal residence: according to the editor of
Cambden, great part, except the towers above-
mentioned, were burnt by *Cromwell*; but the other
towers, with the rest of this magnificent palace, as
it now stands, were executed by Sir *William Bruce,*
by the directions of *Charles* II. within is a beautifull square, with piazzas on every side. It contains
great numbers of fine apartments; some, that are
called the King's, are in great disorder; the rest
are granted to several of the nobility.

In the Earl of *Breadalbane*'s, are some excellent
portraits, particularly three full lengths, remarkably fine, by *Vandyck,* of

Henry Earl of *Holland,*
William Duke of *Newcastle,*
Charles Earl of *Warwick* **,

And by Sir *Peter Lely,* the Duke and Dutchess
of *Lauderdale,* and *Edward* Earl of *Jersey.* There

---

* *In sudore vultus tui vesceris pane.* Anno 1621. These heads are well engraven in *Gordon's* Itinerary, *tab.* iii.

** I am informed that the portraits of the Earls of *Holland* and *Warwick* are now removed to *Taymouth.*

is

is besides a very good head of a boy, by *Morrillio*, and some views of the fine scenes near his Lordship's seat at *Taymouth*.

At Lord *Dunmore*'s lodgings is a very large piece of *Charles* I. and his Queen going to ride, with the sky showering roses on them; a Black holds a grey horse, a boy a spaniel, with several other dogs sporting round: the Queen is painted with a lovelock, and with browner hair and complection, and younger, than I ever saw her drawn. It is a good piece, and said to be done by *Vandyck?* in the same place are two other good portraits of *Charles* II. and *James* VII.

The gallery of this palace takes up one side, and is filled with colossal portraits of the Kings of *Scotland*.

In the old towers are showen the appartments where the murther of *David Rizzo* was committed.

That beautifull piece of *gothic* architecture the church, or chapel, of *Holy-Rood-Abby*, is now a ruin, the roof having fell in, by a most scandalous neglect, notwithstanding money had been granted by Government to preserve it entire. Beneath the ruins lie the bodies of *James* II. and *James* V. *Henry Darnly*, and several persons of rank: and the inscriptions on several of their tombs are preserved by *Maitland*. A gentleman informed me, that some years ago he had seen the remains of the bodies, but in a very decayed state; the beards remained on some; and that the bones of *Henry Darnly* proved their owner, by their great size, for he was said to be seven feet high.

Chapel.

Parks.

Near this palace are the *Parks* first inclosed by *James* V. within are the vast rocks * known by the names of *Arthur*'s Seat and *Salusbury*'s *Craigs*; their fronts exhibit a romantic and wild scene of broken rocks and vast precipices, which from some points seem to over-hang the lower parts of the city. Great columns of stone, from forty to fifty feet in length, and about two feet in diameter, regularly pentagonal, or hexagonal, hang down the face of some of these rocks almost perpendicularly, or with a very slight dip, and form a strange appearance. Considerable quantities of stone from the quarries have been cut and sent to *London* for paving the streets, its great hardness rendering it excellent for that purpose. Beneath these hills are some of the most beautifull walks about *Edinburgh*, commanding a fine prospect over several parts of the country.

On one side of the *Park* are the ruins of St. *Anthony*'s chapel, once the resort of numberless votaries.

Herriot's Hospital.

The south part of the city has several things worth visiting. *Herriot*'s hospital is a fine old building, much too magnificent for the end proposed, that of educating poor children: it was founded by *George Herriot*, jeweller to *James* II. who followed that monarch to *London*, and made a large fortune. There is a fine view of the castle and the sloping part of the city from the front: the gardens were formerly the resort of the gay; and there the *Scotch* Poets often laid, in their comedies, the scenes of intrigue.

* According to *Maitland*, their perpendicular height is 656 feet.

In

In the church-yard of the Grey Friers is the monument of Sir *George Mackenfie*, a rotunda; with a multitude of other tombs; this, and another near the *Cannon-gate* being the only cæmeteries to this populous city.

The college is a mean building; but no one resides in it except the Principal, whose house is supposed to be on the site of that in which *George Darnly* was murdered, then belonging to the Provost of the *Kirk* of *Field*. The students of the university are dispersed over the town, and are about six hundred in number: they wear no habit, nor are they subject to any regulations; but, as they are for the most part volunteers for knowledge, few of them desert her standards. There are twenty-two professors of different sciences, most of whom read lectures: all the chairs are very ably filled; those in particular which relate to the study of medicine, as is evident from the number of ingenious physicians, *eleves* of this university, who prove the abilities of their masters. The *Musæum* had, for many years, been neglected; but, by the assiduity of the present Professor of natural history, bids fair to become a most instructive repository of the *naturalia* of these kingdoms.

The royal infirmary is a spatious and handsome ædifice, capable of containing two hundred patients. The operation-room is particularly convenient, the council-room elegant, with a good picture in it of Provost *Drummond*. From the cupolo of this building is a fine prospect, and a full view of the city.

College.

Infirmary.

Not far from hence are twenty-seven acres of ground, designed for a square, called *George Square*: a small portion is at present built, consisting of small but commodious houses, in the *English* fashion. Such is the spirit of emprovement, that within these three years sixty thousand pounds have been expended in houses in the modern taste, and twenty thousand in the old.

Watson's hospital should not be forgot: a large good building, behind the Grey Friers church; an excellent institution for the educating and apprenticing the children of decayed merchants; who, after having served their time with credit, receive fifty pounds to set up with.

The *meadows*, or public walks, are well planted, and are very extensive: these are the mall of *Edinburgh*, as *Comely Gardens* are its *Vauxhall*.

The *Cowgate* is a long street, running parallel with the *High Street*, beneath the steep southern declivity of the city, and terminates in the *Grass-Market*, a wide street, where cattle are sold, and criminals executed. On several of the houses are small iron crosses, which, I was informed, denoted that they once belonged to the Knights of St. *John*.

On the north side of the city lies the new town, which is planned with great judgement, and will prove a magnificent addition to *Edinburgh*: the houses in St. *Andrew*'s square cost from 1800l. to 2000l. each, and one or two 4000 or 5000l. They are all built in the modern style, and are free from the inconveniences attending the old city.

These

These improvements are connected to the city by a very beautifull bridge, whose highest arch is ninety-five feet high.

In the walk of this evening, I passed by a deep and wide hollow beneath *Calton* Hill, the place where those imaginary criminals, witches and sorcerers, in less enlightened times, were burnt; and where, at festive seasons, the gay and galant held their tilts and tournaments: at one of these, it is said, that the Earl of *Bothwell* made the first impression on the susceptible heart of *Mary Stuart*, having galopped into the ring down the dangerous steeps of the adjacent hill; he seemed to think that

> Women, born to be control'd.
> Stoop to the forward and the bold.

These desperate feats were the humour of the times of chivalry: *Brantome* relates, that the *Duc de Nemours* galopped down the steps of the *Sainte Chappel* at *Paris*, to the astonishment of the beholders. The men cultivated every exercise that could preserve or improve their bodily strength; the ladies, every art that tended to improve their charms: *Mary* is reported to have used a bath of white wine; a custom strange, but not without precedent. *Jaques du Fouilloux*, enraptured with a country girl enumerating the arts which she scorned to use to improve her person, mentions this:

> Point ne portoit de ce linge femelle
> Pour amoindrir son seing et sa mammelle.
> Vasquine nulle, ou aucun pelicon
> Elle ne portoit, ce n'estoit sa façon
> Point ne *prenoit vin blanc pour se 'baigner*,
> Ne drogue encore pour son corps alleger*.

* *L'Adolescence de Jaques du Fouilloux*, 88.

At a small walk's distance from *Colton* Hill lies the new botanic garden*, consisting of five acres of ground, a green-house fifty feet long, two temperate rooms, each twelve feet, and two stoves, each twenty-eight: the ground rises to the north, and defends the plants from the cold winds: the soil a light sand, with a black earth on the surface. It is finely stocked with plants, whose arrangement and cultivation do much credit to my worthy friend Dr. *Hope*, Professor of Botany, who planned and executed the whole. It was begun in 1764, being founded by the munificence of his present Majesty, who granted fifteen hundred pounds for that purpose.

During this week's stay at *Edinburgh*, the prices of provisions were as follow:

Beef, from 5d. to 3d. ¾.
Mutton, from 4d. to 3d. ¾.
Veal, from 5d. to 3d.
Lamb, 2d. ¾.
Bacon, 7d.
Butter, in summer, 8d. in winter, 1s.
Pigeons, *per* dozen, from 8d. to 5s.
Chickens, *per* pair, 8d. to 1s.
A fowl, 1s. 2d.
Green goose, 3s.
Fat goose, 2s. 6d.
Large turky, 4s. or 5s.
Pig, 2s.
Coals, 5d. or 6d. *per* hundred, delivered.

---

* The old botanic garden lies to the east of the new bridge: an account of it is to be seen in the *Museum Balfourianum*.

Many fine excursions may be made at a small distance from this city. *Leith*, a large town, about two miles north, lies on the *Firth*, is a flourishing place, and the port of *Edinburgh*. The town is dirty and ill built, and chiefly inhabited by sailors; but the pier is very fine, and is a much-frequented walk. The races were at this time on the sands, near low-water mark: considering their vicinity to a great city and populous country, the meeting was far from numerous; a proof that dissipation has not generally infected the manners of the *North Britons*.

LEITH.

Craigmellar castle is seated on a rocky eminence, about two miles south of *Edinburgh*, is square, and has towers at each corner. Some few apartments are yet inhabited; but the rest of this great pile is in ruins.

Newbottle, the seat of the Marquiss of *Lothian*, is a pleasant ride of a few miles from the capital. It was once a *Cistercian* abby, founded by *David* I. in 1140; but, in 1591, was erected into a lordship, in favor of Sir *Mark Ker*, son of Sir *Walter Ker*, of *Cessford*. The house lies in a warm bottom, and, like most other of the houses of the *Scotch* nobility, resembles a *French Chateau*, by having a village or little paltry town adjacent. The situation is very favorable to trees, as appears by the vast size of those near the house; and I was informed, that fruit ripens here within ten days as early as at *Chelsea*.

The *Marquiss* possesses a most valuable collection of portraits, many of them very fine, and almost all very instructive: a large half-length of *Henry Darnly* represents him tall, aukward and gauky, with a stupid, insipid countenance; most likely
drawn

drawn after he had loft, by intemperance and debauchery, thofe charms which captivated the heart of the amorous *Mary*.

A head of her mother, *Marie de Guife*; not lefs beautifull than her daughter.

A head of *Madame Monpenfier*, and of feveral other illuftrious perfons, who graced the court of *Louis* XIII.

Prince *Rupert* and Prince *Maurice*, in one piece.

Some fmall portraits, ftudies of *Vandyk*; among which is one of *William* Earl of *Pembroke*, of whom Lord *Clarendon* gives fo advantageous a character.

A beautifull half-length of *Henrietta*, Queen of *Charles* I. her charms almoft apologize for the compliances of the uxorious monarch.

His daughter, the Dutchefs of *Orleans*.

The wife of *Philip* the bold, infcribed *Marga Mala, Lodo Mala*.

Head of *Robert Car*, Earl of *Somerfet*; the countenance effeminate, fmall features, light flaxen or yellowifh hair, and a very fmall beard: is an original of that worthlefs favorite, and proves that the figure given as his among the illuftrious heads is erroneous, the laft being reprefented as a robuft black man.

His father, Sir *Robert Car*.

An Earl of *Somerfet*, of whom I could get no account; handfome, with long light hair inclining to yellow: a head.

A full length of *James* I. by *Jamefon*. Another of *Charles* I. when young, in rich armour, black and gold: a capital piece.

Lady *Tufton*; a fine half length.

Earl

Earl *Morton*, regent: half-length; a yellow beard.

Two very curious half-lengths on wood: one of a man with a long forked black beard; his jacket flashed down in narrow stripes from top to bottom, and the stripes loose: the other with a black full beard, the same sort of stripes, but drawn tight by a girdle.

The Doge of *Venice*, by *Titian*.

Three by *Morillio*; boys and girls in low life.

A remarkable fine piece of our three first circumnavigators, *Drake*, *Hawkins* and *Candish*, half length.

The heads of *Mark* Earl of *Lothian*, and his lady, by Sir *Antonio More*.

Mark Ker, prior of *Newbottle*, who, at the reformation, complied with the times, and got the estate of the abby.

Subterraneous rooms.

In the woods adjacent to this seat are some subterraneous apartments and passages cut out of the live rock. A few miles distant from there, near *Hawthorn-Den*, the residence of the celebrated poet *Drummond* *, are, as I was informed, others of the same nature, but of greater extent, which Doctor *Stukeley* ** calls a *Pictish* castle. These places, in fact, were excavated by the antient inhabitants of the country, either as receptacles for their provisions, or for retreats for themselves or families, in time of war, in the same manner as *Tacitus* relates was the custom of the *Germans* †.

---

* Who is said to have composed his poems in one of these caves: he flourished in the time of *James* VI.

** Vide *Itin. Curiosum*. 50. tab. 38.

† *Solent et subterraneos specus aperire, eosque multo insuper fimo onerant, suffugium hiemi, et receptaculum frugibus, quia rigorem frigorum ejusmodi locis molliunt: et si quando hostis advenit aperta populatur: Abdita autem et defossa aut ignorantur, aut eo ipso fallunt, quod quærenda sunt.* De Moribus Germanor, c. 16.

Two

DALKEITH.

Two or three miles diftant from *Newbottle* is *Dalkeith*, a fmall town, adjoining to *Dalkeith*-houfe, the feat of the Duke of *Buccleugh*: originally the property of the *Douglafes*, and was, when in form of a caftle, of great ftrength; and, during the time of the Regent *Morton*'s retreat, ftyled the *Lion's Den*.

The portraits at *Dalkeith* are numerous, and fome good: among others, the

Firft Duke of *Richmond* and his Dutchefs.

The Dutchefs of *Cleveland*.

Countefs of *Buccleugh*, mother to the Dutchefs of *Monmouth*, and Lady *Egglinton*, her fifter.

The Dutchefs and her two fons: the Dutchefs of *York*; her hand remarkably fine: the Dutchefs of *Lenox*.

Mrs. *Sufanna Waters*, mother of the Duke of *Monmouth*, with his picture in her hand.

Dutchefs of *Cleveland* and her fon, an infant; fhe in character of a *Madonna*: fine.

The Duke of *Monmouth*, in character of a young St. *John*.

Lord *Strafford* and his Secretary; a fmall ftudy of *Vandyk*.

Henry VIII. and Queen *Catherine*, with the divorce in her hand; two fmall pieces, by *Holbein*. *Anna Bullein*, by the fame, dreffed in a black gown, large yellow netted fleeves, in a black cap, peaked behind.

Lady *Jane Gray*, with long hair, black and very thick: not handfome; but the virtues and the intellectual perfections of that fuffering innocent, more than fupplied the abfence of perfonal charms.

A large

A large spirited picture of the Duke of *Monmouth* on horseback. The same in armour. All his pictures have a handsome likeness of his father.

Dutchess of *Richmond*, with a bow in her hand, by Sir *Peter Lely*. A fine head of the late Duke of *Ormond*.

A beautiful head of *Mary Stewart*; the face a sharp face, thin and young; yet has a likeness to some others of her pictures done before misfortunes had altered her; her dress a strait gown, open at the top and reaching to her ears, a small cap, and small ruff, with a red rose in her hand.

In this palace is a room entirely furnished by *Charles* II. on occasion of the marriage of *Monmouth* with the heiress of the house*.

At *Smeton*, another seat of the Duke of *Buccleugh*, a mile distant from the first, is a fine half-length of General *Monk* looking over his shoulder, with his back towards you: he resided long at *Dalkeith*, when he commanded in *Scotland*.

Nell Gwinne, loosely attired.

A fine marriage of St. *Catherine*, by *Vandyk*.

Left *Edinburgh*, and pass'd beneath the castle, JULY 24. whose height and strength, in my then situation, appeared to great advantage. The country I past through was well cultivated, the fields large, but mostly inclosed with stone walls; for hedges are not yet become universal in this part of the kingdom: it is not a century since they were known here. Reach the

---

* Since this, I have been informed that not far from *Dalkeith*, at *Rosslyn*, is a most beautifull and entire chapel of gothic architecture, well worth a visit from a curious Traveller.

South-Ferry, a small village on the banks of the *Firth*, which suddenly is contracted to the breadth of two miles by the jutting out of the land on both shores; but almost instantly widens, towards the west, into a fine and extensive bay. The prospect on each side is very beautifull; a rich country, frequently diversified with towns, villages, castles, and gentlemen's seats *. There is beside a vast view up and down the *Firth*, from its extremity, not remote from *Sterling*, to its mouth near *Mey* isle; in all, about sixty miles.

This Ferry is also called *Queen's-Ferry*, being the passage much used ** by *Margaret*, queen to *Malcom* III. and sister to *Edgar Etheling*, her residence being at *Dumferline*. Cross over in an excellent passage-boat; observe midway the little isle called *Inch-Garvey*, with the ruin of a small castle. An *arctic* gull flew near the boat, pursued by other gulls, as birds of prey are: this is the species that persecutes and pursues the lesser kinds, till they mute through fear, when it catches up their excrements e'er they reach the water: the boatmen, on that account, styled it the dirty *Aulin*.

Granite quarry. Landed in the shire of *Fife* †, at *North Ferry*, near which are the great granite quarries, which help to supply the streets of *London* with paving stones; many ships then waiting near, in order to take in their lading. The granite lies in great perpendicular stacks; above which, a reddish earth

---

* Such as *Seith* castle, *Dumferline* town, Lord *Morris*'s, Lord *Hopetoun*'s, Captain *Dundas*'s.

** Or, as others say, because she, her brother and sister, first landed there, after their escape from *William* the Conqueror.

† Part of the antient *Caledonia*.

filled

filled with friable micaceous nodules. The granite itself is very hard, and is all blasted with gunpowder: the cutting into shape for paving costs two shillings and eight-pence per tun, and the freight to *London* seven shillings.

The country, as far as *Kinross*, is very fine, consisting of gentle risings; much corn, especially *Bear*; but few trees, except about a gentleman's seat, called *Blair*, where there are great and flourishing plantations. Near the road are the last collieries in *Scotland*, except the inconsiderable works in the county of *Sutherland*.

Kinross is a small town, seated in a large plain, bounded by mountains; the houses and trees are so intermixed as to give it an agreeable appearance. It has some manufactures of linnen and cutlery ware. At this time was a meeting of justices, on a singular occasion: a vagrant had been, not long before, ordered to be whipped; but such was the point of honor among the common people, that no one could be persuaded to go to *Perth* for the executioner, who lived there: to press, I may say, two men for that service was the cause of the meeting; so Mr. *Boswell*[*] may rejoice to find the notion of honor prevale in as exalted a degree among his own countrymen as among the virtuous *Corsicans*.

Not far from the town is the house of *Kinross*, built by the famous architect Sir *William Bruce*, for his own residence, and was the first good house in *North Britain*: it is a large, elegant, but plain building; the hall is fifty-two feet long, the grounds about it well planted, the fine lake adjacent; so

---

[*] *Hist. Corsica.*

that

that it is capable of being made as delightfull a place as any in *North Britain*.

Lough-Leven, a magnificent piece of water, very broad, but irregularly indented, is about twelve miles in circumference, and its greatest depth about twenty-four fathoms: is finely bounded by mountains on one side; on the other, by the plain of *Kinross*, and prettily embellished with several groves, most fortunately disposed. Some islands are dispersed in this great expanse of water; one of which is large enough to feed several head of cattle; but the most remarkable is that distinguished by the captivity of *Mary Stuart*, which stands almost in the middle of the lake. The castle still remains; consists of a square tower, a small yard with two round towers, a chapel, and the ruins of a building, where, it is said, the unfortunate Princess was lodged. In the square tower is a dungeon with a vaulted room above, over which had been three other stories. Some trees are yet remaining on this little spot; probably coeval with *Mary*, under whose shade she may have sat, expecting her escape at length effected by the enamoured *Douglas* *. This castle had before been a royal residence, but not for captive monarchs; having been granted from the crown by *Robert* III. to *Douglas*, Laird of *Loch-Leven*; but had been originally a seat of the *Culdees*.

Loch-leven castle.

---

* Historians differ in respect to the cause that influenced him to assist in his sovereign's escape; some attribute it to his avarice, and think he was bribed with jewels, reserved by *Mary*; others, that he was touched by a more generous passion: the last opinion is the most natural; considering the charms of the Queen and the youth of her deliverer.

The

The fish of this lake are Pike, small Perch, fine Eels, and most excellent Trouts; the best and the reddest I ever saw; the largest about six pounds in weight. The fishermen gave me an account of a species they called the *Gally* Trout, which are only caught from *October* to *January*; are split, salted and dried, for winter provision: by the description, they certainly were our Char, only of a larger size than any we have in *England*, or *Wales*, some being two feet and a half long. The birds that breed on the isles are Herring Gulls, Pewit Gulls, and great Terns, called here *Pictarnes*.

Fish & birds.

Lay at a good inn, a single house, about half a mile North of *Kinross*.

Made an excursion about seven miles west, to see the *rumbling brig* at *Glen-devon*, a bridge of one arch, flung over a chasm worn by the river *Devon*, about eighty feet deep, very narrow, and horrible to look down; the bottom, in many parts, is covered with fragments of rocks; in others, the waters are visible, gushing between the stones with great violence: the sides, in many places, project, and almost lock in each other; trees shoot out in various spots, and contribute to encrease the gloom of the glen, while the ear is filled with the cawing of daws, the cooing of wood-pigeons, and the impetuous noise of the waters.

JULY 25.
Rumbling Brig.

A mile lower down is the *Cawdron Glen:* here the river, after a short fall, drops on rocks hollowed in a strange manner into large and deep cylindric cavities, open on one side, or formed into great circular cavities, like cauldrons *; from whence

Cawdron Glen.

* In *Sweden*, and the North of *Germany*, such holes as these are called *Giant's* Pots. *Kalm's Voy.* I. 121. and *Ph. Transf. abridg.* V. 165.

the name of the place: one in particular has the appearance of a vast brewing vessel; and the water, by its great agitation, has acquired a yellow scum, exactly resembling the yesty working of malt liquor. Just beneath this the water darts down about thirty feet in form of a great white sheet: the rocks below widen considerably, and their clifty sides are fringed with wood. Beyond is a view of a fine meadowy vale, and the distant mountains near *Sterling*.

<small>Castle Campbell.</small>

Two miles north is *Castle Campbell*, seated on a steep peninsulated rock between vast mountains, having to the south a boundless view through a deep glen shagged with brush wood; for the forests that once covered the country are now entirely destroyed. Formerly, from its darksome situation, this pile was called the castle of *Gloom*; and all the names of the adjacent places were suitable: it was seated in the parish of *Dolor*, was bounded by the glens of *care*, and washed by the birns of *sorrow*. This castle, with the whole territory belonging to the family of *Argyle*, underwent all the calamities of civil war in 1645; for its rival, the Marquis of *Montrose*, carried fire and sword through the whole estate. The castle was ruined; and its magnificent reliques exist, as a monument of the horror of the times. No wonder then that the *Marquis* experienced so woeful and ignominious a fate, when he fell into the power of so exasperated a chieftain.

Returned to my inn along the foot of the *Ochil* hills, whose sides were covered with a fine verdure, and fed great numbers of cattle and sheep. The country below full of oats, and in a very improving state: the houses of the common people decent, but mostly

mostly covered with sods; some were covered both with straw and sod. The inhabitants extremely civil, and never failed offering brandy, or whey, when I stopt to make enquiries at any of their houses.

In the afternoon crossed a branch of the same hills, which yielded plenty of oats; descended into *Straith-earn*, a beautifull vale, about thirty miles in length, full of rich meadows and corn fields, divided by the river *Earn*, which serpentines finely through the middle, falling into the *Tay*, of which there is a sight at the east end of the vale. It is prettily diversified with groves of trees and gentlemen's houses; among which, towards the west end, is *Castle Drummond*, the forfeited seat of the Earl of *Perth*.

Castle Duplin*; the residence of the Earl of *Kinnoul*, seated on the north side of the vale, on the edge of a steep glen. Only a single tower remains of the old castle, the rest being modernized. The front commands a pleasing view of the vale; behind are plantations, extending several miles in length; all flourish greatly, except those of ash. I remarked in the woods, some very large chesnuts, horse-chesnuts, spruce and silver firs, cedar and arbor vitæ. Broad-leaved *laburnum* thrives in this country greatly, grows to a great size, and the wood is used in fineering.

Fruits succeed here very indifferently; even nonpareils require a wall to ripen: grapes, figs, and late

Straith-earn.

Fruit.

---

* Near this place was the battle of *Duplin*, 1332, between the *English*, under the command of *Baliol*, and the *Scots*. The last were defeated, and such a number of the name of *Hay* slain, that the family would have been extinct, had not several of their wives been left at home pregnant.

peaches, will not ripen: the winters begin early and end late, and are attended with very high winds. I was informed that labor is dear here, notwithstanding it is only eight-pence a day; the common people not being yet got into a method of working, so do very little for their wages. Notwithstanding this, improvements are carried on in these parts with great spirit, both in planting and in agriculture. Lord *Kinnoul* planted last year not fewer than eighty thousand trees, besides *Scotch* firs; so provides future forests for the benefit of his successors, and the embellishment of his country. In respect to agriculture, there are difficulties to struggle with, for the country is without either coal or lime-stone; so that the lime is brought from the estate of the Earl of *Elgin*, near *Dumferline*, who, I was told, drew a considerable revenue from the kilns.

Labor.

In *Castle Duplin* are some very good pictures; a remarkable one of *Luther*, *Bucer*, and *Catherine* the nun, by *Georgiani di Castel franco*.

A fine head of a secular priest, by *Titian*. St. *Nicholas* blessing three children. Two of cattle, by *Rosa di Tivoli*. A head of *Spencer*. *Ruben*'s head, by himself. A fine head of *Butler*, by Sir *Peter Lely*. Of the old Countess of *Desmond*, by *Rembrandt*. Mrs. *Tofts*, in the character of St. *Catherine*, by Sir *Godfrey Kneller*. Sir *George Haye*, of *Maginnis*, in armour, 1640; done at *Rome* by *L. Ferdinand*. *Haye*, Earl of *Carlisle*, in *Charles* the First's time, young and very handsome, by *Cornelius Jansen*. The second Earl of *Kinnoul*, by *Vandyk*. Chancellor *Haye*, by *Mytens*. A good portrait of Lord Treasurer *Oxford*, by *Richardson*. And a beautifull miniature of Sir *John Earnly*. Ascended

Ascended the hill of *Moncrief*; the prospect from thence is the glory of *Scotland*, and well merits the eulogia given it for the variety and richness of its views. On the south and west appear *Straithern*, embellished with the seats of Lord *Kinnoul*, Lord *Rollo*, and of several other gentlemen, the *Carse*, or rich plain of *Gowrie*, *Stormont* hills, and the hill of *Kinnoul*, whose vast cliff is remarkable for its beautifull pebbles. The mæanders of the *Ern*, which winds more than any river I at this time had seen, are most enlivening additions to the scene. The last turn it takes forms a fine peninsula prettily planted, and just beyond it joins the *Tay*, whose æstuary lies full in view, the sea closing the prospect on this side.

To the north lies the town of *Perth*, with a view of part of its magnificent bridge; which, with the fine woods called *Perth* Parks, the vast plain of *Straith-Tay*, the winding of that noble river, its islands, and the grand boundary, formed by the distant highlands, finish this matchless scene. The inhabitants of *Perth* are far from being blind to the beauties of their river; for with singular pleasure they relate the tradition of the *Roman* army, when it came in sight of the *Tay**, bursting into the exclamation of, *Ecce Tiberim*.

On approaching the town are some pretty walks handsomely planted, and at a small distance, the remains of some works of *Cromwel*, called *Oliver's* Mount.

PERTH is large, and in general well built; two of the streets are remarkably fine; in some of the

* Taus, *Taciti vit. Agr.*

lesser are yet a few wooden houses in the old style; but as they decay, the magistrates prohibit the re-building them in the old way. There is but one parish, which has two churches, besides meetings for separatists, who are very numerous. One church, which belonged to a monastery, is very antient: not a vestige of the last is now to be seen; for the disciples of that rough apostle *Knox* made a general desolation of every ædifice that had given shelter to the worshippers of the church of *Rome:* it being one of his maxims, to pull down the nests, and the rooks would fly away.

The flourishing state of *Perth* is owing to two accidents: the first, that of numbers of *Cromwel*'s wounded officers and soldiers chusing to reside here, after he left the kingdom, who introduced a spirit of industry among the people: the other cause was the long continuance of the Earl of *Mar*'s army here in 1715, which occasioned vast sums of money being spent in the place: but this town, as well as all *Scotland*, dates its prosperity from the year 1745, the government of this part of *Great Britain* having never been settled till a little after that time. The rebellion was a disorder violent in its operation, but salutary in its effects.

Trade. The trade of *Perth* is considerable: it exports annually one hundred and fifty thousand pounds worth of linnen, ten thousand of wheat and barley, and about the same in cured salmon. That fish is taken there in vast abundance; three thousand have been caught in one morning, weighing, one with another, sixteen pounds; the whole capture, forty-eight thousand pounds. The fishery begins at St. *Andrew*'s

Andrew's Day, and ends *August* 26th, old style. The rents of the fisheries amount to three thousand pounds *per annum*.

I was informed that smelts come up this river in *May* and *June*.

There has been in these parts a very great fishery of pearl, got out of the fresh-water muscles. From the year 1761 to 1764, 10,000 l. worth were sent to *London*, and sold from 10 s. to 1 l. 16 s. per ounce. I was told that a pearl has been taken there that weighed 33 grains; but this fishery is at present exhausted, from the avarice of the undertakers: it once extended as far as *Lough-Tay*.

Pearl.

Gowrie House is shewn to all strangers; formerly the property and residence of the Earl of *Gowrie*, whose tragical end and mysterious conspiracy (if conspiracy there was) are still fresh in the minds of the people of *Perth*. At present the house is occupied by some companies of artillery. I was shewn the staircase where the unhappy nobleman was killed, the window the frighted monarch *James* roared out of, and that he escaped through, when he was saved from the fury of the populace, by Baily *Roy*, a friend of *Gowrie*'s, who was extremely beloved in the town.

Gowrie conspiracy.

From the little traditions preserved in the palace, it seems as if *Gowrie* had not the least intent of murthering the King: on the day his Majesty came to *Perth*, the Earl was engaged to a wedding-dinner with the Dean of Guild: when the account of the king's design reached him he changed color, on being taken so unprovided; but the Dean forced him to accept the nuptial feast, which was sent over to the Earl's house.

When the king fled he passed by the seat of Sir *William Moncrief*, near *Ern-bridge*, who happening to be walking out at that time, heard from the mouth of his intrepid Majesty the whole relation; but the Knight found it so marvellous and so disjointed, as plainly to tell the King, *that if it was a true story, it was a very strange one.*

Gowrie was a most accomplished gentleman: after he had finished his studies he held the Professor of Philosophy's chair for two years, in one of the *Italian* universities.

Cross the *Tay* on a temporary bridge; the stone bridge, which is to consist of nine arches, being at this time unfinished; the largest arch is seventy-six feet wide; when complete, it promises to be a most magnificent structure. The river here is very violent, and admits of scarce any navigation above; but ships of eighty or ninety tuns come as far as the town.

Scone. *Scone* lies about a mile and half higher up, on the east bank of the river. There was once here an abby of great antiquity*, which was burnt by the reforming zealots of *Dundee*. The present palace was begun by Earl *Gowrie*; but, on his death, being granted by *James* VI. to his favorite, S.r *David Murray*, of *Gospatrie*, was completed by him; who, in gratitude to the king, has, in several parts of the house, put up the royal arms. The house is built round two courts; the dining-room is large and handsome, has an antient but magnificent chimney-piece, the king's arms, with this motto,

Nobis hæc invicta miserunt centum sex Proavi.

---

* Founded by *Alexander* I. 1114, for canons regular of St. *Augustine*.

Beneath

Beneath are the *Murray* arms. In the drawing-room is some good old tapestry, with an excellent figure of *Mercury*. In a small bed-chamber is a medly scripture-piece in needle-work, with a border of animals, pretty well done; the work of *Mary Stuart*, during her confinement in *Loch-leven* castle: but the house in general is in a manner unfurnished.

The gallery is about a hundred and fifty-five feet long; the top arched, divided into compartments, filled with paintings, in water colors, of different sorts of huntings; and that *Nimrod*, *James* VI. and his train, appear in every piece.

Till the destruction of the abby, the kings of *Scotland* were crowned here, sitting in the famous wooden chair, which *Edward* I. transported to *Westminster-Abby*, much to the mortification of the *Scots*, who esteemed it as their palladium. *Charles* II. before the battle of *Worcester*, was crowned in the present chapel. The old Pretender resided at *Scone* for a considerable time in 1715, and his son made it a visit in 1745.

Re-passed the *Tay* at *Bullion*'s Boat; visited the field of *Loncarty*, celebrated for the great victory* obtained by the *Scots* over the *Danes*, by means of the gallant peasant *Hay* and his two sons, who, with no other weapons than the yokes which they snatched from their oxen then at plough, first put a stop to the flight of their countrymen, and afterwards led them on to conquest. The noble family of *Hay* are descended from this rustic hero, and in memory of their action, bear for their arms the instrument

Loncarty.

* In the time of *Kenneth*, who began his reign in 976.

of their victory, with the allusive motto of *Sub jugo*. There are on the spot several *tumuli*, in which are frequently found bones deposited in loose stones, disposed in form of a coffin. Not remote is a spot which supplied me with far more agreeable ideas; a tract of ground, which in 1732 was a meer bog, but now converted into good meadows, and about fifty acres covered with linnen; several other parts with buildings, and all the apparatus of the linnen manufacture, extremely curious and worth seeing, carried on by the industrious family of the *Sandimans*, who annually make four hundred thousand yards of linnen.

The country is good, full of barley, oats, and flax in abundance; but after a few miles travelling, is succeeded by a black heath: ride through a beautifull plantation of pines, and after descending an easy slope the plain beneath suddenly contracts itself into a narrow glen: the prospect before me strongly marked the entrance into the *Highlands*, the hills that bounded it on each side being lofty

Birnam Wood. and rude. On the left was *Birnam* Wood, which seems never to have recovered the march its an-

Dunsinane. cestors made to *Dunsinane*: I was shewn at a great distance a high ridge of hills, where some remains of that famous fortress * (*Macbeth*'s castle) are said yet to exist.

The pass into the *Highlands* is awefully magnificent; high, craggy, and often naked mountains present themselves to view, approach very near each other, and in many parts are fringed with wood, overhanging and darkening the *Tay*, that rolls with great rapidity beneath. After some advance

vance in this hollow, a moſt beautifull knowl, covered with pines, appears full in view; and ſoon
after, the town of *Dunkeld*, ſeated under and en- *Dunkeld.*
vironed by crags, partly naked, partly wooded,
with ſummits of a vaſt height. Lay at *Inver*, a
good inn, on the weſt ſide of the river.

Croſſed it in a boat, attended by a tame ſwan, JULY 28.
which was perpetually folliciting our favours by putting its neck over the ſides of the ferry-boat. Land
in the Duke of *Athol*'s gardens, which are extremely
pleaſing, waſhed by the river, and commanding
from different parts of the walks the moſt beautifull
and pictureſque views of wild and gloomy nature
that can be conceived. Trees of all kinds grow
here extremely well; and even ſo ſouthern a ſhrub
as *Portugal* laurel flouriſhes greatly. In the gardens
are the ruins of the cathedral, once a magnificent
ædifice, as appears by the beautifull round pillars
ſtill ſtanding; but the choir is preſerved, and at
preſent uſed as a church. In the burial-place of
the family is a large monument of the Marquis of
Athol, hung with the arms of the numerous con-
nections of the family. In another part is a tomb
of an old biſhop.

On the other ſide the river is a pleaſing walk
along the banks of the water of *Bran**, a great and
rapid torrent, full of immenſe ſtones. On a rock
at the end of the walk is a neat building, impending over a moſt horrible chaſm, into which the
river precipitates itſelf with great noiſe and fury
from a conſiderable height. The windows of the
pavillion are formed of painted glaſs; ſome of the

* Rivers in *Scotland* are very frequently called *waters*.

panes

panes are red, which makes the water resemble a fiery cataract. About a mile further is another *rumbling brig*, like, but inferior in grandeur, to that near *Kinross*.

The town of *Dunkeld* is small, and has a small linnen manufacture. Much company resorts here, in the summer months, for the benefit of drinking goats milk and whey: I was informed here, that those animals will eat serpents; as it is well known that stags do.

After a ride of two miles along a narrow strait, amidst trees, and often in sight of the *Tay*, was driven by rain into a fisherman's hut, who entertained me with an account of his business: said he paid ten pounds *per ann.* for the liberty of two or three miles of the river; sold the first fish of the season at three-pence a pound; after that, got three shillings *per* fish. The houses in these parts began to be covered with broom, which lasts three or four years: their insides mean, and very scantily furnished; but the owners civil, sensible, and of the quickest apprehensions.

The strait now widens into a vale plentifull in oats, barley and flax, and well peopled: on the right is the junction of the *Tay* and the *Tumel*: the channels of these rivers are wide, full of gravel, the mark of their devastation during floods. Due north is the road to *Blair* and *Fort Augustus*, through the noted pass of *Killicrankie*; turn to the left; ride opposite to *Castle Menzies*: reach *Taymouth*, the seat of the Earl of *Breadalbane*.

Taymouth

Taymouth* lies in a vale scarce a mile broad, very fertile, bounded on each side by high mountains finely planted. Those on the south are covered with trees, or with corn fields, far up their sides. The hills on the north are planted with pines and other trees, and vastly steep, and have a very *alpine* look; but particularly resemble the great slope opposite the *grande Chartreuse* in *Dauphiné*. His Lordship's policy ** surrounds the house, which stands in the park, and is one of the few in which fallow deer are seen.

The ground is in remarkable fine order, owing to his Lordship's assiduity in clearing it from stones, with which it was once covered. A *Blaster* was in constant employ to blast the great stones with gunpowder; for, by reason of their size, there was no other method of removing them.

The *Berceau* walk is very magnificent, composed of great trees, forming a fine *gothic* arch; and probably that species of architecture owed its origin to such vaulted shades. The walk on the bank of the *Tay* is fifty feet wide, and two and twenty hundred yards long; but is to be continued as far as the junction of the *Tay* and the *Lion*, which is about as far more. The first runs on the sides of the walk with great rapidity, is clear, but not colorless, for its pellucidness is like that of brown crystal; as is the case with most of the rivers of *Scotland*, which receive their tinge from the bogs.

---

* Its name, in old maps, is *Balloch*; i. e. the mouth of the loch.
** This word here signifies improvements, or demesne: when used by a merchant, or tradesman, signifies their warehouses, shops, and the like.

The *Tay* has here a wooden bridge two hundred feet long, leading to a white seat on the side of the opposite hill, commanding a fine view up and down *Straith-Tay*. The rich meadows beneath, the winding of the river, the beginning of *Lough-Tay*, the discharge of the river out of it, the neat village and church of *Kenmor*, form a most pleasing and magnificent prospect.

Lough-Tay. The view from the temple of *Venus* is that of the lake, with a nearer sight of the church and village, and the discharge of the river. The lake is about a mile broad, and about fifteen long, bounded on each side by lofty mountains; makes three great bends, which adds to its beauty. Those on the south are well planted, and finely cultivated high up; interspersed with the habitations of the *Highlanders*, not singly, but in small groupes, as if they loved society or clanship: they are very small, mean, and without windows or chimnies, and are the disgrace of *North Britain*, as its lakes and rivers are its glory. *Lough-Tay* is, in many places, a hundred fathoms deep, and within as many yards of the shore, fifty-four.

Till the present year, this lake was supposed to be as incapable of freezing as *Lough-Ness*, *Lough-Earn*, and *Lough-Each*; tho' *Lough-Raynac*, and even *Lough-Fine*, an arm of the sea, often does. But in *March* last, so rigorous and uncommon was the cold, that about the 20th of that month this vast body of water was frozen over, in one part, from side to side, in the space of one night; and so strong was the ice, as greatly to damage a boat which was caught in it.

Lough-

Lough-Tay abounds with Pike, Perch, Eels, Salmon and Trout; of the laſt, ſome have been taken that weighed above thirty pounds. Of theſe ſpecies, the *Highlanders* abhor Eels, and alſo Lampries, fancying, from the form, that they are too nearly related to Serpents *.

The north ſide is leſs wooded, but more cultivated. The vaſt hill of *Laurs*, with beds of ſnow on it, through great part of the year, riſes above the reſt, and the ſtill loftier mountain of *Benmor* cloſes the view far beyond the end of the lake. All this country abounds with game, ſuch as Grous, Ptarmigans **, Stags, and a peculiar ſpecies of Hare, which is found only on the ſummits of the higheſt hills, and never mixes with the common kind, which is frequent enough in the vales †. This ſpecies is grey in ſummer, white in winter; is ſmaller than the brown Hare, and more delicate meat. White Hare.

The *Ptarmigans* inhabit the very ſummits of the higheſt mountains, amidſt the rocks, perching among the grey ſtones, and during ſummer are ſcarce to be diſtinguiſhed from them, by reaſon of their color. They ſeldom take long flights, but fly about like pigeons; are ſilly birds, and ſo tame as to ſuffer a ſtone to be flung at them without riſing. It is not neceſſary to have a dog to find them. They taſte ſo like a Grous, as to be ſcarce Ptarmigan.

---

* I was informed, that at the head of the lake are the remains of an old caſtle, called *Finlarig*, belonging to Lord *Breadalbane*, and of a park finely wooded with old oaks, cheſnuts, and other timber.

** *Br. Zool. illuſtr.* 21. *tab.* xiii.

† The ſame, *p.* 40. *tab.* xlvii.

diſtinguiſhable.

distinguishable. During winter, their plumage, except a few feathers in the tail, are of a pure white, the color of the snow, in which they bury themselves in heaps, as a protection from the rigorous air.

Birds.   *Royston* Crows, called here Hooded Crows, and in the *Erse*, *Feanagh*, are very common, and reside here the whole year. They breed in the hills, in all sorts of trees; lay six eggs; have a shriller note than the common sort; are much more mischievous; pick out the eyes of lambs, and even of horses, when engaged in bogs; but, for want of other food, will eat cranberries, and other mountain berries.

Ring Ouzels breed among the hills, and in autumn descend in flocks to feed on the berries of the wicken trees.

Sea Eagles breed in ruined towers, but quit the country in winter; the black Eagles continue there the whole year.

It is very difficult to leave the environs of this delightfull place: and, before I go within doors, I must recall to mind the fine winding walks on the south side of the hills, the great beech sixteen feet in girth, the picturesque birch with its long streaming branches, the hermitage, the great cataracts adjacent, and the darksome chasm beneath. I must enjoy over again the view of the fine reach of the *Tay*, and its union with the broad water of the *Lion*: I must step down to view the druidical circles of stones, called in the *Erse*, *Tibberd*; and lastly, I

Tay-bridge.   must visit *Tay-bridge*, and, as far as my pen can contribute, extend the fame of our military countrymen,

trymen, who, among other works worthy of the *Romans*, founded this bridge, and left its history inscribed in these terms:

> Mirare
> viam hanc militarem
> Ultra *Romanos* terminos
> M. Passuum CCL. hac illac
> extensam;
> Tesquis et paludibus insultantem
> per Montes rupesque patefactam
> et indignanti TAVO
> ut cernis instratum,
> Opus hoc arduum suâ solertiâ
> Et decennali militum operâ,
> A. Ær. X^{næ} 1733. Posuit G. WADE
> Copiarum in SCOTIA Præfectus.
> Ecce quantum valeant
> Regis GEORGII II. Auspicia.

Taymouth is a large house, a castle modernized. The most remarkable part of its furniture is the works of the famous *Jameson**, the *Scotch Vandyk*, an eleve of this family. That singular performance of his, the genealogical picture, is in good preservation. Sir *Duncan Campbell*, Laird of *Lochon*, is placed recumbent at the foot of a tree, with a branch; on the right is a single head of his eldest son, the chief of the *Argyle* family; but on the

Jameson.

---

* Son of an architect at *Aberdeen*; studied under *Rubens*, at *Antwerp*. *Charles* I. sat to him, and presented him with a diamond ring. He always drew himself with his hat on. His prices were 20l. *Scots*, or 1l. 13s. 4d. *English*, *per* head: was born in 1586; died at *Edinburgh*, 1644. For a further account, consult Mr. *Walpole's* Anecdotes of Painting.'

G various

various ramifications, are the names of his defcendents, and along the body of the tree are nine fmall heads, in oval frames, with the names on the margins, all done with great neatnefs: the fecond fon was firft of the houfe of *Breadalbane*, which branched from the other about four hundred years ago. In a corner is infcribed, *The Geneologie of the houfe of* Glenorquhie *Quhairof is defcendit fundrie nobil & worthie houfes.* Jamefon *faciebat.* 1635. Its fize is eight feet by five. In the fame room are about twenty heads of perfons of the family; among others, that of a lady, fo very ugly, that a wag, on feeing it, with lifted hands pronounced, that fhe was *fearfully and wonderfully made*. There are in the fame houfe feveral heads by *Jamefon*; but many of them unfortunately fpoiled in the mending.

In the library is a fmall book, called, from the binding, the *black book*, with fome beautifull drawings in it, on vellum, of the *Breadalbane* family, in water-colors. In the firft page is old Sir *Duncan*, between two other figures; then follow feveral chiefs of the family, among whom is Sir *Colin*, Knight of *Rhodes*, who died 1480, aged 80. At the end is a manufcript hiftory of the family, ending, I think, in 1633.

JULY 30. Went to divine fervice at *Kinmore* * church, which, with the village, was re-built, in the neateft manner, by the prefent Lord *Breadalbane*: they ftand beautifully on a fmall headland, projecting into the lake. His Lordfhip permits the inhabitants to live rent-free, on condition they exercife fome trade, and keep their houfes clean: fo that,

* Or the Great Head.

by

IN SCOTLAND.

by these terms, he not only saves the expence of sending, on every trifling occasion, to *Perth* or *Crief*, but has got some as good workmen, in common trades, as any in his Majesty's dominions. The congregation was numerous, decent, attentive, still; well and neatly clad, and not a ragged or slovenly person among them. There were two services, one in *English*, the other in *Erse*. After the first, numbers of people, of both sexes, went out of church, and seating themselves in the church-yard, made, in their motly habits, a gay and picturesque appearance. The devotion of the common people, on the usual days of worship, is as much to be admired, as their conduct at the sacrament is to be censured. It is celebrated but once in a year*; when there are, in some places, three thousand communicants, and as many idle spectators. Of the first, as many as possible crowd each side of a long table, and the elements are rudely shoven from one to another; and in some places, before the day is at an end, fighting and other indecencies ensue. It is often made a season for debauchery; so, to this day, *Jack* cannot be persuaded to eat his meat like a christian †.

Every Sunday a collection is made for the sick or necessitous; for poor's rates are unknown in every country parish in *Scotland*. Notwithstanding the common people are but just rouzed from their native indolence, very few beggars are seen in *North Britain*: either they are full masters of the lesson of being content with a very little; or, what is more probable, they are possessed of a spirit that will

* Formerly the sacrament was administered but once in two years.
† *Tale of a Tub.*

struggle hard with necessity before it will bend to the asking of alms.

Visited a pretty little island in *Loch-Tay*, tufted with trees, and not far from the shore: on it are the ruins of a priory dependent on that at *Scone*, founded in 1122, by *Alexander* the First, in which were deposited the remains of his Queen *Sybilla*, natural daughter to *Henry* I. it was founded by *Alexander* to have the prayers of the Monks for the repose of his soul, and that of his royal consort *. To this island the *Campbells* retreated, during the successes of the Marquiss of *Montrose*, where they defended themselves against that hero, which was one cause of his violent resentment against the whole name.

July 31. Rode to *Glen-lion*; went by the side of the river † that gives name to it. It has now lost its antient title of *Duie*, or *Black*, given it on account of a great battle between the *Mackays* and the *Macgregors*; after which, the conquerors are said to have stained the water with red, by washing in it their bloody swords and spears. On the right is a rocky hill, called *Shi-hallen*, or the *Paps*. Enter *Glen-lion* through a strait pass: the vale is narrow, but fertile; the banks of the river steep, rocky, and wooded; through which appear the rapid water of the *Lion*. On the north is a round fortress, on the top of the hill; to which, in old times, the natives retreated, on any invasion. A little farther, on a plain, is a small *Roman* camp ‡, called by the High-

* As appears from a grant made by that Monarch of the isle in *Loch-Tay*, Ut Ecclesia Dei ibi pro me et pro Anima Sybillæ Reginæ ibi defunctæ fabricetur, &c.

† This river freezes; but the *Tay*, which receives it, never does.

‡ It possibly might have been made during the expedition of *Severus*, who penetrated to the extremity of this island: it was the most northern work of the *Romans* I had any intelligence of.

landers

landers *Fortingal,* or the Fort of the Strangers: themselves they style *Na-fian,* or descendents of *Fingal.* In *Fortingal* church are the remains of a prodigious yew-tree, whose ruins measured fifty-six feet and a half in circumference. *Great yew.*

Saw at a gentleman's house in *Glen-lion,* a curious walking-staff, belonging to one of his ancestors: it was iron cased in leather, five feet long; at the top a neat pair of extended wings, like a *caduceus*; but, on being shook, a poniard, two feet nine inches long, darted out.

He also favoured me with the sight of a very antient brotche, which the Highlanders use, like the *fibula* of the *Romans,* to fasten their vest: it is made of silver, is round, with a bar cross the middle, from whence are two tongues to fasten the folds of the garments: one side is studded with pearl, or coarse gems, in a very rude manner; on the other, are certain letters I could not make out.

Return south, and come at once in sight of *Loch-Tay.* The day being very fine and calm, the whole scene was most beautifully repeated in the water. I must not omit that on the north side of this lake is a most excellent road, which runs the whole length of it, leading to *Teindrum* and *Inveraray,* in *Argyleshire,* and is the route which travellers must take, who make what I call the *petit tour** of *Scotland.* This whole road was made at the

---

* Which comprehends the route I have described; adding to it, from *Taymouth,* along the road, on the side of the lake, to *Killin,* 16 miles; from thence to *Teindrum,* 20; *Glenorchie,* 12; *Inveraray,* 16; *Lufs,* on the banks of *Loch-lomond,* 30; *Dunbarton,* 12; *Glasgow,* 15; *Sterling,* 31; *Edinburgh,* by *Hopetoun*-House, 35; a tract unparalleled, for the variety, and frequency of fine and magnificent scenery.

sole expence of the present Lord *Breadalbane*; who, to facilitate the travelling, also erected thirty-two stone-bridges over the torrents that rush from the mountains into the lake. They will find the whole country excell in roads, partly military, partly done by statute labor, and much by the munificence of the great men.

Roads.

I was informed, that Lord *Breadalbane*'s estate was so extensive that he could ride a hundred miles an end on it, even as far as the West Sea, where he has also some islands. These great properties are divided into districts, called *Officiaries*: a ground officer presides over each, and has three, four, or five hundred men under his care: he superintends the duties due from each to their Lord, such as fetching peat, bringing coal from *Perth*, &c. which they do, at their own expence, on horses backs, travelling in strings, the tail of one horse being fastened by a cord, which reaches to the head of the next: the horses are little, and generally white or grey; and as the farms are very small, it is common for four people to keep a plough between them, each furnishing a horse, and this is called a horse gang.

The north side of *Loch-Tay* is very populous; for in sixteen square miles are seventeen hundred and eighty-six souls: on the other side, about twelve hundred. The country, within these thirty years, is grown very industrious, and manufactures a great deal of thread. They spin with rocks *, which they do while they attend their cattle on the hills;

* Their Lord gives among them annually a great number of spinning-wheels.

and,

and, at the three or four fairs in the year, held at *Taymouth*, about sixteen hundred pounds worth of yarn is sold out of *Breadalbane* only.

Much of this may be owing to the good sense and humanity of the chieftain; but much again is owing to the abolition of the feudal tenures, or vassalage; for before that was effected (which was done by the influence of a Chancellor *, whose memory *Scotland* gratefully adores for that service) the Strong oppressed the Weak, the Rich the Poor. Courts indeed were held, and juries called; but juries of vassals, too dependent and too timid to be relied on for the execution of true justice.

Leave *Taymouth*; ford the *Lion*, and ride above it thro' some woods: on the left bursts out a fine cascade, in a deep hollow, covered with trees: at a small distance to the west is *Castle-Garth*, a small castle seated like castle *Campbell*, between two deep glens: keep ascending a steep hill, but the corn country continues for a while: the scene then changes for a wild, black, and mountainous heath: descend into *Raynach*, a meadowy plain, tolerably fertile: the lake of the same name extends from East to West; is about eleven miles long, and one broad: the Northern banks appeared very barren; part of the Southern finely covered with a forest of pine and birch, the first natural woods I had seen of pines: rode a good way into it, but observed no trees of any size, except a birch sixteen feet in circumference: the ground beneath the trees is co-

Aug. 1.

Raynach.

Pine Forest.

---

* Earl of *Hardwick*.

vered with heath, bilberies, and dwarf arbutus, whose glossy leaves make a pretty appearance: this place gives shelter to black game, and is at present the farthest Southern resort of roes; for very few ever straggle lower down: near these woods is a saw-mill, which brings in about 180l. *per ann.* the deal, which is the red sort, is sold in plank to different parts of the country, carried on horses backs, for the trees are now grown so scarce as not to admit of exportation*.

The lake affords no other fish than trouts, and bull trouts; the last, as I was informed, are sometimes taken of the length of four feet and a half: many water fowl breed in the birns or little streams that trickle into the lake; among others different sort of grebes, and divers: I was told of one which the inhabitants call *Turuvachal*, that makes a great noise before storms, and by their description seems to be the *Fluder* of *Gesner*.

The Poet Struan.
This country was once the property of *Robertson*, of *Struan*, who had been in the rebellion of 1715; had his estate restored, but in 1745 rebelling a second time, the country was burnt, and the estate annexed to the crown: he returned a few years after, and died as he lived, a most abandoned sot; notwithstanding which he had a genius for poetry, and left behind him a volume of elegies, and other pieces, in some of which he elegantly laments the ravages of war among his vassals, and the loss of his favourite scenes, and in particular his fountain *Argentine*.

* Some Pot-Ash is also made of the Birch Wood:

IN SCOTLAND.

The country is perfectly highland; and in spite of the intercourse this and the neighboring parts have of late years had with the rest of the world, it still retains some of its antient customs and superstitions; they decline daily, but least their memory should be lost, I shall mention several that are still practised, or but very lately disused in the tract I had passed over. Such a record will have this advantage when the follies are quite extinct, in teaching the unshackled and enlightened mind the difference between the pure ceremonies of religion, and the wild and anile flights of superstition.

Superstitions.

The belief in spectres still exists; of which I had a remarkable proof while I was in the county of *Breadalbane*: a poor visionary, who had been working in his cabbage-garden, imagined that he was raised suddenly into the air, and conveyed over a wall into an adjacent corn-field; that he found himself surrounded by a crowd of men and women, many of whom he knew to have been dead some years, and who appeared to him skimming over the tops of the unbended corn, and mingling together like bees going to hive: that they spoke an unknown language, and with a hollow sound: that they very roughly pushed him to and fro; but on his uttering the name of God, all vanished but a female sprite, who seizing him by the shoulder, obliged him to promise an assignation, at that very hour, that day sevenight: that he then found that his hair was all tied in double knots, and that he had almost lost the use of his speech: that he kept his word with the spectre, whom he soon saw come floating thro' the air towards him: that he spoke to her, but she told

Spectres.

told him at that time she was in too much haste to attend to him, but bid him go away, and no harm should befall him; and so the affair rested when I left the country. But it is incredible the mischief these *Ægri Somnia* did in the neighborhood: the friends and relation of the deceased, whom the old Dreamer had named, were in the utmost anxiety at finding them in such bad company in the other world: the almost extinct belief of the old idle tales began again to gain ground, and the good minister will have many a weary discourse and exhortation before he can eradicate the absurd ideas this idle story has revived.

In this part of the country the notion of witchcraft is quite lost: it was observed to cease almost immediately on the repeal of the witch act; a proof what a dangerous instrument it was in the hands of the vindictive, or of the credulous.

Unlucky day. Among the superstitious customs these are the most singular. A Highlander never begins any thing of consequence on the day of the week on which the 3d of *May* falls, which he styles *Lagh Sheachanna na bleanagh*, or the dismal day.

Bel-tein. On the 1st of *May*, the herdsmen of every village hold their *Bel-tein**, a rural sacrifice: they cut a square trench on the ground, leaving the turf in the middle; on that they make a fire of wood, on which they dress a large caudle of eggs, butter, oatmeal and milk; and bring, besides the ingredients of the caudle, plenty of beer and whisky;

---

* My account of this, and every other ceremony mentioned in this Journal, was communicated to me by gentlemen resident on the spot where they were performed.

for

for each of the company must contribute something. The rites begin with spilling some of the caudle on the ground, by way of libation : on that, every one takes a cake of oatmeal, upon which are raised nine square knobs, each dedicated to some particular being, the supposed preserver of their flocks and herds, or to some particular animal, the real destroyer of them : each person then turns his face to the fire, breaks off a knob, and flinging it over his shoulders, says, *This I give to thee, preserve thou my horses; this to thee, preserve thou my sheep;* and so on. After that, they use the same ceremony to the noxious animals: *This I give to thee, O Fox! spare thou my lambs; this to thee, O hooded Crow! this to thee, O Eagle!*

When the ceremony is over they dine on the caudle; and after the feast is finished, what is left is hid by two persons deputed for that purpose; but on the next *Sunday* they re-assemble, and finish the reliques of the first entertainment *.

On the death of a Highlander, the corps being stretched on a board, and covered with a coarse

Funeral customs.

---

* A custom, favoring of the *Scotch Bel-tein*, prevails in *Gloucestershire*, particularly about *Newent* and the neighboring parishes, on the twelfth day, or on the *Epiphany*, in the evening: all the servants of every particular farmer assemble together in one of the fields that has been sown with wheat; on the border of which, in the most conspicuous or most elevated place, they make twelve fires of straw, in a row; around one of which, made larger than the rest, they drink a chearful glass of cyder to their master's health, success to the future harvest, and then returning home they feast on cakes, made of carraways, &c. soak'd in cyder, which they claim as a reward for their past labors in sowing the grain. This seems to resemble a custom of the antient *Danes*, who, in their addresses to their rural deities, emptied, on every invocation, a cup in honor of them. NIORDI *et* FREJÆ *memoriæ poculis recolebatur, annua ut ipsis contingeret felicitas, frugumque et reliquæ annonæ uberrimus proventus.* Worm. Monum. Dan. lib. i. *p.* 28.

linnen

linnen wrapper, the friends lay on the breast of the deceased a wooden platter, containing a small quantity of salt and earth, separate and unmixed; the earth, an emblem of the corruptible body; the salt, an emblem of the immortal spirit. All fire is extinguished where a corps is kept; and it is reckoned so ominous, for a dog or cat to pass over it, that the poor animal is killed without mercy.

Late-wake. The *Late-wake* is a ceremony used at funerals: the evening after the death of any person, the relations and friends of the deceased meet at the house, attended by bagpipe or fiddle; the nearest of kin, be it wife, son, or daughter, opens a melancholy ball, dancing and greeting; *i. e.* crying violently at the same time; and this continues till day-light; but with such gambols and frolicks, among the younger part of the company, that the loss which occasioned them is often more than supplied by the consequences of that night. If the corps remains unburied for two nights the same rites are renewed. Thus, *Scythian*-like, they rejoice at the deliverance of their friends out of this life of misery.

Coranich. The *Coranich*, or singing at funerals, is still in use in some places: the songs are generally in praise of the deceased; or a recital of the valiant deeds of him, or ancestors. I had not the fortune to be present at any in *North Britain*, but formerly assisted at one in the south of *Ireland*, where it was performed in the fullness of horror. The cries are called by the *Irish* the 'Ulogohne and Hullulu, two words extremely expressive of the sound uttered on these occasions, and being of *Celtic* stock, Etymologists would swear to be the origin of the ἐλολυγων

of

IN SCOTLAND.

of the *Greeks*, and *Ululatus* of the *Latins*. *Virgil* is very fond of using the last, whenever any of his females are distressed; as are others of the *Roman Poets*, and generally on occasions similar to this.

It was my fortune to arrive at a certain town in *Kerry*, at the time that a person of some distinction departed this life; my curiosity led me to the house, where the funeral seemed conducted in the purest classical form.

Quodcunque aspicerem luctus gemitusque sonabant,
Formaque non taciti funeris intùs erat.

In short, the *conclamatio* was set up by the friends in the same manner as *Virgil* describes that consequential of *Dido*'s death.

Lamentis gemituque et fœmines ululatu
Tecta fremunt.

Immediately after this followed another ceremony, fully described by *Cambden*, in his account of the manners of the antient *Irish*; the earnest expostulations and reproaches given to the deceased, for quitting this world, where she enjoyed so many blessings, so good a husband, such fine children. This custom is of great antiquity, for *Euryalus*'s mother makes the same pathetic address to her dead son.

Tune illa senectæ
Sera meæ requies? potuisti relinquere solam
Crudelis?

But when the time approached for carrying out the corps the cry was redoubled.

Tremulis ululatibus æthera complent.

A numerous band of females waiting in the outer court, to attend the herse, and to pay (in chorus) the

the last tribute of their voices. The habit of this sorrowing train, and the neglect of their persons, were admirably suited to the occasion: their robes were black, and flowing, resembling the antient *Palla*; their hair long, and disheveled: I might say,

Vidi egomet nigra succinctam vadere palla
Canidiam; *pedibus nudis, passoque capillo*
Cum Sagana mojore ululantem.

Among these mourners were dispersed the females, who sung the praises of the deceased, and were in the place of the *Mulieres Præficæ* of the *Romans*, and, like them, were a mercenary tribe. I could not but observe that they over-did their parts, as *Horace* acquaints us the mourners of his days did.

Ut qui conducti plorant in funera, dicunt
Et faciunt prope plura dolentibus ex animo.

The corps was carried slowly along the verge of a most beautifull lake, the *ululatus* was continued, and the whole procession ended among the venerable ruins of an old abby. But to return to *North Britain*.

Midwives give new-born babes a small spoonfull of earth and whisky, as the first food they taste.

Before women bake their bannocks, or oatmeal cakes, they make a cross on the last.

Fairies. The notion of second-sight still prevales in a few places: as does the belief of Fairies; and children are watched till the christening is over, least they should be stole, or changed.

Elf-shots, *i. e.* the stone arrow heads of the old inhabitants of this island, are supposed to be weapons shot by Fairies at cattle, to which are attributed

buted any disorders they have: in order to effect a cure, the cow is to be touched by an elf-shot, or made to drink the water in which one has been dipped. The same virtue is said to be found in the crystal gems *, and in the adder-stone, our *Gleix Raidr*; and it is also believed that good fortune must attend the owner; so, for that reason, the first is called *Clach Bhouaigh*, or the happy stone. Captain *Archibald Campbell* shewed me one, a spheroid set in silver, which people came for the use of above a hundred miles, and brought the water it was to be dipt in with them; for without that, in human cases, it was believed to have no effect.

Left *Carrie*, the house of Mr. *Campbell*, factor for the *Struan* estate, where I had a very hospitable reception the preceding night. Went due east; passed over a bridge cross the *Tumel*, which discharges itself out of *Lough Raynach*. Not far off were some neat small houses, inhabited by veteran soldiers, who were settled here after the peace of 1748; had land, and three pounds in money given, and nine pounds lent, to begin the world with. In some few places this plan succeeded; but in general, was frustrated by the dissipation of these new colonists, who could by no means relish an industrious life; but as soon as the money was spent, which seldom lasted long, left their tenements to be possessed by the next comer.

Aug. 2.

Saw a stamping-mill, calculated to reduce limestone to a fine power, in order to save the expence of burning, for manure. The stampers beat it into

---

* *Woodward's* Method of Fossils.

small

small pieces in a trough, which a stream of water passed through, carrying off the fine parts into a proper receptacle, the gross ones being stopped by a grate. I did not find that this project answered; but was told, that the benefit the land was to receive from it would not appear till the third year.

On going up a steep hill have a fine view of the lake. Where the mountains almost close, is *Mount Alexander*, where *Struan* once resided, and which he called his hermitage: it is a most romantic situation, prettily wooded, impending over a fine bason, formed by the *Tumel*, in a deep hollow beneath. At the bottom of this hill is *Argentine*, a little fountain; to which he gave that name from the silvery *mica* it flings up: near this are several rude but beautifull walks amidst the rocks and trees, among which, in clifts and chasms, I was shewn the hard bed of the poor poet, when his disloyalty had made it penal for him to shew his head. Near this the rocks almost meet, and the river rushes with vast violence between. Some outlawed *M'Gregors* were once surprized on the opposite precipice, and all killed; one, who made a desperate leap upon a stone in the middle of the water, and another to the opposite side, had the hard fate to be shot in climbing the opposite rocks.

Argentine.

A mile lower are the falls of the *Tumel*: I have seen higher; but, except that of the *Rhine*, never saw one with more water.

Ascend a very steep and high hill through a great birch wood; a most picturesque scene, from the pendent form of the boughs waving with the wind from the bottom to the utmost summits of the mountain.

mountain. On attaining the top, had a view of a beautifull little *Straith*, fertile, and prettily wooded, with the river in the middle, forming numbers of quick meanders; then suddenly swelling into a lake, that fills the vale from side to side; is about three miles long, and retains the name of the river. After riding along a black moor, in sight of vast mountains, arrive at

Blair *, or *Athol-*House, seated on an eminence above a plain, watered by the *Carrie*, an outrageous stream, whose ravages have greatly deformed the vally, by the vast beds of gravel which it has left behind. The house was once fortified, and held a siege against the Rebels in 1746; but at present it is much reduced in height, and the inside highly finished by the noble owner. The most singular piece of furniture is a chest of drawers made of broom, most elegantly striped in veins of white and brown. This plant grows to a great size in *Scotland*, and furnishes pieces of the breadth of six inches. Great broom trees.

Near the house is a fine walk surrounding a very deep glen finely wooded, but deficient in water at the bottom; but on the side of the walk on the rock is a small crystalline fountain, inhabited at that time by a pair of *Naiads*, in form of golden fish. In a spruce fir was a hang-nest of some unknown bird, suspended at the four corners to the boughs; it was open at top, an inch and a half in diameter, and two deep; the sides and bottom thick, the materials moss, worsted, and birch bark, Hang-nest.

---

* Or the plain where a battle had been fought.

<small>Parr.</small> bark, lined with hair and feathers. The streams afford the *Parr*, a small species of Trout, seldom exceeding eight inches in length, marked on the sides with nine large bluish spots, and on the lateral line with small red ones *.

This country is very mountainous, has no natural woods except of birch; but the vast plantations that begin to cloath the hills will amply supply these defects. There is a great quantity of oats raised in this neighborhood, and numbers of black cattle reared, the resources of the exhausted parts of *South Britain*.

<small>Killicrankie.</small> Visit the pass of *Killicrankie*, about five miles south of *Blair*: near the northern entrance was fought the battle between the Viscount *Dundee* and General *Mackay*, in which the first was killed in the moment of victory. The pass is extremely narrow, between high mountains, with the *Carrie* running beneath in a deep, darksome, and rocky channel, over-hung with trees, forming a scene of horrible grandeur. The road through this strait is very fine, formed by the soldiery lent by the Government, who have sixpence *per* day from the country besides their pay. About a mile beyond the pass, Mr. *Robertson*'s, of *Faskally*, appears like fairy ground amidst these wild rocks, seated in a most beautifull meadow, watered by the river *Tumel*, surrounded with pretty hills finely wooded.

The Duke of *Athol*'s estate is very extensive, and the country populous: while vassalage existed, the chieftain could raise two or three thousand fighting men, and leave sufficient at home to take care of

<small>* Br. Zool. illustr.</small>

the

the ground. Therefores, or rather chases, (for they are quite naked,) are very extensive, and tend vast numbers of Stags, which range, at certain times of the year, in herds of two hundred. Some grow to a great size. I have seen one or one that weighed above seven stone, exclusive of head, entrails and skin. The hunting of these animals was formerly after the manner of an Eastern monarch. Thousands of vassals surrounded a great tract of country, and drove the Deer to the spot where the Chieftains were stationed, who shot them at their leisure. The magnificent chase, made by an Earl of Athol, that this place, for the amusement of James V. and the Queen-mother, is too remarkable to be omitted: it is always therefore given as described by Mr. Hector Boethius, who, in all probability, assisted at it.

" The Earl of Atholl, hearing of the King's " coming, made great provision for him in all " things pertaining to a prince, that he was as well " served and eased, with all such delicious things " that could be gotten at that time in Scotland, as " he had been in his own palace of Edinburgh. For I assure you, this Earl gart " make a curious palace, to the King, his Mo- " ther, and to the Ambassador, where was a shew wor- " thy to be seen, considering it was in a wilderness " . . . . green timber . . . . green bark the ground. The forests, or rather chases, (for they are quite naked) are very extensive, and feed vast numbers of Stags, which range, at certain times of the year, in herds of five hundred. Some grow to a great size: I have heard of one that weighed 18 stone, *Scots*, or 314 lb. exclusive of head, entrails and skin. The hunting of these animals was formerly after the manner of an *Eastern* monarch. Thousands of vassals surrounded a great tract of country, and drove the Deer to the spot where the Chieftains were stationed, who shot them at their leisure. The magnificent hunt, made by an Earl of *Athol*, near this place, for the amusement of *James* V. and the Queen-mother, is too remarkable to be omitted; the relation is therefore given as described by Sir *David Lindsay**, who, in all probability, assisted at it.

Great huntings.

"The Earl of *Athole*, hearing of the King's
"coming, made great provision for him in all
"things pertaining to a prince, that he was as well
"served and eased, with all things necessary to his
"estate, as he had been in his own palace of *Edinburgh*.
"For I heard say, this noble Earl gart
"make a curious palace to the King, to his Mo-
"ther, and to the Embassador, where they were
"so honourably eased and lodged as they had been
"in *England*, *France*, *Italy*, or *Spain*, concerning
"the time and equivalent, for their hunting and
"pastime; which was builded in the midst of a
"fair meadow, a fair palace of green timber,
"wind with green birks, that were green both

---

* *Hist. Scotland,* 266.

"under

" under and above, which was fashioned in four
" quarters, and in every quarter and nuik thereof
" a great round, as it had been a block-house,
" which was lofted and gested the space of three
" house height; the floors laid with green scarets
" spreats, medwarts and flowers, that no man
" knew whereon he zeid, but as he had been in a
" garden. Further, there were two great rounds
" in ilk side of the gate, and a great portculleis
" of tree, falling down with the manner of a bar-
" race, with a draw-bridge, and a great stank of
" water of sixteen foot deep, and thirty foot of
" breadth. And also this palace within was hung
" with fine tapestry and arrasses of silk, and lighted
" with fine glass windows in all airths; that this
" palace was as pleasantly decored, with all neces-
" saries pertaining to a prince, as it had been his
" own palace-royal at home. Further, this Earl
" gart make such provision for the King, and his
" Mother, and the Embassador, that they had all
" manner of meats, drinks, and delicates that were
" to be gotten, at that time, in all *Scotland*, either
" in burgh or land; that is to say, all kind of
" drink, as ale, beer, wine, both white and claret,
" *malvery, muskadel, Hippocras, aquavitæ*. Further,
" there was of meats, wheat-bread, main-bread
" and ginge-bread; with fleshes, beef, mutton,
" lamb, veal, venison, goose, grice, capon, coney,
" cran, swan, partridge, plover, duck, drake,
" brissel-cock and pawnies, black-cock and muir-
" fowl, cappercaillies: and also the stanks, that
" were round about the palace, were full of all
" delicate fishes, as salmonds, trouts, pearches,
                                            " pikes,

" pikes, eels, and all other kind of delicate fishes
" that could be gotten in fresh waters;—and all
" ready for the banket. Syne were there proper
" stewards, cunning baxters, excellent cooks and
" potingars, with confections and drugs for their
" deserts; and the halls and chambers were pre-
" pared with costly bedding, vessel and napery,
" according for a king, so that he wanted none of
" his orders more than he had been at home in his
" own palace. The King remained in this wilder-
" ness, at the hunting, the space of three days and
" three nights, and his company, as I have shewn.
" I heard men say, it cost the Earl of *Athole*, every
" day, in expences, a thousand pounds."

But hunting meetings, among the great men, were often the preludes to rebellion; for under that pretence they collected great bodies of men without suspicion, which at length occasioned an act of parlement prohibiting such dangerous assemblies.

Set out for the county of *Aberdeen*; ride eastward over a hill into *Glen-Tilt*, famous in old times for producing the most hardy warriors; is a narrow glen, several miles in length, bounded on each side by mountains of an amazing height; on the south is the great hill of *Ben y glo*, whose base is thirty-five miles in circumference, and whose summit towers far above the others. The sides of many of these mountains are covered with fine verdure, and are excellent sheep-walks; but entirely woodless. The road is the most dangerous and the most horrible I ever travelled; a narrow path, so rugged that our horses often were obliged to cross their

Aug. 3.
Glen-Tilt.

legs, in order to pick a secure place for their feet; while, at a considerable and precipitous depth beneath, roared a black torrent, rolling through a bed of rock, solid in every part but where the *Tilt* had worn its antient way. Salmon force their passage even as high as this dreary stream, in spite of the distance from the sea, and the difficulties they have to encounter.

Sheelins.   Ascend a steep hill, on the top of which we refreshed ourselves with some goats whey, at a *Sheelin*, or, as it is sometimes called, *Arrie* *, and *Bothay*, a dairy-house, where the Highland shepherds, or graziers, live during summer with their herds and flocks, and during that season make butter and cheese. Their whole furniture consists of a few horn spoons, their milking utensils, a couch formed of sods to lie on, and a rug to cover them. Their food oat-cakes, butter or cheese, and often the coagulated blood of their cattle spread on their bannocks. Their drink milk, whey, and sometimes, by way of indulgence, whisky. Such dairy-houses are common to most mountainous countries: those in *Wales* are called *Vottys*, or Summer-houses; those on the *Swiss Alps*, *Sennes*.

Dined on the side of *Loch-Tilt*, a small piece of water, swarming with Trouts. Continued our journey over a wild, black, moory, melancholy tract. Reached *Brae-mar* †; the country almost instantly changed, and in lieu of dreary wastes, a rich vale, plenteous in corn and grass, succeeded. Cross the *Dee* near its head, which, from an insignificant

* *i. e.* a house made of turf.
† *Brae*, signifies the steep face of any hill.

stream,

stream, in the course of a very few miles, increases to the size of a great river, from the influx of numbers of other waters. The rocks of *Brae-mar*, on the east, are exceedingly romantic, finely wooded with pine. The clifts are very lofty, and their front most rugged and broken, with vast pines growing out of their fissures.

Brae-mar.

This tract abounding with game, was, in old times, the annual resort of numbers of nobility, who assembled here to pass a month or two in the amusements of the chace. Their huntings resembled campaigns; they lived in temporary cottages, called *Lonquhards*, were all dressed in an uniform habit conformable to that of the country, and passed their time with jollity and good chear, most admirably described by *John Taylor*, the water poet, who, in 1618, made there his *Pennilesse Pilgrimage*, p. 135, and describes the rural luxury with all the glee of a *Sancho Panca*.

" I thank my good Lord *Erskin*, (says the Poet)
" hee commanded that I should alwayes bee lodged
" in his lodging, the kitchen being alwayes on the
" side of a banke, many kettles and pots boyling,
" and many spits turning and winding, with great
" variety of cheere: as venison bak'd, sodden, rost
" and stu'de beefe, mutton, goates, kid, hares,
" fresh salmon, pidgeons, hens, capons, chickens,
" partridge, moore-coots, heath-cocks, caperkellies,
" and termagants; good ale, sacke, white and cla-
" ret, tent (or Allegant) and most potent *aqua-
" vitæ**.

" All

---

* The *French*, during the reign of *Charles* IX. seemed not only to have made full as large sacrifices to *Diana* and *Bacchus*, but even though

" All thefe, and more than thefe, we had conti-
" nually, in fuperfluous abundance, caught by
" faulconers, fowlers, fifhers, and brought by my
" Lord's (*Mar*) tenents and purveyors, to victual
" our campe, which confifted of fourteen or fifteen
" hundred men, and horfes. The manner of the
" hunting is this: five or fix hundred men doe rife
" early in the morning, and they doe difperfe them-
" felves divers wayes, and feven, eight, or ten miles

thought their entertainment incomplete without the prefence of *Venus*. *Jacques du Fouilloux*, a celebrated writer on hunting of that age, with much ferioufnefs defcribes all the requifites for the chace, and thus places and equips the jovial crew :— 'L'Affemblee fe
' doit faire en quelque beau lieu foubs des arbres aupres d'une
' fontaine ou Ruiffeau, la ou les veneurs fe doiuent tous rendre
' pour faire leur rapport. Ce pendant le Sommelier doit venir
' avec trois bons chevaux chargez d'inftrumens pour *arroufer le*
' *gofier*, comme coutrets, barraux, barils, flacons et bouteilles:
' lefquelles doiuent eftre pleines de bon vin *d'Arbois, de Beaume, de*
' *Chalofe et de Graue*, luy eftant defcendu du cheval, las metra
' refraifchir en l'eau, ou bien les pourra faire refroidir avec du
' Canfre : apres il eftendra la nappe fur la verdure. Ce fait, le
' cuifinier s'en viendra chargé de plufieurs *bons harnois de gueule*,
' comme jambons, langues de bœuf fumées, groins, et oreilles de
' pourceau, cervelats, efchinées, pieces de bœuf de Saifon, car-
' bonnades, jambons de *Mayence*, paftez, longes de veau froides
' couuertes de poudre blanche, et autres menus fuffrages pour
' remplir le boudin lequel il metra fur la nappe.
' Lors le Roy ou le Seigneur avec ceux de fa table eftrendront
' leurs manteaux fur l'herbe, et fe coucheront de cofté deffus,
' beuuans, mangeans, rians et faifans grand chere;' and that nothing might be wanting to render the entertainment of fuch a fet
of merry men quite complete, honeft *Jacques* adds, ' et s'il y a
' quelque femme de reputation en ce pays qui faffe plaifir aux
' compagnons, elle doit etre alleguée, et fes paffages et remuemens
' de feffes, attendant le rapport a venir.'
' But when the great man fallies out to the chace of foxes and
badgers, he feems not to leave fo important an affair to chance;
fo fets off thus amply provided in his triumphal car, ' Le Seig-
' neur, (fays *Fouilloux*) doit avoir fa petite charrette, la ou il fera
' dedans, avec la Fillette aagée de feize a dix fept ans, laquelle
' luy frottera la tefte par les chemins. Toutes les chevilles et paux
' de la charrette doiuent eftre garnis de flaccons et bouteilles, et
' doit avoir au bout de la charrette un coffre de bois, plein de
' coqs d'inde froids, jambons, langues de Bœufs et autre bons
' harnois de geule. Et fi c'eft en temps d'hiuer, il pourra faire
' porter fon petit pavillon, et faire du feu dedans pour fe chauffer,
' ou bien donner un coup en robbe à la nymphe.' *p*. 35. 75.

" compaffe,

"compasse, they doe bring or chase in the deer in
"many heards (two, three, or four hundred in a
"heard) to such or such a place, as the noblemen
"shall appoint them; then when day is come, the
"lords and gentlemen of their companies doe ride
"or go to the said places, sometimes wading up to
"the middles through bournes and rivers; and
"then they being come to the place, doe lye down
"on the ground till those foresaid scouts, which
"are called the *Tinckhell*, do bring down the deer;
"but, as the proverb says of a bad cooke, so these
"*Tinckhell* men doe lick their own fingers; for,
"besides their bowes and arrows which they carry
"with them, wee can heare now and then a hargue-
"buse, or a musquet, goe off, which doe seldom
"discharge in vaine: then after we had stayed
"three houres, or thereabouts, we might perceive
"the deer appeare on the hills round about us,
"(their heads making a shew like a wood) which
"being followed close by the *Tinckhell*, are chased
"down into the valley where wee lay; then all the
"valley on each side being way-laid with a hun-
"dred couple of strong Irish grey-hounds, they are
"let loose, as occasion serves, upon the heard of
"deere, that with dogs, gunnes, arrowes, durks
"and daggers, in the space of two houres fourscore
"fat deere were slaine, which after are disposed of
"some one way and some another, twenty or thirty
"miles, and more than enough left for us to make
"merry withall at our rendevouze. Being come
"to our lodgings, there was such baking, boyling,
"rosting and stewing, as if Cook Ruffian had been
"there to have scalded the Devill in his feathers."
But to proceed.

Pass by the castle of *Brae-mar*, a square tower, built about a hundred and fifty years ago, to curb the discontented chieftains; but at present unnecessarily garrisoned by a company of foot, being rented by the Government from Mr. *Farquharson*, of *Invercauld*, whose house I reached in less than half an hour.

Invercauld is seated in the centre of the *Grampian* hills, in a fertile vale, washed by the *Dee*, a large and rapid river: nothing can be more beautifull than the different views from the several parts of it. On the northern entrance, immense ragged and broken crags bound one side of the prospect; over whose grey sides and summits is scattered the melancholy green of the picturesque pine, which grows out of the naked rock, where one would think nature would have denied vegetation.

A little lower down is the castle above-mentioned; formerly a necessary curb on the little kings of the country; but at present serves scarce any real purpose, but to adorn the landscape.

The views from the skirts of the plain, near *Invercauld*, are very great; the hills that immediately bound it are cloathed with trees, particularly with birch, whose long and pendent boughs, waving a vast height above the head, surpass the beauties of the weeping willow.

The southern extremity is pre-eminently magnificent; the mountains form there a vast theatre, the bosom of which is covered with extensive forests of pines: above, the trees grow scarcer and scarcer, and then seem only to sprinkle the surface; after which

IN SCOTLAND.

which vegetation ceases, and naked summits of a surprising height succeed, many of them capped with perpetual snow; and, to the country to the N. the great cataract of Cora-Linn, which being at a distance to strike the soul, amidst the dusk forest, rushing from rock to rock to a vast distance.

Some of these hills are supposed to be the highest part of Great Britain; their height has never been taken, but the conjecture is made from the descent of the Dee, which runs from the Cairn Gorm to the sea, above seventy miles in its circuitous course.

"Rode to take a view ... crossed the Tweed at a ... the Dowerton, and ... into a magnificent scene ... except a few of the ... fined for ... (as ... to cut up ... into ... The view of the ... is fine, ... chief town is ... forests now that ... for by the right ... they call it ... mill ... purse ... and sometimes, which led to a distinct ..."

which vegetation ceases, and naked summits * of a surprising height succeed, many of them topped with perpetual snow; and, as a fine contrast to the scene, the great cataract of *Garval-bourn*, which seems at a distance to divide the whole, foams amidst the dark forest, rushing from rock to rock, to a vast distance.

Some of these hills are supposed to be the highest part of *Great Britain*: their height has not yet been taken, but the conjecture is made from the great descent of the *Dee*, which runs from *Brae-mar* † to the sea, above seventy miles, with a most rapid course.

Rode to take a nearer view of the environs; crossed the *Dee* on a good stone-bridge, built by the Government, and entered on excellent roads into a magnificent forest of pines of many miles extent. Some of the trees are of a vast size; I measured several that were ten, eleven, and even twelve feet in circumference, and near sixty feet high, forming a most beautifull column, with a fine verdant capital. These trees are of a great age, having, as is supposed, seen two centuries. The value of these trees is considerable; Mr. *Farquharson* informed me, that by sawing and retailing them, he has got for eight hundred trees five-and-twenty shillings each: they are sawed in an adjacent saw-mill, into plank ten feet long, eleven inches broad, and three thick, and sold for two shillings apiece.

Pine Forest.

---

* The highest is called *Ben y bourd*, under which is a small lough, which I was told had ice the latter end of *July*.
† The most distant from the sea of any place in *North Britain*.

Near

Near this antient forest is another, consisting of smaller trees, almost as high, but very slender; one grows in a singular manner out of the top of a great stone, and notwithstanding it seems to have no other nourishment than what it gets from the dews, is above thirty feet high.

The prospect above these forests is very extraordinary; a distant view of hills over a surface of verdant pyramids of pines.

Stags. This whole tract abounds with game: the Stags at this time were ranging in the mountains; but
Roes. the little Roebucks * were perpetually bounding before us; and the black game often sprung under
Birds. our feet. The tops of the hills swarmed with *Grous* and *Ptarmigans*. Green Plovers, Whimbrels, and Snow-flecks †, breed here: the last assemble in great flocks during winter, and collect so closely in their eddying flight as to give the sportsman opportunity of killing numbers at a shot. Eagles ‡, Peregrine Falcons, and Goshawks, breed here: the Falcons in rocks, the Goshawks in trees: the last pursues its prey an end, and dashes through every thing in pursuit; but if it misses its quarry ceases after two or three hundred yards flight. These birds are proscribed; half a crown is given for an eagle, a shilling for a hawk, or hooded crow.

Foxes are in these parts very ravenous, feeding on roes, sheep, and even she goats.

---

* These animals are reared with great difficulty; even when taken young, eight out of ten generally die.
† *Br. Zool. illustr.* 17. *tab.* xi.
‡ The Ring-tail Eagle, called here the Black Eagle. I suspect, from the description, that the Dotrel breeds here. I heard also of a bird, called here *Snatach na cuirn*, but could not procure it.

Rooks

Rooks visit these vales in autumn, to feed on the different sort of berries; but neither winter nor breed here.

I saw flying in the forests the greater Bulfinch of Mr. *Edwards, tab.* 123, 124. the *Loxia enucleator* of *Linnæus*, whose food is the seed of pine cones; a bird common to the north of *Europe* and *America*.

On our return passed under some high clifts, with large woods of birch intermixed. This tree is used for all sorts of implements of husbandry, roofing of small houses, wheels, fuel; the Highlanders also tan their own leather with the bark; and a great deal of excellent wine is extracted from the live tree. Observed among these rocks a sort of projecting shelf, on which had been a hut, accessible only by the help of some thongs fastened by some very expert climbers, to which the family got, in time of danger, in former days, with their most valuable moveables.

Birch Woods.

The houses of the common people in these parts are shocking to humanity, formed of loose stones, and covered with clods, which they call *devish*, or with heath, broom, or branches of fir: they look, at a distance, like so many black mole-hills. The inhabitants live very poorly, on oatmeal, barley-cakes, and potatoes; their drink whisky sweetened with honey. The men are thin, but strong; idle and lazy, except employed in the chace, or any thing that looks like amusement; are content with their hard fare, and will not exert themselves farther than to get what they deem necessaries. The women are more industrious, spin their own husbands cloaths, and get money by knitting stockings,

Cottages.

the great trade of the county. The common women are in general most remarkably plain, and soon acquire an old look; and by being much exposed to the weather without hats, such a grin, and contraction of the muscles, as heightens greatly their natural hardness of features: I never saw so much plainness among the lower rank of females: but the *ne plus ultra* of hard features is not found till you arrive among the fish-women of *Aberdeen.*

Tenants pay their rent generally in this country in money, except what they pay in poultry, which is done to promote the breed, as the gentry are so remote from any market. Those that rent a mill pay a hog or two; an animal so detested by the Highlanders, that very few can be prevaled on to taste it, in any shape. Labor is here very cheap, the usual pay being fifty shillings a year, and two pecks of oatmeal a week.

Aug. 6. Pursued my journey east, along a beautifull road by the river side, in sight of the pine forests. The vale now grows narrow, and is filled with woods of birch and alder. Saw on the road-side the seats of gentlemen high built, and once defensible. The peasants cultivate their little land with great care to the very edge of the stony hills. All the way are vast masses of granite, the same which is called in *Cornwall,* Moor-stone.

Pass of *Bollitir.* The Glen contracts, and the mountains approach each other. Quit the *Highlands,* passing between two great rocks, called the Pass of *Bollitir,* a very narrow strait, whose bottom is covered with the tremendous ruins of the precipices that bound the road. I was informed, that here the wind rages with

with great fury during winter, and catching up the snow in eddies, whirls it about with such impetuosity, as makes it dangerous for man or beast to be out at that time. Rain also pours down sometimes in deluges, and carries with it stone and gravel from the hills in such quantity, that I have seen these *spates*, as they are called, lie cross the roads, as the *avelenches*, or snow-falls, do those of the *Alps*. In many parts of the *Highlands* were *hospitia* for the reception of travellers, called by the *Scotch*, *Spittles*, or hospitals: the same were usual in *Wales*, where they are styled *Yspitty*; and, in both places, were maintained by the religious houses: as similar *Asylums* are to this day supported, in many parts of the *Alps*.

This pass is the eastern entrance into the Highlands. The country now assumes a new face: the hills grow less; but the land more barren, and is chiefly covered with heath and rock. The edges of the *Dee* are cultivated, but the rest only in patches, among which is generally a groupe of small houses. There is also a change of trees, oak being the principal wood, but not much of that. Refreshed my horses at a hamlet called *Tulloch*, and looking west, saw the great mountain *Lagbin y gair*, which is always covered with snow.

Observed several vast plantations of pines, planted by gentlemen near their seats: such a laudable spirit prevails, in this respect, that in another half-century it never shall be said, that to spy the nakedness of the land are you come.

Dine at the little village of *Kincaird*. Hereabouts the common people cultivate a great deal of cabbage.

cabbage. The oat-fields are inclosed with rude low mounds of stone.

Lay at a mean house at *Banchorie*. The country, from *Bollitir* to this place, dull, unless where varied with the windings of the river, or with the plantations.

Aug. 7. The nearer to *Aberdeen*, the lower the country grows, and the greater quantity of corn: in general, oats and barley; for there is very little wheat sown in these parts. Reach

Aberdeen. *Aberdeen*, a fine city, lying on a small bay formed by the *Dee* *, deep enough for ships of two hundred tuns. The town is about two miles in circumference, and contains thirteen thousand souls, and about three thousand in the suburbs. It once enjoyed a good share of the tobacco trade, but was at length forced to resign it to *Glasgow*, which was so much more conveniently situated for it. At present, its imports are from the *Baltic*, and a few merchants trade to the *West-Indies* and *North America*. Its exports are stockings, thread, salmon, and oat-meal: the first is a most important article, as appears by the following state of it. For this manufacture, 20,800 pounds worth of wool is annually imported, and 1600 pounds worth of oil. Of this wool is annually made 69,333 dozen pairs of stockings, worth, at an average, 1l. 10s. *per* dozen. These are made by the country people, in almost all parts of this great county, who get 4s. *per* dozen for spinning, and 14s. *per* dozen for knitting; so that there is annually paid

Stocking trade.

* The bridge lies about two miles south of the town, and consists of seven neat arches.

them

them 62,329 l. 14 s. And besides, there is about 2000 l. value of stockings manufactured from the wool of the county, which encourages the breed of sheep much; for even as high as *Invercauld*, the farmer sells his sheep at twelve shillings apiece, and keeps them till they are four or five years old, for the sake of the wool. About 200 combers are also employed constantly. The thread manufacture is another considerable article, tho' trifling in comparison of the woollen.

The salmon fisheries on the *Dee* and the *Don*, are a good branch of trade: about 46 boats, and 130 men, are employed on the first; and in some years, 167,000 lb. of fish have been sent pickled to *London*, and about 930 barrels of salted fish exported to *France*, *Italy*, &c. The fishery on the *Don* is far less considerable.

Salmon.

The town of *Aberdeen* is in general well built, with granite from the neighboring quarries. The best street, or rather *place*, is the Castle-street: in the middle is an octogon building, with neat bas relievos of the Kings of *Scotland*, from *James* I. to *James* VII. The Town-house makes a good figure, and has a handsome spire in the centre.

The east and west churches are under the same roof; for the *North Britons* observe œconomy even in their religion: in one I observed a small ship hung up; a common thing in *Scotland*, a sort of votive offering frequent enough in *Popish* churches, but appeared very unexpectedly here.

In the church-yard lies *Andrew Cant*, minister of *Aberdeen*, from whom the spectator derives the word to *cant*; but, in all probability, *Andrew* canted no

Andrew Cant.

more than the rest of his brethren, for he lived in a whining age *; the word therefore seems to be derived from *canto*, from their singing out their discourses.

In the same place are multitudes of long-winded epitaphs; but the following, though short, has a most elegant turn:

Si fides, si humanitas, multoque gratus lepore candor;
Si suorum amor, amicorum charitas, omniumque Benevolentia spiritum reducere possent,
Haud heic situs esset Johannes Burnet *a* Elrick, 1747.

College. The college is a large old building, founded by George Earl of *Marechal*, 1593. On one side is this strange inscription; probably alluding to some scoffers at that time:

>They have seid,
>Quhat say thay?
>Let Yame say.

In the great room are several good pictures. A head of the Founder. The present Lord *Marechal* when young, and General *Keith*, his brother. Bishop *Burnet* in his robes, as Chancellor of the Garter. A head of *Mary Stuart*, in black, with a crown in one hand, a crucifix in the other. *Arthur Jonston*, a fine head, by *Jameson*. *Andrew Cant*, by the same. *Gordon*, of *Strakloch*, publisher of the maps, and several others, by *Jameson*.

In the library is the alcoran on vellum, finely illuminated.

* In *Charles* the First's time.

Aretine,

A *Hebrew* Bible, Manuscript, with Rabinical notes, on vellum.

Isidori excerpta ex libro: a great curiosity, being a complete natural history, with figures, richly illuminated on squares of plated gold, on vellum.

A Paraphrase on the Revelation, by *James* VI. with notes, in the King's own hand.

A fine missal*.

There are about a hundred and forty students belonging to this college.

The grammar-school is a low but neat building. Gordon's hospital is handsome; in front is a good statue of the founder: it maintains forty boys, children of the inhabitants of *Aberdeen,* who are apprenticed at proper ages.

School.
Hospital.

The infirmary is a large plain building, and sends out between eight and nine hundred cured patients annually.

On the side of the Great Bleachery, which is common to the town, are the publick walks. Over a road, between the Castle-street and the river, is a very handsome arch, which must attract the attention of the traveller.

On the east of the town is a work begun by *Cromwel,* from whence is a fine view of the sea: beneath is a small patch of ground, noted for producing very early barley, which was then reaping.

Prices of provisions in this town were these: Beef, (16 ounces to the pound) 2d. ½. to 5d. mutton the same; butter, (28 ounces to the pound) 6d.

Provisions.

* There is also a very curious silver chain six feet long, found in the ruins of the White Fryers; at one end is a round flat plate, on the other a pear-shaped appendage.

to 8d. cheese, ditto, 4d. to 4d. ½. a large pullet, 6d. or 10d. duck, the same; goose, 2s. 3d.

Granite quarry. Cross the harbor to the granite quarries that contribute to supply *London* with paving-stones: the stone lies either in large nodules or in shattery beds, are cut into shape; and the small pieces for the middle of the streets are put on board for seven shillings *per* tun, the long stones at ten-pence *per* foot.

Aug. 8. Old Aberdeen. Visited old *Aberdeen*, about a mile north of the new; a poor town, seated not far from the *Don*. The college is built round a square with cloisters. The chapel is very ruinous within; but there still remains some wood-work of exquisite workmanship. This was preserved by the spirit of the Provost, at the time of the reformation, who armed his people and checked the blind zeal of the populace.

The library is large. The most remarkable things are, *John Trevisa's* translation of *Higden's Polychronicon*, in 1387; the manuscript excellently wrote, and the language very good, for that time. A very neat *Dutch* missal, with elegant paintings on the margin. Another of the angels appearing to the shepherds, with one of the men playing on the bagpipes. A manuscript catalogue of the old treasury of the college.

Hector Boethius was the first principal of the college, and sent for from *Paris* for that purpose, on an annual salary of forty marks, *Scots*, at thirteen-pence each. The square tower on the side of the college was built by *Cromwel*, for the reception of students; of which there are about a hundred belonging to the college, who lie in it.

In

In Bishop *Elphinston*'s hall, who was the founder, is a picture of Bishop *Dunbar*, who finished what the other left incomplete. *Forbes*, Bishop of *Aberdeen*, and Professors *Sandiland* and *Gordon*, by *Jameson*. The *Sybils*: said to be done by the same hand, but seemed to me in too different a style to be his; but the *Sybilla Ægyptiaca* and *Erythræa* are in good attitudes.

The cathedral is very antient; no more than the two very antique spires and one isle, which is used as a church, are now remaining.

From a *tumulus*, called *Tillie dron*, now covered with trees, is a fine view of an extensive and rich corn country; once a most barren spot, but by the industry of the inhabitants brought to its present state. A pretty vale bordered with wood, the cathedral soaring above the trees, and the river *Don*, form all together a most agreeable prospect.

Beneath are some cruives, or wears, to take salmon in. The owners are obliged by law to make the rails of the cruives* of a certain width, to permit fish of a certain size to pass up the river; but as that is neglected, they pay an annual sum to the owners of the fisheries which lie above, to compensate the loss.

In the *Regiam Majestatem* are preserved several antient laws relating to the salmon fisheries, couched in terms expressive of the simplicity of the times.

From *Saturday* night till *Monday* morning, they were obliged to leave a free passage for the fish, which is styled the *Saterdayes Sloppe* †.

* Cruives, &c. shall have their hecke two inches wide, that the fry may pass. *Rob.* I.
† *Alex.* I.

Alexander

Alexander I. enacted, 'That the streame of the water sal be in all parts swa free, that ane swine of the age of three zeares, well feed, may turne himself within the streame round about, swa that his snowt nor taill fall not touch the bank of the water.

'Slayers of reide fishe or smoltes of salmond, the thirde time are punished with death. And sic like he quha commands the samine to be done.' *Jac.* IV. *parl.* 6. *stat. Rob.* III.

Aug. 9. Continue my journey: pass over the bridge of *Don*; a fine gothic arch flung over that fine river, from one rock to the other: ride for some miles on the sea sands; pass through *Newburgh*, a small village, and at low water ford the *Ythen*, a river productive of the pearl muscle: go through the parish of *Furvie*, now entirely overwhelmed with sand, (except two farms) and about 500l. *per ann.* lost to the *Errol* family, as appears by the oath of the factor, made before the court of sessions in 1600, to ascertain the ministers salary. It was at that time all arable land, now covered with shifting sands, like the deserts of *Arabia*, and no vestiges remain of any buildings, except a small fragment of the church.

Inundation of sand.

The country now grows very flat; produces oats; but the crops are considerably worse than in the preceding country. Reach

Bowness, or *Buchaness*, the seat of the Earl of *Errol*, perched like a falcon's nest, on the edge of a vast clift above the sea. The drawing-room, a large and very elegant apartment, hangs over it; the waves run in wild eddies round the rocks beneath,

neath, and the sea fowl clamor above and below, forming a strange prospect and singular chorus. The place was once defensible, there having been a ditch and draw-bridge on the accessible side; but now both are destroyed.

Above five miles south is *Slains*, the remains of the old family castle, seated strongly on a peninsulated rock; but demolished in 1594, by *James* VI. on the rebellion of the Earl of *Huntly*. Near this place are some vast caverns, once filled with curious stalactical incrustations, but now destroyed, in order to be burnt into lime; for there is none in this country, that usefull commodity being imported from the Earl of *Elgin*'s works on the *Firth* of *Forth*.

Here the shore begins to grow bold and rocky, and indented in a strange manner with small and deep creeks, or rather immense and horrible chasms. The famous *Bullers* of *Buchan* lie about a mile north of *Bowness*: are a vast hollow in a rock, projecting into the sea, open at top, with a communication to the sea through a noble natural arch, thro' which boats can pass, and lie secure in this natural harbor. There is a path round the top, but in some parts too narrow to walk on with satisfaction, as the depth is about thirty fathom, with water on both sides, being bounded on the north and south by small creeks.

Bullers of *Buchan*.

Near this is a great insulated rock, divided by a narrow and very deep chasm from the land. This rock is pierced through midway between the water and the top, and in great storms the waves rush through it with vast noise and impetuosity. On the sides,

Kittiwakes. sides, as well as those of the adjacent cliffs, breed multitudes of *Kittiwakes* *. The young are a favorite dish in *North Britain*, being served up a little before dinner, as a whet for the appetite; but, from the rank smell and taste, seem as if they were more likely to have a contrary effect. I was told of an honest gentleman who was set down for the first time to this kind of whet, as he supposed; and after demolishing half a dozen, with much impatience declared, that he had eaten *sax*, and did not find himself a bit *more* hungry than before he began.

Fishery of sea dogs. On this coast is a great fishery of Sea Dogs †, which begins the last week of *July*, and ends the first in *September*. The livers are boiled for oil; the bodies split, dried, and sold to the common people, who come from great distances for them. There are very fine Turbot taken on this coast; and towards *Peterhead*, good fisheries of Cod and Ling. The Lord of the Manour has 3l. 6s. 8d. *per annum* from every boat, (a six-man boat) but if a new crew sets up, the Lord, by way of encouragement, finds them a boat. Besides these, they have little yawls for catching bait at the foot of the rocks. Muscles are also much used for bait, and many boats loads are brought for that purpose from the mouth of the *Ythen*. Of late years, a very successfull salmon fishery has been set up in the sandy bays below *Slains*. This is performed by long nets, carried out to sea by boats, a great compass taken, and then hawled on shore. It is re-

* Br. Zool. illustr. 26. tab. xxiii.
† The Picked Dog, Br. Zool. III. 77.

marked,

marked, these fish swim against the wind, and are much better tasted than those taken in fresh waters.

Most of the labor on shore is performed here by the women: they will carry as much fish as two men can lift on their shoulders, and when they have sold their cargo and emptied their basket, will replace part of it with stones: they go sixteen miles to sell or barter their fish; are very fond of finery, and will load their fingers with trumpery rings, when they want both shoes and stockings. The fleet was the last war supplied with great numbers of men from this and other parts of *Scotland,* as well as the army: I think near 70,000 engaged in the general cause, and assisted in carrying our glory through all parts of the globe: of the former, numbers returned; of the latter, very few.

The houses in this country are built with clay, Houses. tempered in the same manner as the *Israelites* made their bricks in the land of *Ægypt:* after dressing the clay, and working it up with water, the laborers place on it a large stratum of straw, which is trampled into it and made small by horses: then more is added, till it arrives at a proper consistency, when it is used as a plaister, and makes the houses very warm. The roofs are *sarked, i. e.* covered with inch-and-half deal, sawed into three planks, and then nailed to the joists, on which the slates are pinned.

The land prospect is extremely unpleasant; for no trees will grow here, in spite of all the pains that have been taken: not but in former times it must have been well wooded, as is evident from the numbers of trees dug up in all the bogs. The same nakedness prevales over great part of this coast, even far beyond *Bamff*, except in a few warm bottoms.

The corn of this tract is oats and barley; of the last I have seen very good close to the edges of the cliffs. Rents are paid here partly in cash, partly in kind; the last is commonly sold to a contractor. The land here being poor, is set cheap. The people live hardly: a common food with them is *sowens*, the husks of oats, first put into a barrel with water, in order to grow sour, and then boiled.

Aug. 11. Crossed the country towards *Bamff*, over oat-lands, a coarse sort of downs, and several black heathy moors, without a single tree for numbers of miles. See *Craigston* castle, a good house, once defensible, seated in a snug bottom, where the plantations thrive greatly. Saw here a head of *David Lesly*, by *Jameson*, and another of Sir *Alexander Frazier*, by the same. Passed by a small ruined castle, at a place called *Castleton*, seated on a round hill in a deep glen, and scarce accessible. Ford the *Devron*, a fine river, over which had been a beautifull bridge, now washed away by the floods. Reach

Craigston Castle.

Bamff. *Bamff*, pleasantly seated on the side of a hill; has several streets; but that with the town-house in it, adorned with a new spire, is very handsome: the harbor is very bad, as the entrance at the mouth of the *Devron* is very uncertain, being often stopped by the shifting of the sands, which are continually changing, in great storms; the pier is therefore placed on the outside. Much salmon is exported

exported from hence. About *Troop* head, some kelp is made; and the adventurers pay the Lord of the Manour 50l. *per ann.* for the liberty of collecting the materials.

The Earl of *Finlater* has a house, prettily seated on an eminence, near the town, with some plantations of shrubs and small trees, which have a good effect in so bare a country. The prospect is very fine, commanding the fine meadows near the town, *Down* a small but well-built fishing-town, the great promontory of *Troop-head*, and to the north the hills of *Rossshire*, *Sutherland*, and *Cathness*.

The house once belonged to the *Sharps*; and the violent archbishop of that name was born here. In one of the apartments is a picture of *Jameson*, by himself, sitting in his painting-room, dressed like *Rubens*, and with his hat on, and his pallet in his hand. On the walls are represented hung up, the pictures of *Charles* I. and his Queen; a head of his own wife; another head; two sea views, and *Perseus* and *Andromeda*, the productions of his various pencil.

Duff House a vast pile of building, a little way from the town, is a square, with a square tower at each end; the front richly ornamented with carving, but, for want of wings, has a naked look: the rooms within are very small, and by no means answer the magnificence of the case.

Duff House.

In the apartments are these pictures: *Frances*, Dutchess of *Richmond*, full length, in black, with a little picture at her breast. Æt. 57, 1633, by *Vandyk*. Fine heads of *Charles* I. and his Queen. A head of a *Duff*, with short grey hair, by *Alexander*
of

of *Corfenday*. Near the house is a shrubery, with a walk two miles long leading to the river.

AUG. 12. About two miles west of *Bamff*, not far from the sea, is a great stratum of sand and shells, used with success as a manure. Sea tang is also much used for corn-lands, sometimes by itself, sometimes mixed with earth, and left to rot: it is besides often laid fresh on grass, and answers very well. Passed by the house of *Boyne*, a ruined castle, on the edge of a steep glen, filled with some good ash and maples.

Near *Portsoy*, a small town, is a large stratum of marble, a coarse sort of *Verd di Corsica*, used in some houses for chimney-pieces. Reach

Cullen House. *Cullen* House, seated at the edge of a deep glen full of very large trees, which being out of the reach of the sea winds prosper greatly. This spot is very prettily laid out in walks, and over the entrance is a magnificent arch sixty feet high, and eighty-two in width. The house is large, but irregular. The most remarkable pictures are, a full length of *James* VI. by *Mytens*: at the time of the revolution, the mob had taken it out of *Holyrood* House, and were kicking it about the streets, when the Chancellor, the Earl of *Finlater*, happening to pass by, redeemed it out of their hands. A portrait of *James* Duke of *Hamilton*, beheaded 1649, in a large black cloak, with a star, by *Vandyk*. A half-length of his brother, by the same, killed at the battle of *Worcester*. *William* Duke of *Hamilton*, president of the revolution parlement, by *Kneller*. Old Lord *Bamff*, aged 90, with a long white square beard,

beard, who is said to have incurred the censure of the church, at that age, for his galantries *.

The country round *Cullen* has all the marks of improvement, owing to the † indefatigable pains of the late noble owner, in advancing the art of agriculture and planting, and every other usefull business, as far as the nature of the soil would admit. His success in the first was very great; the crops of beans, peas, oats, and barley, were excellent; the wheat very good, but, through the fault of the climate, will not ripen till it is late, the harvest in these parts being in *October*. The plantations are very extensive, and reach to the top of the hill of *Knock*; but the farther they extend from the bottoms the worse they succeed.

The town of *Cullen* is mean; yet has about a hundred looms in it, there being a flourishing manufacture of linnen and thread, of which near fifty thousand pounds worth is annually made.

Near this town the Duke of *Cumberland*, after his march from *Bamff*, joined the rest of his forces from *Straithbogie*, and encamped at *Cullen*.

In a small sandy bay are three lofty spiring rocks, formed of flinty masses, cemented together very

---

* Among other pictures of persons of merit, that of the admirable *Crichton* must not be overlooked. I was informed, that there is one of that extraordinary person in the possession of *Alexander Morrison*, Esq; of *Bagnie*, in the county of *Bamff*; it is in the same apartment with some of *Jameson*'s, but seems done by a superior hand: came into Mr. *Morrison*'s possession from the family of *Crichton*, Viscount *Frendraught*, chief of the name to whom *Crichton* probably sent it from *Italy*, where he spent the last years of his short life.

† His Lordship collected together near 2000 souls, to his new town at *Keith*, by *feuing*; i. e. giving in perpetuity, on payment of a slight acknowlegement, land sufficient to build a house on, with gardens and back-yard.

differently from any stratum in the country. These are called the three Kings of *Cullen*. A little farther is another vast rock, pierced quite through, formed of pebbly concretions lodged in clay, which had subsided in thick but regular layers.

Aug. 13.

Stone marle.

Passed through a fine open country, full of gentle risings, and rich in corn, with a few clumps of trees sparingly scatered over it. Great use is made here of stone marle, a gritty indurated marle, found in vast strata, dipping pretty much: it is of different colors, blue, pale brown, and reddish; is cut out of the quarry, and laid very thick on the ground in lumps, but will not wholly dissolve under three or four years. In the quarry is a great deal of sparry matter, which is laid apart, and burnt for lime. Arrive at

Castle Gordon.

Castle-Gordon, a large old house, the seat of the Duke of *Gordon*, lying in a low wet country, near some large well-grown woods, and a considerable one of great hollies. The principal pictures in *Castle-Gordon* are, the first Marquiss of *Huntly*. Fourth Marquiss of *Huntly*, beheaded by the Covenanters. His son, the gallant Lord *Gordon*, *Montrose*'s friend, killed at the battle of *Auldfort*. Lord *Lewis Gordon*, a less generous warrior; the plague[*] of the people of *Murray*, (then the seat of the Covenanters) whose character, with that of the

---

[*] Whence this proverb,

'The Guil, the *Gordon*, and the Hooded Craw,
'Were the three worst things *Murray* ever saw.'

Guil is a weed that infests corn. It was from the castle of *Rothes*, on the *Spey*, that Lord *Lewis* made his plundering excursions into *Murray*.

brave

brave *Montrofe*, is well contrafted in thefe old lines:

> If ye with *Montrofe* gae, ye'l get fic and wae enough;
> If ye with Lord *Lewis* gae, ye'l get rob and rave enough.

The head of the fecond Countefs of *Huntly*, daughter of *James* I. A fine fmall portrait of the *Abbè d'Aubignè*, fitting in his ftudy. A very fine head of St. *John* receiving the revelation; a beautifull expreffion of attention and devotion.

The Duke of *Gordon* ftill keeps up the diverfion of falconry, and had feveral fine Hawks, of the Peregrine and gentle Falcon fpecies, which breed in the rocks of *Glenmore*. I faw alfo here a true Highland gre-hound, which is now become very fcarce: it was of a very large fize, ftrong, deep chefted, and covered with very long and rough hair. This kind was in great vogue in former days, and ufed in vaft numbers, at the magnificent ftag-chafes, by the powerfull Chieftains. *Falconry.*

The *Spey* is a dangerous neighbor to *Caftle-Gordon*; a large and furious river, overflowing very frequently in a dreadfull manner, as appears by its ravages far beyond its banks. The bed of the river is wide and full of gravel, and the channel very fhifting. *The Spey.*

The Duke of *Cumberland* paffed this water at *Beily* church, near this place, when the channel was fo deep as to take an officer, from whom I had the relation, and who was fix feet four inches high, up to the breaft. The oppofite banks are very high and fteep; fo that, had not the Rebels been providentially fo infatuated as to neglect oppofition,

the

the passage must have been attended with considerable loss.

The salmon fishery on this river is very great: about seventeen hundred barrels full are caught in the season, and the shore is rented for about 1200l. per annum.

Aug. 14.
Forchabus.

Passed through *Forchabus*, a wretched town, close to the castle. Crossed the *Spey* in a boat, and landed in the county of *Murray*.

The peasants houses, which, throughout the shire of *Bamff*, were very decent, were now become very miserable, being entirely made of turf: the country partly moor, partly cultivated, but in a very slovenly manner.

Elgin.

Dine at *Elgin**, a good town, with many of the houses built over piazzas; has little trade; but is remarkable for its ecclesiastical antiquities. The cathedral † had been a magnificent pile, but is now in ruins. *Jonston*, in his *encomia urbium*, celebrates the beauty of *Elgin*, and laments the fate of this noble building:

Arcibus heroum nitidis urbs cingitur, intus
   Plebeii radiant, nobiliumque Lares:
Omnia delectant, veteris sed rudera templi
   Dum spectas, lachrymis, Scotia tinge genas.

The west door is very elegant, and richly ornamented. The choir very beautifull, and has a fine

---

* *Celticè* Belle ville.
† Founded by *John*, second son of the house of *Innes*, and Bishop of *Murray*, 1406; of whose epitaph is this fragment:
Hic jacet in Xto pater et Dominus, Dominus Johannes de Innes *hujus Ecclesiæ episcopus---Qui hoc notabile opus incepit, et per septennium edificavit.*

and

and light gallery running round it; and at the east end are two rows of narrow windows in an excellent gothic taste. The chapter-house is an octagon, the roof supported by a fine single column, with neat carvings of coats of arms round the capital. There is still a great tower on each side of this cathedral; but that in the centre, with the spire and whole roof, are fallen in, and form most awefull fragments, mixed with the battered monuments of Knights and Prelates. *Boethius* says that *Duncan*, who was killed by *Macbeth* at *Inverness*, lies buried here. Numbers of modern tomb-stones also crowd the place; a proof how difficult it is to eradicate the opinion of local sanctity, even in a religion that affects to despise it.

About a mile from hence is the castle of *Spinie*; a large square tower, and a vast quantity of other ruined buildings, still remain, which shews its antient magnificence whilst the residence of the Bishops of *Murray*: the lake of *Spinie* almost washes the walls; is about five miles long, and half a mile broad, seated in a flat country. During winter, great numbers of wild swans migrate hither; and I have been told, that some have bred here. *Boethius* * says they resort here for the sake of a certain herb called after their name.

Spinie.

Between this and *Elgin* is a ruined chapel, called *Maison dieu*. Near it is a large gravelly cliff, from whence is a beautifull view of the town, cathedral, a round hill with the remains of a castle, and beneath is the gentle stream of the *Lossie*, the *Loxia* of *Ptolomy*.

* *Scotorum* Regni descr. ix.

K.   Three

Pluscairdin Abby.

Three miles south is the Abby of *Pluscairdin*, in a most sequestred place; a beautifull ruin, the arches elegant, the pillars well turned, and the capitals rich *.

Cross the *Lossie*, ride along the edge of a vale, which has a strange mixture of good corn and black turberies: on the road-side is a mill-stone quarry.

Arrive in the rich plain of *Murray*, fertile in corn. The view of the *Firth* of *Murray*, with a full prospect of the high mountains of *Rossshire* and *Sutherland*, and the magnificent entrance into the bay of *Cromartie* between two lofty hills, form a fine piece of scenery.

Kinloss Abby.

Turn about half a mile out of the road to the north, to see *Kinloss* Abby †, the burying-place of many a *Scottish* monarch. The Prior's chamber, two semicircular arches, the pillars, the couples of several of the roofs, afford specimens of the most beautifull gothic architecture in all the elegance of simplicity, without any of its fantastic ornaments. Near the abby is an orchard of apple and pear trees, at least coeval with the last Monks; numbers lie prostrate; their venerable branches seem to have taken fresh roots, and were loaden with fruit, beyond what could be expected from their antique look.

Great column.

Near *Forres*, on the road-side, is a vast column, three feet ten inches broad, and one foot three inches thick: the height, above ground is twenty-three feet; below, as is said, twelve or fifteen. On one

---

* As I was informed, for I did not see this celebrated abby.
† Founded about 1124, by *David* I.

side

side are numbers of rude figures of animals and armed men, with colors flying: some of the men seemed bound like captives. On the opposite side was a cross, included in a circle, and raised a little above the surface of the stone. At the foot of the cross are two gigantic figures, and on one of the sides is some elegant fret-work.

This is called King *Sueno*'s stone; and seems to be, as Mr. *Gordon* * conjectures, erected by the *Scots*, in memory of the final retreat of the *Danes:* it is evidently not *Danish*, as some have asserted; the cross disproves the opinion, for this nation had not at that time received the light of christianity.

On a moor not far from *Forres*, *Boethius*, and *Shakespear* from him, places the rencountre of *Macbeth* and the three wayward sisters, or witches. It was my fortune to meet with but one, which was somewhere in the last county: she was of a species far more dangerous than these, but neither *withered nor wild in her attire*, but so fair,

She look'd not like an inhabitant o' th' Earth!

Lay at *Forres*, a very neat town, seated under some little hills, which are prettily divided. In the great street is the town-house with a handsome cupolo, and at the end is an arched gateway, which has a good effect. On a hill west of the town are the poor remains of the castle, from whence is a fine view of a rich country, interspersed with groves, the bay of *Findorn*, a fine bason, almost round, with a narrow strait into it from the sea, and a melancholy prospect of the parish of the same name,

Forres.

* *Itin. Septentr.* 158.

Inundation of sand. now nearly overwhelmed with sand. This strange inundation is still in motion, but mostly in the time of a west wind: it moves along the surface with an even progression, but is stopped by water, after which it forms little hills: its motion is so quick, that a gentleman assured me he had seen an apple-tree so covered with it, in one season, as to leave only a few of the green leaves of the upper branches appear above the surface. An estate of about 300 l. *per ann.* has been thus overwhelmed; and it is not long since the chimnies of the principal houses were to be seen: it began about eighty years ago, occasioned by the cutting down the trees and pulling up the bent, or starwort, which gave occasion at last to the act 15th G. II. to prevent its farther ravages.

Aug. 15. Cross the *Findorn*; land near a friable rock of whitish stone, much tinged with green, an indication of copper. The stone is barren for lime. From an adjacent eminence is a picturesque view of *Forres*. About three miles farther is *Tarnaway* Castle, the antient seat of the Earls of *Murray*. The hall, called *Randolph*'s Hall, from its founder Earl *Randolph*, one of the great supporters of *Robert Bruce*, is timbered at top like *Westminster-Hall*: its dimensions are 79 feet by 35, 10 inches, and seems a fit resort for Barons and their vassals. In the rooms are some good heads: one of a youth, with a ribband of some order hanging from his neck. One unknown, with a black body to his vest, and brown sleeves. The Fair, or Bonny Earl of *Murray*, as he is commonly called, who was murdered, as supposed, on account of

Tarnaway Castle.

of a jealousy *James* VI. entertained of a passion the Queen had for him: at left such was the popular opinion, as appears from the old ballad on the occasion:

> He was a braw Gallant,
> And he played at the Gluve;
> And the bonny Earl of *Murray*,
> Oh! he was the Queene's Love.

There are besides, the heads of his lady and daughter; all are on wood except that of the Earl. To the south-east of the castle are large birch woods, abounding with Stags and Roes.

Continued my journey west to *Auldearne*. Am now arrived again in the country where the *Erse* service is performed. Just beneath the church is the place where *Montrose* obtained a signal victory over the Covenanters, many of whose bodies lie in the church, with an inscription, importing, according to the cant of the time, that they died fighting for their religion and their king. I was told this anecdote of that hero: That he always carried with him a *Cæsar's* Commentaries, on whose margins were written, in *Montrose's* own hand, the generous sentiments of his heart; verses out of the *Italian* Poets, expressing contempt of every thing but glory.

Have a distant view of *Nairn*, a small town near the sea. Ride through a rich corn country, mixed with deep and black turberies, which shew the original state of the land. Reach *Calder* Castle, or *Cawdor*, as *Shakespear* calls it, once the property of its *Thanes*. The antient part is a great square tower;

Auldearne.

Cawdor.

tower; but there is a large and more modern building annexed, with a draw-bridge.

All the houses in these parts are castles, or at least defensible; for, till the year 1745, the Highlanders made their inroads, and drove away the cattle of their defenceless neighbors. There are said to exist some very old marriage articles of the daughter of a chieftain, in which the father promises for her portion, 200 *Scots* marks, and the half of a *Michaelmas moon*, i. e. half the plunder, when the nights grew dark enough to make their excursions.

Rode into the woods of *Calder*, in which were very fine birch trees and alders, some oak, great broom, and juniper, which gave shelter to the Roes. Deep rocky glens, darkened with trees, bound each side of the wood: one has a great torrent roaring at its distant bottom; called the Brook of *Achneem*: it well merits the name of that of *Acheron*, being a most fit scene for witches to celebrate their nocturnal rites in.

A joug. Observed on a pillar of the door of *Calder* church, a *joug*, i. e. an iron yoke, or ring, fastened to a chain; which was, in former times, put round the necks of delinquents against the rules of the church, who were left there exposed to shame during the time of divine service: but these penalties are now *Scotch clergy.* happily abolished. The clergy of *Scotland*, the most decent and consistent in their conduct of any set of men I ever met with of their order, are at present much changed from the furious, illiterate, and enthusiastic teachers of the old times, and have taken up the mild method of persuasion, instead of the cruel discipline of corporal punishments.

ments. Science almoſt univerſally flouriſhes among them; and their diſcourſe is not leſs improving than the table they entertain the ſtranger at is decent and hoſpitable. Few, very few of them, permit the bewitchery of diſſipation to lay hold of them, notwithſtanding they allow all the innocent pleaſures of others, which, though not criminal in the layman, they know, muſt bring the taint of levity on the churchman. They never ſink their characters by midnight brawls, by mixing with the gaming world, either in cards, cocking, or horſe-races, but preſerve, with a narrow income, a dignity too often loſt among their brethren ſouth of the *Tweed.*

The *Scotch* livings are from 40 l. *per ann.* to 150 l. *per ann.* a decent houſe is built for the miniſter on the glebe, and about ſix acres of land annexed. The church allows no curate, except in caſe of ſickneſs or age, when one, under the title of helper, is appointed; or, where the livings are very extenſive, a miſſionary or aſſiſtant is allotted; but ſine-cures, or ſine-cured preferments, never diſgrace the church of our ſiſter kingdom. The widows and children of thoſe who die in poor circumſtances are of late provided for out of a fund eſtabliſhed by two acts, 17th and 22d, G. II.*

Scotch livings.

Croſs the *Nairn*; the bridge large, but the ſtream inconſiderable, except in floods. On the weſt is *Kilravoch* Caſtle, and that of *Dalcroſs*. Keep due north, along the military road from *Perth*; paſs

* An account of the government of the church of *Scotland*, as collected from a worthy and ſenſible miniſter, will be given in the Appendix, No. I.

along a narrow low piece of land, projecting far into the *Firth*, called *Arderfier*, forming a strait scarce a mile over, between this county and that of *Cromartie* *. At the end of this point is *Fort George*, a small but strong and regular fortress, built since 1745, as a *place d'armes*: it is kept in excellent order; but, by reason of the happy change of the times, seemed almost deserted: the barracks are very handsome, and form several regular and good streets.

Fort George.

Lay at *Cambeltown*, a place consisting of numbers of very mean houses, owing its rise and support to the neighboring fort.

Aug. 16.
Culloden.

Passed over *Culloden Moor*, the place that *North Britain* owes its present prosperity to, by the victory of *April* 16, 1746. On the side of the Moor are the great plantations of *Culloden* House, the seat of *Duncan Forbes*, a warm and active friend to the house of *Hanover*, who spent great sums in its service, and by his influence, and by his persuasions, diverted numbers from joining in rebellion; at length he met with a cool return, for his humane but unpolitical attempt to sheath, after victory, the unsatiated sword. But let a veil be flung over a few excesses consequential of a day productive of so much benefit to the united kingdoms.

The young adventurer lodged here the evening preceding the battle; distracted with the dissensions among his officers, even when they were at the brink of destruction, he seemed incapable of acting, could be scarcely persuaded to mount his horse,

* Between which plies a ferry-boat.

never

never came into the field of battle, as might have been expected from a prince who had his last stake to play, but fled ingloriously to the old traitor *Lovat*, who, I was told, did execrate him, on hearing that he approached as a fugitive.

The Duke of *Cumberland*, when he found that the barges of the fleet attended near the shore for the safety of his person, in case of a defeat, immediately ordered them away, to convince his men of the resolution he had taken of either conquering or perishing with them.

After descending from the Moor, got into a well cultivated country; and after riding some time under low but pleasant hills, not far from the sea, reach

INVERNESS, finely seated on a plain, between the Firth of the same name and the river *Ness*: the first, from the narrow strait of *Arderfier*, instantly widens into a fine bay, and again as suddenly contracts opposite *Inverness*, at the ferry of *Kessock*, the pass into *Rossshire*. The town is large and well built, and very populous, being the last of any note in *North Britain*. On the north is *Oliver*'s Fort, a pentagon; but only the form remains to be traced by the ditches and banks. Near it is a very considerable rope manufacture. On an eminence south of the town is old *Fort George*, which was taken and blown up by the Rebels: it had been no more than a very antient castle, the place where *Boethius* says that *Duncan* was murdered: from thence is a most charming view of the *Firth*, the passage of *Kessock*, the river *Ness*, the strange shaped hill of *Tommin heurich*, and various groupes of distant mountains. That

INVERNESS.

That singular *Tommin* is of an oblong form, broad at the base, and sloping on all sides towards the top; so that it looks like a great ship with its keel upwards. Its sides and part of the neighboring plains are planted, so it is both an agreeable walk and a fine object. It is perfectly detached from any other hill; and if it was not for its great size, might pass * for a work of art. The view from it is such, that no traveller will think his labor lost, after gaining the summit.

At *Inverness*, and I believe at other towns in *Scotland*, is an officer, called *Dean* of the *Guild*, who, assisted by a council, superintends the markets, regulates the price † of provisions; and if any house falls down, and the owner lets it lie in ruins for three years, the *Dean* can absolutely dispose of the ground to the best bidder.

Cross the *Ness* on a bridge of seven arches, above which the tide flows for about a mile.

Proceed north; have a fine view of the Firth, which now widens again from *Kessock* into a large bay some miles in length. The hills slope down to the water-side, and are finely cultivated; but the distant prospect is of rugged mountains of a stupendous height, as if created as guards to the rest of the island from the fury of the boisterous north.

---

* Its length at top about 300 yards; I neglected measuring the base or the height, which are both considerable; the breadth of the top only 20 yards.

† Beef, (22 ounces to the pound) 2d. to 4d. Mutton, 2d. to 3d. Veal, 3d. to 5d. Pork, 2d. to 3d. Chickens, 3d. to 4d. a couple. Fowl, 4d. to 6d. apiece. Goose, 12d. to 14d. Ducks, 1s. a couple. Eggs, seven a penny. Salmon, of which there are several great fisheries, 1d. and 1d. halfpenny per pound.

Ride

Ride close to the water-edge thro' woods of alder, pass near several houses of the *Fraziers*, and reach *Castle Dunie*, the site of the house of their chieftain Lord *Lovat*.

Castle Dunie.

The old house, which was very mean, was burnt down in 1746; but a neat box, the residence of the hospitable factor, is built in its stead on a high bank well wooded, over the pretty river *Bewley*, or *Beaulieu*. The country, for a certain circuit, is fertile, well cultivated, and smiling. The bulk of Lord *Lovat*'s estate was in these parts; the rest, to the amount of 500 l. *per ann.* in *Straitherick*. He was a potent chieftain, and could raise about 1000 men: but I found his neighbors spoke as unfavorably of him, as his enemies did in the most distant parts of the kingdom. His property is one of the annexed estates, *i. e.* settled unalienably on the crown, as all the forfeited fortunes in the Highlands are: the whole value of which brought in at that time about 6000 l. *per ann.* and those in the Lowlands about the same sum; so that the power and interest of a poor twelve thousand *per ann.* terrified and nearly subverted the constitution of these powerfull kingdoms.

Forfeited estates.

The profits of these estates are lodged in the hands of Trustees, who apply their revenue for the founding of schools for the instruction of children in spinning; wheels are given away to poor families, and flax-seed to farmers. Some money is given in aid of the roads, and towards building bridges over the torrents; by which means a ready intercourse is made to parts before inaccessible to strangers.

strangers*: And in 1753, a large sum was spent on an *Utopian* project of establishing colonies (on the forfeited estates) of disbanded soldiers and sailors: comfortable houses were built for them, land and money given, and some lent; but the success by no means answered the intentions of the projectors.

Aug. 17. Ford the *Bewley*, where a salmon fishery, belonging to the *Lovat* estate, rents at 120l. *per annum*.

Leornamonach. The country on this side the river is called *Leornamonach,* or the Monk's Land, having formerly been the property of the Abby of *Bewly*; and the opposite

Airds. side bears the name of *Airds*, or the Heights. Pass by some excellent farms, well enclosed, improved, and planted; the land produces wheat and other corn. Much cattle are bred in these parts, and there are several linnen manufactures.

Castle *Braan.* Ford the *Conan* to Castle *Braan*, the seat of Lord *Fortrose*; a good house, pleasantly situated on the side of a hill, commands a view of a large plain, and to the west a wild prospect of broken and lofty mountains.

There is here a fine full length of *Mary Stuart*, with this inscription, *Maria D. G. Scotiæ piiſſima regina. Franciæ Dotaria. Anno Ætatis Regni* 38. 1580. Her dress is black, with a ruff, cap, handkerchief, and a white veil down to the ground, beads and prayer-book, and a cross hanging from her neck; her hair dark brown, her face handsome, and considering the difference of years, so much resembling her portrait by *Zuccbero,* in *Chiswick*

* The factors, or agents of these estates, are also allowed all the money they expend in planting.

House,

House, as to leave little doubt as to the originality of the last.

A small half-length on wood of *Henry Darnly*, inscribed *Henricus Stuardus Dominus Darnly, Æt.* IX. M.D.LV. dressed in black, with a sword; it is the figure of a pretty boy.

A fine portrait of Cardinal *Richlieu*. General *Monk*, in a buff coat. Head of Sir *George Mackenfie*. The Earl of *Seaforth*, called, from his size, *Kenneth More*. Dutchess of *Beaufort*, daughter of the Marquiss of *Powis*. Earl of *Castlemaine*, admiral in the time of *Charles* II.

Near the house are some very fine oaks and horse-chesnuts: in the garden, Turky apricots, orange nectarines, and a small soft peach, ripe; other peaches, nectarines, and green gages, far from ripe.

Pass through *Dingwall*, a small town, the capital of *Rossshire*, situated near the head of the Firth of *Cromartie*: an antient cross, and an obelisk over the burying-place of the Earls of *Cromartie*'s family, were all I saw remarkable in it. *Dingwall.*

Ride along a very good road cut on the side of a hill with the country very well cultivated above and below, with several small woods interspersed near the water's edge. There is a fine view of almost the whole bay, the most capacious and secure of any in *Great Britain*; its whole navy might lie there with ease, and ships of two hundred tuns may sail up above two-thirds of its length, which extends thirty miles, from the *Sutters** of *Cromartie* *Firth of Cromartie.*

---

* *Sutters*, or Shooters; two hills that form its entrance, projecting considerably into the water.

to a small distance beyond *Dingwall*: the entrance is narrow; the projecting hills defend this fine bay from all winds; so it justly merits the name given it of *Portus salutis*.

FOULES. FOULES, the seat of Sir *Henry Monro*, lies about a mile from the *Firth*, near vast plantations on the flats, as well as on the hills. Those on the hills are six miles in length, and in a very flourishing state. On the back of these are extensive vallies full of oats, bounded by mountains, which here, as well as in the Highlands, in general run from east to west. Sir *Henry* holds a forest from the crown by Singular tenure. a very whimsical tenure, that of delivering a snow-ball on any day of the year that it is demanded; and he seems to be in no danger of forfeiting his right by failure of the quit-rent, for snow lies in form of a *glaciere* in the chasms of *Benwewish*, a neighboring mountain, throughout the year.

AUG. 18. Continue my journey along the low country, which is rich and well cultivated.

Pass near *Invergordon* [*], a handsome house, amidst fine plantations. Near it is the narrowest part of the Firth, and a ferry into the shire of *Cromarty*, now a country almost destitute of trees; yet, in the time of *James* V. was covered with timber, and over-run with wolves [†].

---

[*] At *Culraen*, three miles from this place, is found, two feet beneath the surface, a stratum of white soapy marle filled with shells, and is much used as a manure.

[†] These animals have been long extinct in *North Britain*, notwithstanding M. *de Buffon* asserts the contrary. There are many antient laws for their extirpation: that of *James* I. *parlem*. 7. is the most remarkable: " The Schireffs & Barons suld hunt the wolf four or thrie times in the Zear, betwixt St. *Marks* day & *Lambes*, quhich is the time of their quhelpes, & all tenents sall rise with them under paine of ane wadder."

Near

Near the summit of the hill, between the Firths *Ballinagouan.*
of *Cromartie* and *Dornoch*, is *Ballinagouan*, the seat
of a gentleman, who has most successfully converted
his sword into a plough-share; who, after a series
of disinterested services to his country, by clearing
the seas of privateers, the most unprofitable of cap-
tures, has applied himself to arts not less deserving
of its thanks. He is the best farmer and the
greatest planter in the country: his wheat and his
turneps shew the one, his plantations of a million
of pines each year the other *. It was with great
satisfaction that I observed characters of this kind
very frequent in *North Britain*; for during the interval of peace, every officer possessed of any pa-
trimony was fond of retiring to it, assumed the farmer without flinging off the gentleman, enjoyed
rural quiet; yet ready to undergo the fatigues of
war the moment his country clamed his services.

About two miles below *Ballinagouan* is a melancholy instance of a reverse of conduct: the ruins
of *New Tarbat*, once the magnificent seat of an *New Tarbat.*
unhappy nobleman, who plunged into a most un-
gratefull rebellion, destructive to himself and family. The tenants, who seem to inhabit it *gratis*,
are forced to shelter themselves from the weather
in the very lowest apartments, while swallows make
their nests in the bold stucco of some of the upper.

While I was in this county, I heard a singular
but well-attested relation of a woman disordered in

---

* Pine, or *Scotch* fir-seed, as it is called, sells from four to six
shillings per pound. Rents are payed here in kind: the landlord
either contracts to supply the forts with the produce of the land,
or sells it to the merchant, who comes for it. The price of labor
is 6d. per day to the men, 3d. to the women.

her

her health, who fafted for a fupernatural fpace of time; but the length of the narrative obliges me to fling it into the Appendix *.

Ride along a tedious black moor to *Tain*, a fmall town on the Firth of *Dornoch*; diftinguifhed for nothing but its large fquare tower, decorated with five fmall fpires. The place appeared very gay at this time; for all the gaudy finery of a little fair was difplayed in the fhew of hard ware, painted linnens, and ribbands. Kept along the fhore, for about two miles, through an open corn country, and croffing the great ferry, in breadth near two miles, thro' a rapid tide, and in a bad boat, land in the county of *Sutherland*, and in lefs than an hour reach its capital,

DORNOCH. Dornoch, a fmall town, half in ruins; once the refidence of the Bifhops of *Cathnefs*, and, like *Durham*, the feat of Ecclefiaftics: many of the houfes ftill are called after the titles of thofe that inhabited them: the Bifhop lodged in the caftle: the Dean's houfe is at prefent the inn: the cathedral was in form of a crofs, is now a ruin, except part, which is the prefent church. On the doors and window-fhutters were painted (as is common in many parts of *North Britain*) white tadpole-like figures on a black ground, defigned to exprefs the tears of the country for the lofs of any perfon of diftinction. Thefe were occafioned by the affecting end of that amiable pair the young Earl and Countefs of *Sutherland*, who were lovely in their lives, and in their deaths they were not divided, for their happinefs was interrupted by a very fhort feparation; *fanè ubi*

* No. II.

idem

idem et maximus et honestissimus amor est, aliquando præstat morte jungi, quam vita distrahi.

Ride on a plain not far from the sea; pass by a small cross, called the *Thane's* Cross; and not far from thence the spot where an unhappy creature had been burnt, if I mistake not, in *June* 1727, for the imaginary crime of *witchcraft* *.

Cross a very narrow inlet to a small bay at *Porth-beg*, or the little ferry, in a boat as dangerous as the last; for horses can neither get in or out without great risque, from the vast height of the sides and their want of slips. Keep along the shore, pass by the small village of *Golspic*, and reach

Dunrobin castle, the antient seat of the Earls of *Sutherland*, founded about the year 1100, situated on a round hill at a small distance from the sea. The few paintings here are; an Earl of *Murray*, an

Dunrobin.

---

* This is the last instance of these frantic executions in the north of *Scotland*, as that in the south was at *Paisly* in 1696, where, among others, a woman, young and handsome, suffered, and with a reply to her enquiring friends, worthy a *Roman* matron, being asked why she did not make a better defence on her tryal, answered, *My persecutors have destroyed my honor, and my life is not now worth the pains of defending.* The last instance of national credulity on this head was the story of the witches of *Thurso*, who tormenting for a long time an honest fellow under the usual form of cats, at last provoked him so, that one night he put them to flight with his broad sword, and cut off the leg of one less nimble than the rest; on his taking it up, to his amazement he found it belonged to a female of his own species, and next morning discovered the owner, an old hag, with only the companion leg to this. The horrors of this tale were considerably abated in the place I heard it, by an unlucky enquiry made by one in company, viz. In what part would the old woman have suffered, had the man cut off the cat's tail? But these relations of almost obsolete superstitions must never be thought a reflection on this country, as long as any memory remains of the tragical end of the poor people at *Tring*, who, within a few miles of our capital, in 1751, fell a sacrifice to the belief of the common people in witches, or of that ridiculous imposture in the capital itself, in 1762, of the *Cock-Lane* ghost, which found credit with all ranks of people.

L old

old man, on wood. His son and two daughters, by *Co. G.* 1628. A fine full length of *Charles* I. *Angus Williamson*, a heroe of the *clan Chattan*, who rescued the *Sutherlands* in the time of distress. A very singular picture of the Duke of *Alva* in council, with a cardinal by his side, who puts a pair of bellows blown by the Devil into his ear: the Duke has a chain in one hand, fixed to the necks of the kneeling *Flemings*; in the other he shews them a paper of recantation for them to sign, behind whom are the reformed Clergy.

The demesn is kept in excellent order, and I saw here (*lat.* 58.) a very fine field of wheat, which would be ripe about the middle of next month. This was the last wheat which had been sown this year in *North Britain*.

Sutherland is a country abounding in cattle, and sends out annually 2500 head, which sold about this time from 2 l. 10 s. to 3 l.* *per* head. These are very frequently without horns, and both they and the horses are very small. Stags abound in the hills, there being reckoned not less than 1600 on the *Sutherland* estate, which, in fact, is the greatest part of the county. Besides these are Roes, Grous, black game and Ptarmigans in plenty, and during winter multitudes of water-fowl on the coast.

Pictish Castles: Not far from *Dunrobin* is a very entire antiquity of the kind known in *Scotland* by the name of the *Pictish* Castles, and called here *Cairn Lean*, or a grey tower: that I saw was about 130 yards in circumference, round, and raised so high above the

* Lean.

ground as to form a considerable mount: on the top was an extensive but shallow hollow; within were three low concentric galleries, at small distances from each other, covered above with large stones; and the side-walls were about four or five feet thick, rudely made. There are generally three of these places near each other, so that each may be seen from any one. Whether these were the *suffugia hiemi* aut *receptacula frugibus* of the *Picts*, as they were of the *Germans*, or whether they might not have been used for religious purposes, as such hollows have been in *Norway**, I will not pretend to decide: if the last, I would suppose some of the galleries to be for the priests, the others for the victims, who were chosen by lot, and who might be brought to be sacrificed in the concave area above, which was well adapted to retain their blood, that was to be sprinkled on the spectators, on the posts of their houses, and on the sails of their ships †.

Kept along the shore northward. About a mile from the castle are some small cliffs of free-stone; in one is *Straith-leven* Cove, an artificial cave, with seats and several shallow circular hollows cut within-side. At some distance, and near the sea, are small strata of coal three feet thick dipping to the east, and found at the depth of about 14 to 24 yards. Sometimes it takes fire on the bank, which has given it so ill a name, that people are very fearfull of taking it aboard their ships. I am sur-

Aug. 19.

Coal.

---

† *Wormii* Monumenta Danicorum, *lib.* I. *p.* 6.
* *Worm. Monum. lib.* V. *p.* 24.

prized

that they will not run the rifque, confidering the miraculous quality it poffeffes of driving away rats wherever it is ufed. This is believed by the good people of *Sutherland*, who affured me ferioufly of its virtues; and they farther attributed the fame to the earth and very heath of their county. They add too, that not a rat will live with them, notwithftanding they fwarm in the adjacent fhires of *Rofs* and *Cathnefs* *.

In *Affynt*, a part of this county, far weft of *Dunrobin*, are large ftrata of a beautifull white marble, equal, as I was told, to the *Parian*. I afterwards faw fome of the fame kind found at *Glenavon* in *Badenoch*.

Crofs the water of *Brora*, which runs along a deep chafm, over which is a handfome bridge of a fingle arch. Near is a cave, where the Salmon-fifhers lie during the feafon: the roof is pierced through to the furface, which ferves for a natural chimney. They take annually about 10 or 12 lafts of fifh. In a bank not far from the bridge are found abundance of *Belemnitæ*.

---

* Some years ago I bought of the Monks, at the great *Benedictine* convent at *Augfburg*, fome papers of St. *Ulric*'s earth, which I was affured, by *Lutheran* and *Papift*, had the fame rat-expelling quality with that above-mentioned; but whether for want of due faith, or neglect of attending to the forms of the printed prefcription given with them, (here copied at full length) I know not, but the audacious animals haunt my houfe in fpite of it:—*Venerabiles Reliquiæ de Terra Sepulchrali, five de refoluta deintùs carne S. Udalrici Conf. & Epifcopi* Auguftani; *quæ fi honorificè ad inftar aliarum Reliquiarum habeantur, & ad Dei laudem, Divique Præfulis honorem, pium quoddam opus, v. g. Oratio, Jejunium, Eleemofyna* &c. *præftetur, mirum eft, qua polleant efficaciâ, ad profcribendos præfertim è domibus, & vicinia Glires, qui fubfiftere minimè valent, ubicunque fimiles Reliquiæ cum fiduciâ fuerint appenfæ, vel affervatæ. Idque ex fpeciali prærogativâ, quâ omnipotens Deus infignia tanti Patroni merita perpetuo miraculo ftatuit condecorare.*

The

The country is very sandy, and the arable, or cultivated part, very narrow, confined on the east by the sea, on the west by lofty black mountains, which approach nearer and nearer to the water, till at length they project into it at the great promontory the *Ord of Cathness*, the boundary between that county and *Sutherland*, after which the coast is bold and rocky, except a small bay or two.

Ford the very dangerous water of *Hemsdale*, rapid and full of great stones. Very large Lampries are found here, fish detested by the Highlanders. Beneath the stones on the sea-shore are abundance of spotted and viviparous Blennies, Father Lashers, and Whistle Fish. Mackrel appear here this month, but without their roes. I thought them far inferior in goodness to those of our country. Much salmon is taken here. *Hemsdale.*

The grey Water-wagtail quits this country in the winter; with us it resides.

Dined at the little village of *Hemsdale*; near which are the ruins of a square tower.

Passed through a rich vale full of good barley and oats between the hill of *Hemsdale* and the *Ord*. Ascend that vast promontory on a good road winding up its steep sides, and impending in many parts over the sea, infinitely more high and horrible than our *Penmaen Mawr*. Beneath were numbers of Seals floating on the waves, with sea-fowl swimming among them with great security. Observed projecting from one part of the *Ord*, far below, a small and verdant hill, on which, tradition says, was fought a single combat between an Earl of *Cathness* and a son of the Earl of *Sutherland*, while their two armies *Ord of Cathness.*

armies looked on from above: the first was killed on the spot, the last died of his wounds.

Beneath this cape are immense caves, the resort of Seals* and Sea-fowls: the sides and top are chiefly covered with heath and morassy earth, which gives it a black and melancholy look. Ride over some boggy and dreary moors. Pass thro' *Ausdale*, a little highland village. Descend into a deep bottom covered with alders, willows, birch and wicken trees, to *Langwall*, the seat of Mr. *Sutherland*, who gave me a very hospitable reception. The country abounds with Stags and Roes, and all sorts of feathered game, while the adjacent river brings Salmon almost up to his door.

Lavellan.   I enquired here after the *Lavellan* †, which, from description, I suspect to be the Water Shrew-mouse. The country people have a notion that it is noxious to cattle: they preserve the skin, and, as a cure for their sick beasts, give them the water in which it has been dipt. I believe it to be the same animal which in *Sutherland* is called the Water Mole.

Aug. 20.   Proceed on my journey. Pass near *Berridale*. On a peninsula jutting into the sea is the ruin of the castle; between it and the land is a deep chasm, where there had been a draw-bridge. On this castle are stationed, in the salmon season, persons who are to observe the approach of the fish to the fresh waters.

* During spring great quantities of Lump-fish resort here, and are the prey of the Seals, as appears from the numbers of their skins, which at that season float ashore. The Seals, at certain times, seem visited with a great mortality; for at those times multitudes of them are seen dead in the water.
† *Sibbald hist. Scotland. Br. Zool. illust.* cii.

Near

Near *Clathron* is a druidical stone set an end, and of a most stupendous size.

Saw *Dunbeth*, the seat of Mr. *Sinclair*, situated on a narrow neck of land; on one side impending over the sea, on the other over a deep chasm, into which the tide flows: a small narrow garden, with billows beating on three sides, fills the rest of the land between the house and the sea. Numbers of old castles in this county have the same tremendous situation. On the west side of this house are a few rows of tolerable trees; the only trees that I saw from *Berridale* to the extremity of *Cathness**. On the right inland are the small remains of *Knackennan* castle, built by an Earl of *Cathness*. From these parts is a full view of the lofty naked mountain of *Scaraben* and *Morven*. The last Ptarmigans in *Scotland* are on the first; the last Roes about *Langwall*, there being neither high hills nor woods beyond. All the county on this side, from *Dunbeth* to the extremity, is flat, or at left very seldom interrupted with hills, and those low; but the coasts rocky, and composed of stupendous cliffs.

Dunbeth.

Scaraben.

Refreshed our horses at a little inn at the hamlet of *Clythe*, not far from the headland, called *Clytheness*. Reach *Thrumster*, a seat of Mr. *Sinclair*'s. It is observable, that the names of places in this county often terminate in *ter* and *dale*, which favors of *Danish* origin.

The *Sinclairs* are very numerous, and possess considerable fortunes in these parts; but *Boethius*

---

* But vast quantity of subterraneous timber in all the moors. Near *Dunbeth* is an entire *Pict's* castle, with the hollow in the top, and is called the *Bourg* of *Dunbeth*.

says

says, that they, the *Fraziers, Campbells, Boswels,* and many others, came originally from *France.*

Aug. 21. *Wick.*
Pass through *Wick*, a small burrough town with some good houses, seated on a river within reach of the tide, and at a distance lies the old castle. Somewhat farther, close to the sea, is *Archringal* tower, the seat of Sir *William Dunbar.* Ride over the Links of *Keith*, on the side of *Sinclair* bay. These were once a morass, now covered with sand, finely turfed over; so in this instance the land has been obliged by the instability of the sand. The old castle of *Keiss* is seated on a rock, with a good house of the same name near it.

Near *Freswick* castle the cliffs are very lofty; the strata that compose them lie quite horizontally in such thin and regular layers, and so often intersected by fissures, as to appear like masonry. Beneath are great insulated columns, called here *Stacks,* composed of the same sort of natural masonry as the cliffs; many of them are hollowed quite thro', so as to form most magnificent arches, which the sea rushes thro' with vast noise and impetuosity, affording a most august piece of scenery to such who are steady enough to survey it from the narrow and almost impending paths.

Freswick castle.
Freswick castle is seated on a narrow rock projecting into the sea, with just room enough for it to stand on: the access to it while the draw-bridge was in being, was over a deep chasm cut thro' the little isthmus that connected it to the main land. These dreadful situations are strongly expressive of the jealous and wretched condition of the tyrant owners.

After

After riding near *Fresswick* bay, the second sandy bay in the county, pass over a very bad morass, and after a few miles travel arrive at *Dungsby* bay *, a low tract, consisting of oat-lands and grazing land: the *ultima Thule* of Mr. *Wallace*, whose description it answers in this particular.

Dungsby bay.

Quam juxta infames scopuli, et petrosa vorago
Asperat undisonis saxa pudenda vadis †.

The beach is a collection of fragments of shells; beneath which are vast broken rocks, some sunk, others apparent, running into a sea never pacific. The contrary tides and currents form here a most tremendous contest; yet, by the skilfulness of the people, are passed with great safety in the narrow little boats I saw lying on the shore.

The points of this bay are *Dungsby*-head and St. *John*'s head, stretching out into the sea to the east and west, forming a pair of horns; from the resemblance to which it should seem that this country was antiently styled *Cornuna*.

From hence is a full view of several of the *Orkney* islands, such as *Flota*, *Waes*, *Ronaldsa*, *Swanna*, to the west the *Skerries*, and within two miles of land *Stroma*, famous for its natural mummies, or the entire and uncorrupted bodies of persons who had been dead sixty years. I was informed that they were very light, had a flexibility in their limbs, and were of a dusky color ‡. This isle is fertile in corn,

Orkneys.

Mummies.

---

* *John a Grout*'s house is now known only by name. The proper name of the bay is *Duncan*'s.
† Vide WALLACE's *Orkney isles*, 33.
‡ In the *Philosophical Transactions abridged*, viii. 705. is an almost parallel instance of two corpses, found in a moor in *Derbyshire*, that had for 49 years resisted putrefaction, and were in much the same state as those in *Stroma*.

is inhabited by about thirty families, who know not the use of a plough, but dig every part of their corn land.

Dine at the good minister's of *Cannesby*. On my return saw at a distance the *Stacks* of *Dungsby*, a vast insulated rock, over-topping the land, and appearing like a great tower.

<small>Second sight.</small> Passed near the seat of a gentleman not long deceased; the last who was believed to be possessed of the *second sight*. Originally he made use of the pretence, in order to render himself more respectable with his clan; but at length, in spite of fine abilities, was made a dupe to his own artifices, became possessed with a serious belief of the faculty, and for a considerable number of years before his death was made truely unhappy by this strange opinion, which originally arose from the following accident. A boat of his was on a very tempestuous night at sea; his mind, filled with anxiety at the danger his people were in, furnished him with every idea of the misfortune that really befell them: he suddenly starting up pronounced that his men would be drowned, for that he had seen them pass before him with wet garments and dropping locks. The event was correspondent, and he from that time grew confirmed in the reality of spectral predictions.

There is another sort of divination, called *Sleinanachd*, or reading the *speal-bone*, or the blade-bone of a shoulder of mutton well scraped. When Lord *Loudon* was obliged to retreat before the Rebels to the isle of *Skie*, a common soldier, on the very moment the battle of *Culloden* was decided, proclaimed the

GANNET

the victory at that distance, pretending to have discovered the event by looking through the bone.

I heard of one instance of second sight, or rather of foresight, which was well attested, and made much noise about the time the prediction was fulfilled. A little after the battle of *Preston Pans*, the president, *Duncan Forbes*, being at his house of *Culloden* with a nobleman, from whom I had the relation, fell into discourse on the probable consequences of the action: after a long conversation, and after revolving all that might happen, Mr. *Forbes* suddenly turning to a window, said, *All these things may fall out; but depend on it, all these disturbances will be terminated on this spot.*

Returned the same road. Saw multitudes of *Gannets*, or *Soland* Geese, on their passage northward: they went in small flocks from five to fifteen in each, and continued passing for hours: it was a stormy day; they kept low and near the shore; but never passed over the land, even when a bay with promontories intervened, but followed (preserving an equal distance from shore) the form of the bay, and then regularly doubled the Capes. I saw many parties make a sort of halt for the sake of fishing; they soared to a great height, then darting down headlong into the sea made the water foam and spring up with the violence of their descent; after which they pursued their route.

Gannets.

Swans resort in *October* to the Loughs of *Hemprigs* and *Waster*, and continue there till *March*. Abundance of Land-rails are found throughout the county. Multitudes of Sea-fowl breed in the cliffs: among others, the *Lyre*; but the season being past, I neither

I neither saw it, nor could underſtand what ſpecies it was.

Sinclair bay and caſtle.

Went along a fine hard ſand on the edge of *Sinclair* bay. On the ſouth point, near *Roſs-head*, on the ſame rock, are *Sinclair* and *Carnego* caſtles; but, as if the joint tenants, like beaſts of prey, had been in fear of each other, there was between them a draw-bridge; the firſt too had an iron door, which dropped from above through grooves ſtill viſible.

Produce of Cathneſs.

Cathneſs may be called an immenſe moraſs, mixed with ſome fruitfull ſpots of oats and barley, much coarſe graſs, and here and there ſome fine, almoſt all natural, there being as yet very little artificial. At this time was the hay harveſt both here and about *Dunrobin*: the hay on this rough land is cut with very ſhort ſcythes, and with a briſk and ſtrong ſtroke. The country produces and exports great quantities of *oatmeal*, and much whiſky is diſtilled from the barley: the great thinneſs of inhabitants throughout *Cathneſs* enables them to ſend abroad much of its productions. No wheat had been raiſed this year in the county; and I was informed that this grain is ſown here in the ſpring, by reaſon of the wet and fury of the winters.

Cattle.

The county is ſuppoſed to ſend out, in ſome years, 2200 head of cattle; but in bad ſeaſons, the farmer kills and ſalts numbers for ſale. Great numbers of ſwine are reared here: they are ſhort, high-backed, long-briſtled, ſharp, ſlender and long-noſed; have long erect ears, and moſt ſavage looks, and are ſeen tethered in almoſt every field. The reſt of the commodities of *Cathneſs* are butter, cheeſe,

cheese, tallow, hides, the oil and skins of seals, and the feathers of geese.

Here are neither barns or graineries; the corn is thrashed out and preserved in the chaff in *bykes*, which are stacks in shape of bee-hives, thatched quite round, where it will keep good for two years.

Much Salmon is taken at *Castle-hill, Dunet, Wick*, and *Thurso*. The miraculous draught at the last place is still talked of; not less than 2500 being taken at one tide, within the memory of man. At a small distance from *Sinclair* castle, near *Staxigo* creek, is a small herring-fishery, the only one on the coast: Cod and other white fish abound here; but the want of ports on this stormy coast is an obstacle to the establishment of fisheries on this side the country. *Salmon.*

In the month of *November* numbers of Seals * are taken in the vast caverns that open into the sea and run some hundreds of yards under ground. Their entrance is narrow, their inside lofty and spacious. The Seal-hunters enter these in small boats with torches, which they light as soon as they land, and then with loud shouts alarm the animals, which they kill with clubs as they attempt to pass. This is a hazardous employ; for should the wind blow hard from sea, these adventurers are inevitably lost †. *Seals.*

Much lime-stone is found in this country, which when burnt is made into a compost with turf and tang. The tender sex (I blush for the *Cathnesians*) *Servitude.*

---

* Sometimes a large species near twelve feet long has been killed on the coast; and I have been informed that the same kind are found on the rock *Hiskir*, one of the western isles.
† For a fuller account, *vide Br. Zool. illustr.* 38.

are

are the only animals of burden: they turn their patient backs to the dunghills, and receive in their *keizes*, or baskets, as much as their lords and masters think fit to fling in with their pitchforks, and then trudge to the field in droves of sixty or seventy. The common people are kept here in great servitude, and most of their time is given to their Lairds, an invincible impediment to the prosperity of this county.

Of the ten parishes in *Cathness*, only the four that lie S. E. speak *Erse*; all the others speak *English*, and that in greater purity than most part of *North Britain*.

Inoculation is much practised by an ingenious physician (Dr. *Mackenzie*, of *Wick*) in this county, and also the *Orkneys* *, with great success, without any previous preparation The success was equally great at *Sanda*, a poor isle, where there was no sort of fuel but what was got from dried cow-dung: but in all these places, the small-pox is very fatal in the natural way. Other diseases in *Cathness* are colds, coughs, and very frequently palsies.

Long days.   I came here too late † to have any benefit from the great length of days; but from *June* to the middle of *July*, there is scarce any night; for even at what

---

* At this time a person was employed in the same business in the *Shetland* islands.

† Besides the missing so singular a phænomenon, I found that the bad weather, which begins earlier in the north, was setting in: I would therefore recommend to any traveller, who means to take this distant tour, to set out from *Edinburgh* a month sooner than myself.

is

is called midnight the smallest print may be read, so truely did *Juvenal* style these people.

 Minima contentos nocte BRITANNOS.

 On my way between *Thrumster* and *Dunbeth*, again saw numbers of flocks of *Gannets* keeping due north, and the weather being very calm they flew high. It has not been observed that they ever return this way in the spring; but seem to make a circuit of the island, till they again arrive at the *Bass*, their only breeding-place on the eastern coast.

 On descending a steep hill is a romantic view of the two bridges over the waters of *Berridale* and *Langwall*, and their wooded glens, and of the castle of *Berridale**, over the sea, where the Salmon-fishers station themselves to observe the approach of those fish out of the ocean. After a tedious ascent up the King's road of four miles gain the top of the *Ord*, and lie at *Hemsdale*.

 Re-visit the same places, till I pass *Dingwall*. Cross the *Conan* in a boat, a very beautifull river, not remote from *Castle Braan*. Was in this neighborhood informed of other singular customs of the Highlanders.

 On New-year's day they burn juniper before their cattle, and on the first *Monday* in every quarter sprinkle them with urine.

 In some parts of the country is a *Bel-tein*, different from that before-mentioned. A cross is cut on some sticks, which is dipped in pottage, and the *Thursday* before *Easter* one of each placed over

Aug. 23.
Gannets.

Berridale.

Aug. 24. to 29.

Singular customs.

A Bel-tein.

---

* A little up the land is the ruin of *Ach-castle*.

the

the sheep-cot, the stable, or the cow-house. On the 1st of *May* they are carried to the hill where the *Bel-tein* is celebrated; all decked with wild flowers, and after the feast is over, re-placed over the spots they were taken from. These follies are now seldom practised, and that with the utmost secrecy; for the Clergy are indefatigable in discouraging every species of superstition.

In certain places, the death of people is supposed to be foretold by the cries and shrieks of *Benshi*, or the Fairies wife, uttered along the very path where the funeral is to pass; and what in *Wales* are called *corps candles*, are often imagined to appear, and foretell mortality.

Marriage customs. The courtship of the Highlander has these remarkable circumstances attending it: after privately obtaining the consent of the Fair, he formally demands her of the father. The Lover and his friends assemble on a hill allotted for that purpose in every parish, and one of them is dispatched to obtain permission to wait on the daughter: if he is succefsfull, he is again sent to invite the father and his friends to ascend the hill and partake of a whisky cask, which is never forgot: the Lover advances, takes his future Father-in-law by the hand, and then plights his troth, and the Fair-one is surrendered up to him. During the marriage ceremony, great care is taken that dogs do not pass between them, and particular attention is payed to the leaving the Bridegroom's left-shoe without buckle or latchet, to prevent witches* from de-

---

* An old opinion. *Gesner* says that the witches made use of toads as a charm, *Ut vim coeundi, ni fallor, in viris tollerent.* Gesner de quad. ovi. p. 72.

priving him, on the nuptial night, of the power of loosening the virgin zone. As a test, not many years ago a singular custom prevaled in the *western* Highlands the morning after a wedding: a basket was fastened with a cord round the neck of the bridegroom by the female part of the company, who immediately filled it with stones, till the poor man was in great danger of being strangled: if his bride did not take compassion on him, and cut the cord with a knife given her to use at discretion. But such was the tenderness of the *Caledonian* spouses, that never was an instance of their neglecting an immediate relief of their good man.

Pass near the abby* of *Beaulieu*, a large ruin: cross the ferry, and again reach *Inverness*.

Make an excursion ten miles south of *Inverness* to *Moy-hall*, pleasantly seated at the head of a small but beautifull lake of the same name, full of Trout, and *Char*, called in the *Erse*, *Tariar-kinich*, and in the *Scotch*, Red Weems. This water is about two miles and a half long, and half a mile broad, adorned with two or three isles prettily wooded. Each side is bounded by hills cloathed at the bottom with trees; and in front, at the distance of thirty miles, is the great mountain of *Karn Goran*, patched with snow.

Aug. 30.
Moy-hall.

This place is called *Stasach na gail*, or the threshold of the Highlands, being a very natural and strongly marked entrance from the north. This is the seat of the *Clan Chattan*, or the *M'Intoshes*, once a powerfull people: in the year 1715, fifteen

Clan Chattan.

---

* Founded about 1219, by Lord *Patrick Bisset*, for the monks of *Vall'ombrosa*.

M

hundred

hundred toke the field; but in 1745, scarce half that number: like another *Absalom*, their fair mistress was in that year supposed to have stolen their hearts from her *Laird* their chieftain: but the severest loyalist must admit some extenuation of their error, in yielding to the insinuations of so charming a seducer.

Boethius relates, that in his time *Inverness* was greatly frequented by merchants from *Germany*, who purchased here the furs of several sorts of wild beasts*; and that wild horses were found in great abundance in its neighborhood: that the country yielded a great deal of wheat and other corn, and quantities of nuts and apples. At present there is a trade in the skins of Deer, Roes, and other beasts, which the Highlanders bring down to the fairs. There happened to be one at this time: the commodities were skins, various necessaries brought in by the Pedlars, coarse country cloths, cheese, butter and meal; the last in goat-skin bags; the butter lapped in cawls, or leaves of the broad *alga* or tang; and great quantities of birch wood and hazel cut into lengths for carts, &c. which had been floated down the river from *Lough-Ness*.

Highland dress.

The fair was a very agreeable circumstance, and afforded a most singular groupe of Highlanders in all their motly dresses. Their *brechan*, or plaid, consists of twelve or thirteen yards of a narrow

---

* *Ad Nessæ lacus longi quatuor et viginti passuum millia, lati duodecim latera, propter ingentia nemora ferarum ingens copia est cervorum, equorum indomitorum, capreolorum et ejusmodi animantium magna vis: ad hæc martirillæ, Fouinæ, ut vulgo vocantur, vulpes, mustellæ, Fibri, Lutræque incomparabili numero quorum tergora exteræ gentes ad luxum immenso pretio coemunt.* Scot. Regni Descr. ix. Hist. Scot. xxx.

stuff,

stuff, wrapt round the middle, and reaches to the knees: is often fastened round the middle with a belt, and is then called *brechan-feal*; but in cold weather, is large enough to wrap round the whole body from head to feet; and this often is their only cover, not only within doors, but on the open hills during the whole night. It is frequently fastened on the shoulders with a pin often of silver, and before with a brotche (like the *fibula* of the *Romans*), which is sometimes of silver, and both large and expensive; the old ones have very frequently mottos.

The stockings are short, and are tied below the knee. The *cuoranen* is a sort of laced shoe made of a skin with the hairy side out, but now seldom worn. The *truish* were worn by the gentry, and were breeches and stockings made of one piece.

The *fillebeg*, i. e. little plaid, also called *kelt*, is a sort of short petticoat reaching only to the knees, and is a modern substitute for the lower part of the plaid, being found to be less cumbersome, especially in time of action, when the Highlanders used to tuck their *brechan* into their girdle. Almost all have a great pouch of badger and other skins, with tassels dangling before. In this they keep their tobacco and money.

Their antient arms were the *Lochaber* ax, now Arms. used by none but the town-guard of *Edinburgh*; a tremendous weapon, better to be expressed by a figure than words.

The broad-sword and target; with the last they covered themselves, with the first reached their enemy at a great distance. These were their antient weapons, as appears by *Tacitus*; but since the disarming act, are scarcely to be met with; partly owing to that, partly to the spirit of industry now rising among them, the Highlanders in a few years will scarce know the use of any weapon.

Bows and arrows were used in war as late as the middle of the last century, as I find in a manuscript life of Sir *Ewin Cameron*.

The *dirk* was a sort of dagger stuck in the belt. I frequently saw this weapon in the shambles of *Inverness*, converted into a butcher's knife, being, like *Hudibras*'s dagger,

A serviceable dudgeon,
Either for fighting or for drudging.

The dirk was a weapon used by the antient *Caledonians*, for *Dio Cassius*, in his account of the expedition of *Severus*, mentions it under the name of *Pugio*.

The *Mattucashlash*, or arm-pit dagger, was worn there ready to be used on coming to close quarters. These, with a pistol stuck in the girdle, completely armed the Highlander †.

Fiery cross.

It will be fit to mention here the method the Chieftains toke formerly to assemble the clans for any military expedition. In every clan there is a known place of rendezvous, styled *Carn a whin*,

---

* *Simul constantia, simul arte Britanni ingentibus gladiis et brevibus cetris, missilia nostrorum vitare vel excutere.* — Vita Agricolæ. c. 36.
† *Major*, who wrote about the year 1518, thus describes their arms: *Arcum et sagittas, latissimum ensem cum parvo halberto, pugionem grossum ex solo latere sciudentem, sed acutissimum sub zonam semper ferunt. Tempore belli loricam ex toris ferreis per totum corpus induunt.* Lib. I. c. viii.

to which they must resort on this signal. A person is sent out full speed with a pole burnt at one end and bloody at the other, and with a cross at the top, which is called *Crosh-tairie*, the cross of shame, or the fiery cross; the first from the disgrace they would undergo if they declined appearing; the second from the penalty of having fire and sword carried thro' their country, in case of refusal. The first bearer delivers it to the next person he meets, he running full speed to the third, and so on. In the late rebellion, it was sent by some unknown disaffectd hand thro' the county of *Breadalbane*, and passed through a tract of thirty-two miles in three hours, but without effect.

The women's dress is the *kirch*, or a white piece of linnen, pinned over the foreheads of those that are married, and round the hind part of the head, falling behind over their necks. The single women wear only a ribband round their head, which they call a snood. The *tanac*, or plaid, hangs over their shoulders, and is fastened before with a brotche; but in bad weather is drawn over their heads. In the county of *Breadalbane*, many wear, when in high dress, a great pleated stocking of an enormous length, called *ossan*. In other respects, their dress resembles that of women of the same rank in *England*: but their condition is very different, being little better than slaves to our sex.

Women's dress.

The manners of the native Highlanders may justly be expressed in these words: indolent to a high degree, unless rouzed to war, or to any animating amusement; or I may say, from experience, to lend any disinterested assistance to the distressed traveller,

Character of the Highlanders.

traveller, either in directing him on his way, or affording their aid in paſſing the dangerous torrents of the Highlands: hoſpitable to the higheſt degree, and full of generoſity: are much affected with the civility of ſtrangers, and have in themſelves a natural politeneſs and addreſs, which often flows from the meaneſt when leſt expected. Thro' my whole tour I never met with a ſingle inſtance of national reflection! their forbearance proves them to be ſuperior to the meanneſs of retaliation. I fear they pity us; but I hope not indiſcriminately. Are exceſſively inquiſitive after your buſineſs, your name, and other particulars of little conſequence to them: moſt curious after the politicks of the world, and when they can procure an old news-paper, will liſten to it with all the avidity of *Shakeſpear*'s blackſmith. Have much pride, and conſequently are impatient of affronts, and revengefull of injuries. Are decent in their general behaviour; inclined to ſuperſtition, yet attentive to the duties of religion, and are capable of giving a moſt diſtinct account of the principles of their faith. But in many parts of the Highlands, their character begins to be more faintly marked; they mix more with the world, and become daily leſs attached to their chiefs: the clans begin to diſperſe themſelves through different parts of the country, finding that their induſtry and good conduct afford them better protection (ſince the due execution of the laws) than any their chieftain can afford; and the chieftain taſting the ſweets of advanced rents, and the benefits of induſtry, diſmiſſes from his table the crowds of retainers, the

former

former instruments of his oppression and freakish tyranny.

Most of the antient sports of the Highlanders, such as archery, hunting, fowling and fishing, are now disused: those retained are, throwing the *putting*-stone, or stone of *strength**, as they call it, which occasions an emulation who can throw a weighty one the farthest. Throwing the *penny*-stone, which answers to our coits. The *shinty*, or the striking a ball of wood or of hair: this game is played between two parties in a large plain, and furnished with clubs; which-ever side strikes it first to their own goal wins the match. *Highland sports.*

The amusements by their fire-sides were, the telling of tales, the wildest and most extravagant imaginable: musick was another: in former times, the harp was the favorite instrument, covered with leather and strung with wire †, but at present is quite lost. Bagpipes are supposed to have been introduced by the *Danes*; the oldest are played with the mouth, the loudest and most ear-piercing of any wind musick; the other, played with the fingers only, are of *Irish* origin: the first suited the genius of this warlike people, rouzed their courage to battle, alarmed them when secure, and collected them when scattered. This instrument is become scarce since the abolition of the power of the chieftains, and the more industrious turn of the common people. *Bagpipes.*

---

* *Cloch neart.*
† Major says, *Pro musicis instrumentis et musico concentu, Lyra sylvestres utuntur, cujus chordas ex aere, et non ex animalium intestinis faciunt, in qua dulcissimè modulantur.*

Vocal

Vocal musick was much in vogue amongst them, and their songs were chiefly in praise of their antient heroes. I was told that they still have fragments of the story of *Fingal* and others, which they carrol as they go along; these vocal traditions are the foundation of the works of *Ossian*.

Aug. 31. Leave *Inverness*, and continue my journey west for some time by the river-side: have a fine view of the plain, the *Tommin*, the town and the distant hills. After a ride of about six miles reached *Lough-Ness**, and enjoyed along its banks a most romantic and beautifull scenery, generally in woods of birch, or hazel, mixed with a few holly, white-thorn, aspin, ash and oak, but open enough in all parts to admit a sight of the water. Sometimes the road was strait for a considerable distance, and resembled a fine and regular avenue; in others it wound about the sides of the hills which overhung the lake: the road was frequently cut thro' the rock, which on one side formed a solid wall; on the other, a steep precipice. In many parts we were immersed in woods; in others, they opened and gave a view of the sides and tops of the vast mountains soaring above: some of these were naked, but in general covered with wood, except on the meer precipices, or where the grey rocks denied vegetation, or where the heath, now glowing with purple blossoms, covered the surface. The form of these hills was very various and irregular, either broken into frequent precipices, or towering into rounded summits cloathed with trees; but not so

---

* This beautifull lake has a great resemblance to some parts of the lake of *Lucerne*, especially towards the east end.

close

close but to admit a sight of the sky between them. Thus, for many miles, there was no possibility of cultivation; yet this tract was occupied by diminutive cattle, by Sheep, or by Goats: the last were pied, and lived most luxuriously on the tender branches of the trees. The wild animals that possessed this picturesque scene were Stags and Roes, black game, and Grous; and on the summits, white Hares and Ptarmigans. Foxes are so numerous and voracious that the farmers are sometimes forced to house their Sheep, as is done in *France*, for fear of the Wolves*.

The north side of *Lough-Ness* is far less beautifull than the south. In general, the hills are less high, but very steep; in a very few places covered with brush-wood, but in general very naked, from the sliding of the strata down their sloping sides. About the middle is Castle *Urquhart*, a fortress founded on a rock projecting into the lake, and was said to have been the seat of the once powerfull *Cummins*. Near it is the broadest part of the Lough, occasioned by a bay near the castle.

<small>Castle Urquhart.</small>

Above is *Glen-Moriston*, and east of that *Straith-Glas*, or the *Chisolm*'s country; in both of which

---

* It is to me matter of surprize that no mention is made, in the Poems of *Ossian*, of our greater beasts of prey, which must have abounded in his days; for the Wolf was a pest to the country so late as the reign of Queen *Elizabeth*, and the Bear existed there at least till the year 1057, when a *Gordon*, for killing a fierce Bear, was directed by the King to carry three Bears heads in his banner. Other native animals are often mentioned in several parts of the work; and in the five little poems on night, compositions of as many Bards, every modern *British* beast of chace is enumerated, the howling Dog and howling Fox described; yet the howling Wolf omitted, which would have made the Bards night much more hideous.

are forests of pines, where that rare bird the Cock of the Wood is still to be met with. At *Glen-Moriston* is a manufacture of linnen, where forty girls at a time are taught for three months to spin, and then another forty taken in: there are besides six looms, and all supported out of the forfeited lands.

Above is the great mountain *Meal Fourvounich*, the first land sailors make from the east sea; on the top is a lake said to be 100 fathoms deep.

I was informed that in that neighborhood are glens and cascades of surprising beauty, but my time did not permit me to visit them.

Dined at a poor inn near the *General's Hut*, or the place where General *Wade* resided when he inspected the great work of the roads, and gave one rare example of making the soldiery usefull in time of peace. Near is a fine glen covered at the bottom with wood, through which runs a torrent rising southward. The country also is prettily varied with woods and corn-fields.

Fall of *Fyers*. About a mile farther is the fall of *Fyers*, a vast cataract, in a darksome glen of a stupendous depth; the water darts far beneath the top thro' a narrow gap between two rocks, then precipitates above forty feet lower into the bottom of the chasm, and the foam, like a great cloud of smoke, rises and fills the air. The sides of this glen are vast precipices mixed with trees over-hanging the water, through which, after a short space, the waters discharge themselves into the lake.

About half a mile south of the first fall is another passing through a narrow chasm, whose sides

it

it has undermined for a confiderable way: over the gap is a true *Alpine* bridge of the bodies of trees covered with fods, from whofe middle is an awefull view of the water roaring beneath.

At the fall of *Fyers* the road quits the fide of the lake, and is carried for fome fpace through a fmall vale on the fide of the river *Fyers*, where is a mixture of fmall plains of corn and rocky hills. Then fucceeds a long and dreary moor, a tedious afcent up the mountain *See-whinnin*, or *Cummin's* Seat, whofe fummit is of a great height and very craggy. Defcend a fteep road, leave on the right *Lough-Taarf*, a fmall irregular piece of water, decked with little wooded ifles, and abounding with *Char*. After a fecond fteep defcent, reach

Fort Auguftus *, a fmall fortrefs, feated on a plain at the head of *Lough-Nefs*, between the rivers *Taarf* and *Oich*; the laft is confiderable, and has over it a bridge of three arches. The fort confifts of four baftions; within is the Governor's houfe, and barracks for 400 men: it was taken by the Rebels in 1746, who immediately deferted it, after demolifhing as much as they could.

Fort Auguftus.

Lough-Nefs is twenty-two miles in length; the breadth from one to two miles, except near Caftle *Urqhuart*, where it fwells out to three. The depth is very great; oppofite the rock called the *Horfe-fhoe*, near the weft end, it has been found to be 140 fathoms. From an eminence near the fort is a full view of its whole extent, for it is perfectly

Lough-Nefs.

---

* Its *Erfe* name is *Kil-whinnin*, or the burial-place of the *Cummins*. It lies on the road to the Ifle of *Skie*, which is about 52 miles off; but on the whole way there is not a place fit for the reception of man or horfe.

ftrait,

strait, running from east to west, with a point to the south. The boundary from the fall of *Fyers* is very steep and rocky, which obliged General *Wade* to make that *detour* from its banks; partly on account of the expence in cutting through so much solid rock, partly through an apprehension that in case of a rebellion the troops might be destroyed in their march, by the tumbling down of stones by the enemy from above: besides this, a prodigious arch must have been flung over the Glen of *Fyers*.

<small>Never freezes.</small> This lake, by reason of its great depth, never freezes, and during cold weather a violent steam rises from it as from a furnace. Ice brought from other parts, and put into *Lough-Ness*, instantly thaws; but no water freezes sooner than that of the lake when brought into a house. Its water is esteemed very salubrious; so that people come or send thirty miles for it: old Lord *Lovat* in particular made constant use of it. But it is certain, whether it be owing to the water, or to the air of that neighborhood, that for seven years the garrison of Fort *Augustus* had not lost a single man.

The fish of this lake are Salmon, which are in season from *Christmas* to *Midsummer*, Trouts of about 2 lb. weight, Pikes and Eels. During winter it is frequented by Swans and other wild fowls.

The greatest rise of water in *Lough-Ness* is fourteen feet. The lakes from whence it receives its supplies are *Lough-Oich*, *Louch-Garrie*, and *Lough-Quich*. There is but very little navigation on it; the only vessel is a gally belonging to the fort, to bring the stores from the east end, the river *Ness* being too shallow for navigation.

It

It is violently agitated by the winds, and at times the waves are quite mountainous. *November* 1ſt, 1755, at the ſame time as the earthquake at *Liſbon*, theſe waters were affected in a very extraordinary manner: they roſe and flowed up the lake from eaſt to weſt with vaſt impetuoſity, and were carried above 200 yards up the river *Oich*, breaking on its banks in a wave near three feet high; then continued ebbing and flowing for the ſpace of an hour: but at eleven o'clock a wave greater than any of the reſt came up the river, broke on the north ſide, and overflowed the bank for the extent of 30 feet. A boat near the *General's Hut*, loaden with bruſh-wood, was thrice driven aſhore, and twice carried back again; but the laſt time, the rudder was broken, the wood forced out, and the boat filled with water and left on ſhore. At the ſame time, a little iſle, in a ſmall lough in *Badenoch*, was totally reverſed and flung on the beach. But at both theſe places no agitation was felt on land.

Its agitations in 1755.

Rode to the caſtle of *Tor-down*, a rock two miles weſt of Fort *Auguſtus*: on the ſummit is an antient fortreſs. The face of this rock is a precipice; on the acceſſible ſide is a ſtrong dyke of looſe ſtones; above that a ditch, and a little higher a terraſs ſupported by ſtones: on the top a ſmall oval area, hollow in the middle: round this area, for the depth of near twelve feet, are a quantity of ſtones ſtrangely cemented with almoſt vitrified matter, and in ſome places quite turned into black *ſcoria*: the ſtones were generally granite mixed with a few gritſtones of a kind not found nearer the place than 40 miles. Whether this was the antient ſite of ſome forge,

SEPT. 1. Caſtle of *Tor-down*.

forge, or whether the stones which form this fortress* had been collected from the strata of some *Vulcano*, (for the vestiges of such are said to have been found in the Highlands) I submit to farther enquiry.

From this rock is a view of *Ben-ki*, a vast craggy mountain above *Glen-Garrie*'s country. Towards the south is the high mountain *Coryarich*: the ascent from this side is nine miles, but on the other into *Badenoch* is very rapid, and not above one, the road being, for the ease of the traveller, cut in a zigzag fashion. People often perish on the summit of this hill, which is frequently visited during winter with dreadfull storms of snow.

SEPT. 2. After a short ride westward along the plain, reach *Lough-Oich*, a narrow lake; the sides prettily indented, and the water adorned with small wooded *Glen-Garrie*. isles. On the shore is *Glen-Garrie*, the seat of Mr. M‘Donald, almost surrounded with wood, and not far distant is the ruin of the old castle. This lake is about four miles long; the road on the south side is excellent, and often carried through very pleasant woods.

After a small interval arrive on the banks of *Lough-Lochy*. *Lough-Lochy*, a fine piece of water, fourteen miles long, and from one to two broad. The distant mountains on the north were of an immense height; those on the south had the appearance of fine sheep-walks. The road is continued on the side of the lake about eight miles. On the opposite shore was *Achnacarrie*, once the seat of *Cameron* of *Lochiel*,

---

* I was informed that at *Arisaig* is an old castle formed of the same materials.

but

but burnt in 1746. He was esteemed by all parties the honestest and most sensible man of any that embarked in the pernicious and absurd attempt of that and the preceding year. By his influence he prevented the Rebels from committing several excesses, and even saved the city of *Glasgow* from being plundered, when their army returned out of *England*, irritated with their disappointment, and enraged at the loyalty that city had shewn. The Pretender came to him as soon as ever he landed. *Lochiel* seeing him arrive in so wild a manner and so unsupported, entreated him to desist from an enterprize from which nothing but certain ruin could result to him and his partizans. The Adventurer grew warm, and reproached *Lochiel* with a breach of promise. This affected him so deeply, that he instantly went and took a tender and moving leave of his lady and family, foreseeing he was on the point of parting with them for ever. The income of his estate was at that time, as I was told, not above 700 l. *per ann.* yet he brought fourteen hundred men into the field.

The waters of this lake form the river *Lochy*, and discharge themselves into the western sea, as those of *Lough-Oich* do through *Lough-Ness* into the eastern. About the beginning of this lake enter *Lochaber* *; stop at *Low-bridge*, a poor house; travel over a black moor for some miles; see abundance of cattle, but scarce any corn. Cross

Lochaber.

High-bridge, a fine bridge of three arches flung over the torrent *Spean*, founded on rocks; two of

---

* So called from a lake not far from Fort *William*, near whose banks *Banquo* was said to have been murthered.

the

the arches are 95 feet high. This bridge was built by General *Wade*, in order to form a communication with the country. These publick works were at first very disagreeable to the old Chieftains: it lessened their influence greatly; for by admitting strangers among them their clans were taught that the Lairds were not the first of men. But they had another reason much more solid: *Lochaber* had been a den of thieves; and as long as they had their waters, their torrents and their bogs, in a state of nature, they made their excursions, could plunder and retreat with their booty in full security. So weak were the laws in many parts of *North Britain*, till after the late rebellion, that no stop could be put to this infamous practice. A contribution, called the *black meal*, was raised by several of these plundering chieftains over a vast extent of country: whoever payed it had their cattle ensured, but those who dared to refuse were sure to suffer. Many of these free-booters were wont to insert an article, by which they were to be released from their agreement, in case of any civil commotion: thus, at the breaking out of the last rebellion, a *M'Gregor* *, who had with the strictest honor (till that event) preserved his friends cattle, immediately sent them word, that from that time they were out of his protection, and must now take care of themselves. *Barrisdale* was another of this class, chief of a band of robbers, who spread terror over the whole country: but the Highlanders at that time esteemed the open theft of cattle, or the making a *spreith* (as

---

* Who assumed the name of *Graham*.

they

they called it) by no means dishonorable; and the young men considered it as a piece of gallantry, by which they recommended themselves to their mistresses. On the other side there was often as much bravery in the pursuers; for frequent battles ensued, and much blood has been spilt on those occasions. They also shewed great dexterity in tracing the robbers, not only through the boggy land, but over the firmest ground, and even over places where other cattle had passed, knowing well how to distinguish the steps of those that were wandering about from those that were driven hastily away by the Free-booters.

From the road had a distant view of the mountains of *Arisaig*, beyond which were *Moydart*, *Kinloch*, &c. At the end of *Lough Shiel* the Pretender first set up his standard in the wildest place that imagination can frame. The inhabitants of this country are mostly Papists, and here the strength of the rebellion lay.

Pass by the side of the river *Lochy*, now considerable. See *Inverlochy Castle* with four large round towers *, which, by the mode of building, seems to have been the work of the *English*, in the time of *Edward* I. who laid large fines on the *Scotch* Barons for the purpose of erecting new castles. Reach *Fort William*, built in King *William*'s reign; as was a small town near it, called *Mary-*

Inverlochy.

* The largest is called *Cummin*'s tower. These towers so greatly resemble those built by the same monarch in *North Wales*, that I scarce hesitate to attribute this castle to him. By several accounts it appears that there had been a castle on the same spot, built many centuries prior to this ruin; and it is also asserted, that the league between *Charlemagne* and *Achaius*, King of *Scotland*, was signed by the latter in it.

N

borough,

borough, in honor of his Queen; but prior to that, had been a small fortress, erected by order of *Cromwel*, with whose people the famous Sir *Ewen Cameron** had numerous contests. The present fort is a triangle, has two bastions, and is capable of admitting a garrison of eight hundred men. It was well defended against the Rebels in 1746, who raised the siege with much disgrace. The fort lies on a narrow arm of the sea, called *Loch-yell*, which extends some miles higher up the country, making a bend to the north, and extends likewise westward towards the isle of *Mull*, near twenty-four *Scotch* miles.

This fort on the west, and *Fort Augustus* in the centre, and *Fort George* on the east, form what is called the *chain*, from sea to sea. This space is called *Glen-more*, or the great Glen, which, including water and land, is almost a level of seventy miles. There is, in fact, but little land, but what is divided by firth, lough, or river; except the two miles which lie between *Lough Oich* and *Lough Lochy*. By means of *Fort George*, all entrance up the Firth towards *Inverness* is prevented, *Fort Augustus* curbed the inhabitants midway, and *Fort William* is a check to any attempts on the west. Detachments are made from all these garrisons to *Inverness*, *Bernera* barracks opposite to the Isle of *Skie*, and Castle *Duart* in the Isle of *Mull* †. Other

The Chain.

---

* Who is said to have killed the last Wolf in *Scotland*, about the year 1680.

† I was informed that coal has been lately discovered in this island. What advantage may not this prove, in establishments of manufactures, in a country just rouzed from the lap of indolence!

small

small parties are also scattered in huts throughout the country, to prevent the stealing of cattle.

Fort William is surrounded by vast mountains, which occasion almost perpetual rain: the loftiest are on the south side; *Benevish* soars above the rest, and ends, as I was told, in a point, (at this time concealed in mist) whose height from the sea is said to be 1450 yards. As an antient *Briton*, I lament the disgrace of *Snowdon*; once esteemed the highest hill in the island, but now must yield the palm to a *Caledonian* mountain. But I have my doubts whether this might not be rivaled, or perhaps surpassed by others in the same country; for example, *Ben y bourd*, a central hill, from whence to the sea there is a continued and rapid descent of seventy miles, as may be seen by the violent course of the *Dee* to *Aberdeen*. But their height has not yet been taken, which to be done fairly must be from the sea. *Benevish*, as well as many others, harbor snow throughout the year.

Benevish.

The bad weather which reigned during my stay in these parts prevented me from visiting the celebrated parallel roads in *Glen-Roy*. As I am unable to satisfy the curiosity of the Reader from my own observation, I shall deliver in the Appendix * the informations I could collect relating to these amazing works.

The great produce of *Lochaber* is cattle: that district alone sends out annually 3000 head; but if a portion of *Invernessshire* is included, of which this properly is part, the number is 10,000. There are

Trade of *Lochaber*.

* *No.* III.

N 2

also

also a few horses bred here, and a very few sheep; but of late several have been imported. Scarce any arable land, for the excessive wet which reigns here almost totally prevents the growth of corn, and what little there is fit for tillage sets at ten shillings an acre. The inhabitants of this district are therefore obliged, for their support, to import six thousand bolls of oatmeal annually, which cost about 4000l. the rents are about 3000l. *per ann.* the return for their cattle is about 7500l. the horses may produce some trifle; so that the tenants must content themselves with a very scanty subsistence, without the prospect of saving the least against unforeseen accidents. The rage of raising rents has reached this distant country: in *England* there may be reason for it, (in a certain degree) where the value of lands is encreased by accession of commerce, and by the rise of the price of provisions; but here (contrary to all policy) the great men begin at the wrong end, with squeezing the bag, before they have helped the poor tenant to fill it, by the introduction of manufactures. In many of the isles this already shews its unhappy effect, and begins to depopulate the country; for numbers of families have been obliged to give up the strong attachment the *Scots* in general have for their country, and to exchange it for the wilds of *America.*

The houses of the peasants in *Lochaber* are the most wretched that can be imagined; framed of upright poles, which are wattled; the roof is formed of boughs like a *wigwam*, and the whole is covered with sods; so that in this moist climate

their

their cottages have a perpetual and much finer verdure than the rest of the country.

Salmons are taken in these parts as late as *May*; about 50 tuns are caught in the season. These fish never appear so early on this coast as on the eastern.

Phinocs are taken here in great numbers, 1500 having been taken at a draught. They come in *August* and disappear in *November*. They are about a foot long, their color grey spotted with black, their flesh red; rise eagerly to a fly. The fishermen suppose them to be the young of what they call a great Trout, weighing 30 lb. which I suppose is the Grey*.

Sept. 4. Left *Fort William*, and proceeded south along the military road on the side of a hill, an awefull height above *Loch-Leven*†, a branch of the sea, so narrow as to have only the appearance of a river, bounded on both sides with vast mountains, among whose winding bottoms the tide rolled in with solemn majesty. The scenery begins to grow very romantic; on the west side are some woods of birch and pines: the hills are very lofty, many of them taper to a point, and my old friend, the late worthy Bishop *Pocock*, compared the shape of one to mount *Tabor*. Beneath them is *Glen-Co*, infamous for the massacre of its inhabitants in 1691, and celebrated for having (as some assert) given birth to *Ossian*; towards the north is *Morvan*, the country of his hero *Fingal*.

Glen-Co.

---

* *Br. Zool.* III. 248.

† The country people have a most superstitious desire of being buried in the little isle of *Mun*, in this Lough.

Leave on the left a vast cataract, precipitating itself in a great foaming sheet between two lofty perpendicular rocks, with trees growing out of the fissures, forming a large stream, called the water of *Boan*.

Kinloch-Leven. Breakfast at the little village of *Kinloch-Leven* on most excellent minced stag, the only form I thought that animal good in.

Near this village is a single farm fourteen miles long, which sets for only 35 l. *per ann.* and from the nature of the soil, perhaps not very cheap.

A Quern. Saw here a *Quern*, a sort of portable mill, made of two stones about two feet broad, thin at the edges, and a little thicker in the middle. In the centre of the upper stone is a hole to pour in the corn, and a peg by way of handle. The whole is placed on a cloth; the grinder pours the corn into the hole with one hand, and with the other turns round the upper stone with a very rapid motion, while the meal runs out at the sides on the cloth. This is rather preserved as a curiosity, being much out of use at present. Such are supposed to be the same with what are common among the *Moors*, being the simple substitute of a mill.

Immediately after leaving *Kinloch-Leven* the mountains soar to a far greater height than before; the sides are covered with wood, and the bottoms of the glens filled with torrents that roar amidst the loose stones. After a ride of two miles begin to ascend the *black mountain*, in *Argyleshire*, on a steep road, which continues about three miles almost to the summit, and is certainly the highest publick road in *Great Britain*. On the other side the

The black mountain.

the descent is scarce a mile, but is very rapid down a zigzag way. Reach the *King*'s house, seated in a plain: it was built for the accommodation of His Majesty's troops, in their march through this desolate country, but is in a manner unfurnished.

Pass near *Lough-Tulla*, a long narrow piece of water, with a small pine-wood on its side. A few weather-beaten pines and birch appear scattered up and down, and in all the bogs great numbers of roots, that evince the forest that covered the country within this half century. These were the last pines which I saw growing spontaneously in *North Britain*. The pine-forests are become very rare! I can enumerate only those on the banks of *Lough-Raynach*, at *Invercauld*, and *Brae-mar*; at *Coygach* and *Dirry-Monach*: the first in *Straithnavern*, the last in *Sutherland*. Those about *Lough-Loyn*, *Glen-Moriston*, and *Straith-Glas*; a small one near *Lough-Garrie*, another near *Lough-Arkig*, and a few scattered trees above *Kinloch-Leven*, all in *Invernessshire*; and I was also informed that there are very considerable woods about *Castle Grant*. I saw only one species of Pine in those I visited; nor could I learn whether there was any other than what is vulgarly called the *Scotch Fir*, whose synonyms are these:

Pinus sylvestris foliis brevibus glaucis, conis parvis albentibus. Raii hist. Pl. 1401. syn. stirp. Br. 442.

Pinus sylvestris. Gerard's herb. 1356. Lin. sp. Pl. 1418. Flora Angl. 361.

Pin d'Ecoſſe, ou de Geneve. Du Hamel Traitè des Arbres. II. 125. No. 5.

Fyrre, Strom. Sondmor. 12.

Moſt of this long day's journey from the *black mountain* was truly melancholy, almoſt one continued ſcene of duſky moors, without arable land, trees, houſes, or living creature, for numbers of miles.

The roads are excellent; but from *Fort William* to *Kinloch-Leven,* very injudiciouſly planned, often carried far about, and often ſo ſteep as to be ſcarce ſurmountable; whereas had the engineer followed the track uſed by the inhabitants, thoſe inconveniences would have been avoided.

Theſe roads, by rendering the highlands acceſſible, contributed much to their preſent improvement, and were owing to the induſtry of our ſoldiery; they were begun in 1723 *, under the directions of Gen. *Wade,* who, like another *Hannibal,* forced his way through rocks ſuppoſed to have been unconquerable: many of them hang over the mighty lakes of the country, and formerly afforded no other road to the natives than the paths of ſheep or goats, where even the Highlander crawled with difficulty, and kept himſelf from tumbling into the far ſubjacent water by clinging to the plants and buſhes of the rock. Many of theſe rocks were too hard to yield to the pick-ax, and the miner was obliged to ſubdue their obſtinacy with gunpowder, and often in places where nature had denied him footing, and where he was forced to begin his labors, ſuſpended from above by ropes on the face of the horrible precipice.

* *Vide p.* 81.

precipice. The bogs and moors had likewise their difficulties to overcome; but all were at length constrained to yield to the perseverence of our troops.

In some places I observed, that, after the manner of the *Romans*, they left engraven on the rocks the names of the regiment each party belonged to, who were employed in these works; nor were they less worthy of being immortalized than the *Vexillatio's* of the *Roman* legions; for civilization was the consequence of the labors of both.

These roads begin at *Dunkeld*, are carried on thro' the noted pass of *Killicrankie*, by *Blair*, to *Dalnacardoch*, *Dalwhinie*, and over the *Coryarich*, to *Fort Augustus*. A branch extends from thence eastward to *Inverness*, and another westward, over *Highbridge*, to *Fort William*. From the last, by *Kinloch-Leven*, over the *Black Mountain*, by the King's house, to *Teindrum*, and from thence, by *Glen-urqhie*, to *Inveraray*, and so along the beautifull boundaries of *Lough-Lomond*, to its extremity.

Another road begins near *Crief*, passes by *Aberfeldy*, crosses the *Tay* at *Tay-bridge*, and unites with the other road at *Dalnacardoch*; and from *Dalwhinie* a branch passes through *Badenoch* to *Inverness*.

These are the principal military roads; but there may be many others I may have over-looked.

Rode through some little vales by the side of a small river; and from the appearance of fertility, have some relief from the dreary scene of the rest of the day. Reach

Tyendrum, a small village. The inn is seated the highest of any house in *Scotland*. The *Tay* runs east,

Tyendrum.

east, and a few hundred yards further is a little lake, whose waters run west. A lead-mine is worked here by a level to some advantage; was discovered about thirty years ago: the veins run S. W. and N. E.

SEPT. 5. Continue my tour on a very fine road on a side of a narrow vale, abounding with cattle, yet destitute both of arable land and meadow; but the beasts pick up a sustenance from the grass that springs up among the heath. The country opens on approaching *Glen-Urqhie*, a pretty vally, well cultivated, fertile in corn, the sides adorned with numbers of pretty groves, and the middle watered by the river *Urqhie:* the church is seated on a knowl, in a large isle, formed by the river: the *Manse*, or minister's house, is neat, and his little demesn is decorated in the most advantageous places with seats of turf, indicating the content and satisfaction of the possessor in the lot Providence has given him.

Glen-Urqhie.

In the church-yard are several grave-stones of great antiquity, with figures of a warrior, each furnished with a spear, or two-handed sword: on some are representations of the chase; on others, elegant fret-work; and on one, said to be part of the coffin of a *M'Gregor*, is a fine running pattern of foliage and flowers, and excepting the figures, all in good taste.

On an eminence on the south side of this vale dwells *M'Nabb*, a smith, whose family have lived in that humble station since the year 1440, being always of the same profession. The first of the line was employed by the Lady of Sir *Duncan Campbell*,

who

who built the castle of *Kilchurn* when her husband was on a croisade: some of their tombs are in the church-yard of *Glen-Urqbie*; the oldest has a hammer and other implements of his trade cut on it. I here was favored with several translations of some *English* poetry into the *Erse* language; an epitaph, and an elegy, to be found in the Appendix*, by those whose turn leads them to peruse performances of that kind. After breakfast, at a good inn near the village, was there present at a christening, and became sponsor to a little *Highlander*, by no other ceremony than receiving him for a moment into my arms.

Pursue my journey, and have a fine view of the meanders of the river before its union with *Lough-Aw*: in an isle in the beginning of the lake is the castle of *Kilchurn*, which had been inhabited by the present Lord *Breadalbane*'s grandfather. The great tower was repaired by his Lordship, and garrisoned by him in 1745, for the service of the government, in order to prevent the Rebels from making use of that great pass cross the kingdom; but is now a ruin, having lately been struck by lightening.

Castle of Kilchurn.

At a place called *Hamilton*'s Pass, in an instant burst on a view of the lake, which makes a beautifull appearance; is about a mile broad, and shews at lest ten miles of its length. This water is prettily varied with isles, some so small as meerly to peep above the surface; yet even these are tufted with trees; some are large enough to afford hay and pasturage; and in one, called *Inch-hail*, are the

Lough-Aw.

* No. IV.

remains

remains of a convent*. On *Fraoch-Elan***, the *Hesperides* of the Highlands, are the ruins of a castle. The fair *Mego* longed for the delicious fruit of the isle, guarded by a dreadfull serpent: the hero *Fraoch* goes to gather it, and is destroyed by the monster. This tale is sung in the *Erse* ballads, and is translated and published in the manner of *Fingal*.

Mount Crouachan. The whole extent of *Lough-Aw* is thirty miles, bounded on the north by *Lorn*, a portion of *Argyleshire*, a fertile country, prettily wooded near the water-side. On the N. E. are vast mountains: among them *Crouachan* † towers to a great height; it rises from the lake, and its sides are shagged with woods impending over it. At its foot is the discharge of the waters of this Lough into *Lough-Etive*, an arm of the sea, after a turbulent course of a series of cataracts for the space of three miles. At *Bunaw*, near the north end, is a large salmon-fishery; also a considerable iron-foundery, which I fear will soon devour the beautifull woods of the country.

Scotstown. Pass by *Scotstown*, a single house. Dine at the little village of *Cladish*. About two miles hence, on an eminence in sight of the convent on *Inch-hail*, is a spot, called *Croisch an Tsleachd*, or the cross of bowing, because, in *Popish* times, it was always customary to kneel or make obeisance on first sight of any consecrated place ‡.

---

* The country people are still fond of burying here. Insular interments are said to owe their origin to the fear people had of having their friends corpses devoured by wolves on the main land.

** This island was granted by *Alexander* III. in 1267, to *Gillcrist M'Nachdan* and his heirs for ever, on condition they should entertain the King whenever he passed that way.

† Or the Great Heap.

‡ Druidical stones and temples are called *Clachan*, churches having often been built on such places: to go to *Clachan* is a common *Erse* phrase for going to church.

Pass

Pass between hills finely planted with several sorts of trees, such as *Weymouth* pines, &c. and after a picturesque ride, reach

Inveraray; the castle the principal seat of the Dukes of *Argyle*, chief of the *Campbells*; was built by Duke *Archibald*; is quadrangular with a round tower at each corner, and in the middle rises a square one glazed on every side to give light to the staircase and galleries, and has from without a most disagreeable effect. In the attic story are eighteen good bed-chambers: the ground-floor was at this time in a manner unfurnished, but will have several good apartments. The castle is built of a coarse *lapis ollaris*, brought from the other side of *Lough-Fine*, and is the same kind with that found in *Norway*, of which the King of *Denmark*'s palace at *Copenhagen* is built. Near the new castle are some remains of the old.

Inveraray.

This place will in time be very magnificent; but at present the space between the front and the water is disgraced with the old town, composed of the most wretched hovels that can be imagined. The founder of the castle designed to have built a new town on the west side of the little bay the house stands on: he finished a few houses, a custom-house, and an excellent inn: his death interrupted the completion of the plan, which, when brought to perfection, will give the place a very different appearance to what it now bears.

From the top of the great rock *Duniquaich* is a fine view of the castle, the lawn sprinkled with fine trees, the hills covered with extensive plantations, a country fertile in corn, bordering the Lough,

and

and the Lough itself covered with boats. The trees on the lawn about the castle are said to have been planted by the Earl of *Argyle:* they thrive greatly; for I observed beech from nine to twelve feet and a half in girth, pines nine, and a lesser maple between seven and eight.

But the busy scene of the herring-fishery gave no small improvement to the magnificent environs of *Inveraray.* Every evening * some hundreds of boats in a manner covered the surface of *Lough-Fine,* an arm of the sea, which, from its narrowness and from the winding of its shores, has all the beauties of a fresh-water lake: on the week-days, the chearfull noise of the bagpipe and dance ecchoes from on board: on the sabbath, each boat approaches the land, and psalmody and devotion divide the day; for the common people of the north are disposed to be religious, having the example before them of a gentry untainted by luxury and dissipation, and being instructed by a clergy, who are active in their duty and who preserve respect, amidst all the disadvantages of a narrow income.

Lough-Fine. The length of *Lough-Fine,* from the eastern end to the point of *Lamond,* is above thirty *Scotch* miles; but its breadth scarce two measured: the depth from sixty to seventy fathoms. It is noted *Herrings.* for the vast shoals of herrings that appear here in *July* and continue till *January.* The highest season is from *September* to *Christmas,* when near six hun-

---

* The fishery is carried on in the night, the herrings being then in motion.

dred

dred boats, with four men in each, are employed. A chain of nets is used (for several are united) of a hundred fathoms in length. As the herrings swim at very uncertain depths, so the nets are sunk to the depth the shoal is found to take: the success therefore depends much on the the judgement or good fortune of the fishers, in taking their due depths; for it often happens that one boat will take multitudes, while the next does not catch a single fish, which makes the boatmen perpetually enquire of each other about the depth of their nets. These are kept up by buoys to a proper pitch; the ropes that run through them are fastened with pegs, and by drawing up or letting out the rope (after taking out the pegs) they adjust their situation, and then replace them. Sometimes the fish swim in twenty fathom water, sometimes in fifty, and oftentimes even at the bottom.

It is computed that each boat gets about 40l. in the season. The fish are either salted, and packed in barrels for exportation, or sold fresh to the country people, two or three hundred horses being brought every day to the water-side from very distant parts. A barrel holds 500 herrings, if they are of the best kind; at a medium, 700: but if more, for sometimes a barrel will hold 1000, they are reckoned very poor. The present price 1l. 4s. *per* barrel; but there is a drawback of the duty on salt for those that are exported.

The great rendezvous of vessels for the fishery off the western isles is at *Cambeltown*, in *Cantyre*, where they clear out on the 12th of *September*, and sometimes three hundred busses are seen there at a time: they

they must return to their different ports by *January* 13th, where they ought to receive the præmium of 2 l. 10 s. *per* tun of herrings; but it is said to be very ill paid, which is a great discouragement to the fishery.

The herrings of *Lough-Fine* are as uncertain in their migration as they are on the coast of *Wales.* They had for numbers of years quitted that water; but appeared again there within these dozen years. Such is the case with the loughs on all this western coast, not but people despair too soon of finding them, from one or two unsuccessfull tryals in the beginning of the season; perhaps from not adjusting their nets to the depth the fish happen then to swim in: but if each year a small vessel or two was sent to make a thorough tryal in every branch of the sea on this coast, they would undoubtedly find shoals of fish in one or other.

Tunnies. *Tunnies* [*], called here *Mackrel-Sture*, are very frequently caught in the herring season, which they follow to prey on. They are taken with a strong iron hook fastened to a rope and baited with a herring: as soon as hooked lose all spirit, and are drawn up without any resistance: are very active when at liberty, and jump and frolick on the surface of the water.

Sept: 7. Crossed over an elegant bridge of three arches upon the *Aray*, in front of the castle, and kept riding along the side of the Lough for about seven miles: saw in one place a shoal of herrings, close to the surface, perfectly piled on one another, with a flock of Gulls, busied with this offered booty.

[*] *Br. Zool. illustr.* 33.

After

After quitting the water-side the road is carried for a considerable way through the bottoms of naked, deep and gloomy glens. Ascend a very high pass with a little lough on the top. Reach the end of *Lough-Long*, another narrow arm of the sea, bounded by high hills, and after a long course terminates in the *Firth* of *Clyde*.

Near this place see a house, very pleasantly situated, belonging to Colonel *Campbell*, amidst plantations, with some very fertile bottoms adjacent. On ascending a hill not half a mile farther, appears Lough-Lomond. *North-Britain* may well boast of its waters; for so short a ride as thirty miles presents the traveller with the view of four most magnificent pieces. *Lough-Aw, Lough-Fine, Lough-Long*, and *Lough-Lomond*. Two indeed are of salt-water; but, by their narrowness, give the idea of fresh-water lakes. It is an idle observation of travellers, that seeing one is the same with seeing all of these superb waters; for almost every one I visited has its proper characters.

Review of the Lakes.

Lough-Leven is a broad expanse, with isles and cultivated shores.

Lough-Tay makes three bold windings, has steep but sloping shores, cultivated in many parts, and bounded by vast hills.

Lough-Raynach, is broad and strait, has more wildness about it, with a large natural pine wood on its southern banks.

Lough-Tumel is narrow, confined by the sloping sides of steep hills, and has on its western limits a flat, rich, woody country, and is watered by a most serpentine stream.

The

The *Lough* of *Spinie* is almoſt on a flat, and its ſides much indented.

Lough-Moy is ſmall, and has ſoft features on its banks, amidſt rude environs.

Lough-Neſs is ſtrait and narrow; its ſhores abound with a wild magnificence, lofty, precipitous and wooded, and has all the greatneſs of an *Alpine* lake.

Lough-Oich has lofty mountains at a ſmall diſtance from its borders; the ſhores indented, and the water decorated with iſles.

Lough-Locky wants the iſles; its ſhores ſlope, and ſeveral ſtraiths terminate on its banks.

Lough-Aw is long and waving: its little iſles tufted with trees, and juſt appearing above the water, its two great feeds of water at each extremity, and its ſingular lateral diſcharge near one of them, ſufficiently mark this great lake.

Lough-Lomond.   *Lough-Lomond*, the laſt, the moſt beautifull of the *Caledonian* lakes. The firſt view of it from *Tarbat* preſents an extenſive ſerpentine winding amidſt lofty hills: on the north, barren, black and rocky, which darken with their ſhade that contracted part of the water. Near this gloomy tract, beneath *Craig Roſ-*

M'Gregors.   *ton*, was the principal ſeat of the *M'Gregors*, a murderous clan, infamous for exceſſes of all kinds; at length, for a horrible maſſacre of the *Colquhuns*, or *Cahouns*, in 1602, were proſcribed, and hunted down like wild beaſts; their very name ſuppreſſed by act of council; ſo that the remnant, now diſperſed like *Jews*, dare not even ſign it to any deed. Their poſterity are ſtill ſaid to be diſtinguiſhed among the clans in which they have incorporated themſelves,

themselves, not only by the redness of their hair, but by their still retaining the mischievous disposition of their ancestors.

On the west side, the mountains are cloathed near the bottoms with woods of oak quite to the water edge; their summits lofty, naked and craggy.

On the east side, the mountains are equally high, but the tops form a more even ridge parallel to the lake, except where *Ben-Lomond* *, like *Saul* amidst his companions, overtops the rest. The upper parts were black and barren; the lower had great marks of fertility, or at least of industry, for the yellow corn was finely contrasted with the verdure of the groves intermixed with it.

This eastern boundary is part of the *Grampian* hills, which extend from hence through the counties of *Perth, Angus, Mearns,* and *Aberdeen*. They take their name from only a single hill, the *Mons Grampius* of *Tacitus*, where *Galgacus* waited the approach of *Agricola*, and where the battle was fought so fatal to the brave *Caledonians*. Antiquarians have not agreed upon the particular spot; but the able Mr. *Gordon* † places it near *Comerie*, at the upper end of *Straithern*, at a place to this day called *Galgachan Moor*. But to return.

Grampian hills.

The road runs sometimes through woods, at others is exposed and naked; in some, so steep as to require the support of a wall: the whole the work of the soldiery: blessed exchange of instruments of destruction for those that give safety to the traveller, and a polish to the once inaccessible native.

---

* Its height is 3240 feet.
† *Itin. Septent.* 39.

A great headland covered with trees separates the first scene from one totally different. On passing this cape an expanse of water bursts at once on your eye, varied with all the softer beauties of nature. Immediately beneath is a flat covered with wood and corn: beyond, the headlands stretch far into the water, and consist of gentle risings; many have their surfaces covered with wood, others adorned with trees loosely scattered either over a fine verdure, or the purple bloom of the heath. Numbers of islands are dispersed over the lake of the same elevated form as the little capes, and wooded in the same manner; others just peep above the surface, and are tufted with trees; and numbers are so disposed as to form magnificent vistos between.

Opposite *Luss,* at a small distance from shore, is a mountainous isle almost covered with wood; is near half a mile long, and has a most fine effect. I could not count the number of islands, but was told there are twenty-eight: the largest two miles long, and stocked with Deer.

The length of this charming lake is 24 *Scotch* miles; its greatest breadth eight: its greatest depth a hundred and twenty fathoms. Besides the fish common to the Loughs are *Guiniads,* called here *Poans.*

The country from *Luss* * to the southern extremity of the lake continually improves; the mountains sink gradually into small hills; the land is highly cultivated, well planted, and well inhabited.

---

* A tolerable inn on the borders of the lake.

bited. I was ftruck with rapture at a fight fo long new to me: it would have been without alloy, had it not been dafhed with the uncertainty whether the mountain virtue, hofpitality, would flourifh with equal vigor in the fofter fcenes I was on the point of entering on; for in the *Highlands* every houfe gave welcome to the traveller.

The vale between the end of the lake and *Dunbarton* is unfpeakably beautifull, very fertile, and finely watered by the great and rapid river *Levin*, the difcharge of the lake, which, after a fhort courfe, drops into the Firth of *Clyde* below *Dunbarton*: there is fcarcely a fpot on its banks but what is cultivated with bleacheries, plantations and *villas*. Nothing can equal the contraft in this day's journey, between the black barren dreary glens of the morning ride, and the foft fcenes of the evening, iflands worthy of the retreat of *Armida*, and which *Rinaldo* himfelf would have quitted with a figh.

Before I take my laft leave of the *Highlands*, it would be proper to obferve that every entrance into them is ftrongly marked by nature. *Entrances into the Highlands.*

On the fouth, the narrow and wooded glen near *Dunkeld* inftantly fhews the change of country.

On the eaft, the craggy pafs of *Bollitir* gives a contracted admiffion into the *Grampian* hills.

On the north, the mountains near *Lough-Moy* appear very near, and form what is properly ftyled the threfhold of the country; and on the

Weft, the narrow road impending over *Lough-Lomond* forms a moft characteriftic entrance to this mountainous tract.

But the *Erse* language is not confined within these limits; for it is spoken on all sides beyond these mountains. On the eastern coast it begins at *Nairn*; on the western, extends over all the isles. It ceases in the north of *Cathness*, the *Orkneys*, and the *Shetland* islands *; but near *Lough-Lomond*, is heard at *Luss*, at *Buchanan*, east of the lake, and at *Roseneth*, west of it.

Cross the ferry over the *Levin* at *Bonnel*, and after a ride of three miles reach

Dunbarton.   *Dunbarton*, a small but good old town, seated on a plain near the conflux of the *Levin* with the Firth of *Clyde*; it consists principally of one large street in form of a crescent. On one side is the *Tolbooth*, and at the south end the church with a small spire steeple. The waites of the town are bagpipes, which go about at nine o'clock at night and five in the morning.

Its castle.   The castle is seated a little south of the town on a two-headed rock of a stupendous height, rising in a strange manner out of the sands, and totally detached from every thing else. On one of the summits are the remains of an old light-house; on the other, the powder magazine: in the hollow between is a large well of excellent water fourteen feet deep. The sides of the rocks are immense precipices, and often over-hang, except on the side where the governor's house stands, which is defended by walls and a few cannon, and garrisoned by a few invalids. From its natural strength, it was in former times deemed impregnable; so that the

* In the *Shetland isles* are still some remains of the *Norse*, or old *Norwegian* language.

desperate

desperate but succesfull scalado of it 1571* may vie with the greatest attempts of that kind, with the capture of the *Numidian* fortress, in the *Jugurthine* war, by *Marius*; or the more horrible surprize of *Fescamp* †, by the gallant *Bois-rosè*.

From the summits of this rock is a fine view of the country, of the town of *Dunbarton*, the river *Levin*, the Firth of *Clyde*, (the *Glota* of *Tacitus*) here, about a mile broad, and of the towns of *Greenock* and *Port Glasgow*, on the opposite shore. The business of this country is the spinning of thread, which is very considerable. There is also a great Fish: salmon-fishery: but in this populous country, so great is the demand for them that none can be spared for curing. *Gilses* come up the river in *June*, and continue in plenty about twenty days; and many Salmon Trout are taken from *March* to *July*. *Phinocs*, called here Yellow Fins, come in *July*, and continue about the same space of time as the Gilses: the fishermen call them the young of some great Sea Trout. During *May*, *Parrs* appear in such numbers in the *Levin*, that the water seems quite animated with them. There are besides in that river Perch and a few *Poans* ‡.

Pass by the ruins of *Dunglas* castle, near the Sept. 8. banks of the *Clyde*, which meanders finely along a rich plain full of barley and oats, and much inclosed with good hedges, a rarity in *North Britain*.

---

* *Robertson's hist. Scotland*, II. 15. *octavo*. *Guthrie's*, VII. 331.
† *Sully's Memoirs*, *Vol*. I. Book VI.
‡ At *Dunbarton* I was informed by persons of credit, that Swallows have often been taken in midwinter, in a torpid state, out of the steeple of the church, and also out of a sand-bank over the river *Endrick*, near *Lough-Lomond*.

At a diſtance are ſome gentle riſings, interſperſed with woods and villas belonging to the citizens of *Glaſgow*.

GLASGOW.

The beſt built of any modern ſecond-rate city I ever ſaw: the houſes of ſtone, and in a good taſte. The principal ſtreet runs eaſt and weſt, and is near a mile and a half long; but unfortunately, is not ſtrait. The *Tolbooth* is large and handſome. Next to that is the Exchange: within is a ſpacious room with full-length portraits of all our monarchs ſince *James* I. and an excellent one, by *Ramſay*, of *Archibald* Duke of *Argyle*, in a Judge's robe. Before the Exchange is a large equeſtrian ſtatue of King *William*. This is the broadeſt and fineſt part of the ſtreet: many of the houſes are built over piazzas, but too narrow to be of much ſervice to walkers. Numbers of other ſtreets croſs this at right angles, and are in general well built.

Market-places.

The market-places are great ornaments to this city, the fronts being done in a very fine taſte, and the gates adorned with columns of one or other of the orders. Some of theſe markets are for meal, greens, fiſh, or fleſh. There are two for the laſt, which have conduits out of ſeveral of the pillars; ſo that they are conſtantly kept ſweet and clean.

Near the meal-market is a publick grainary, to be filled on any apprehenſion of ſcarceneſs.

The guard-houſe is in the great ſtreet, which is kept by the inhabitants, who regularly do duty. An excellent police is obſerved here, and proper officers attend the markets to prevent any abuſes.

The old bridge over the *Clyde* conſiſts of eight arches, and was built 400 years ago by Biſhop *Rea*;

Rea; two others are now building. The tide flows three miles higher up the country; but at low water is fordable. There is a plan for deepening the channel; for at prefent the tide brings up only very fmall veffels; and the ports belonging to this city lie fourteen miles lower, at *Port Glafgow* and *Greenock*, on the weft fide of the *Firth*.

Near the bridge is a large alms-houfe, a vaft nailery, a ftone-ware manufacture, and a great porter brewery, which fupplies fome part of unin-duftrious *Ireland*. Within fight, on the fouth fide, are collieries; and much coal is exported into the laft-mentioned ifland, and into *America*.

The great imports of this city are tobacco and fugar: of the former, above 40,000 hogfheads have been annually imported, and near 20,000 again exported into *France*. The manufactures here are linnens, cambricks *, lawns, tapes, fuftians, and ftriped linnens; fo that it already begins to rival *Manchefter*, and has in point of the conveniency of its ports, in refpect to *America*, a great advantage over it. {Trade.}

The college is a large building, with a handfome front to the ftreet, refembling fome of the old colleges in *Oxford*. *Charles* I. fubfcribed 200l. towards this work, but was prevented by the troubles from paying it; but *Cromwell* afterwards fulfilled the defign of the royal donor. It was founded in 1450, by *James* II. Pope *Nicholas* I. gave the bull, but Bifhop *Turnbull* fupplied the money. There are about 400 ftudents belonging to the col- {College.}

---

* The greateft cambrick manufacture is now at *Paifly*, a few miles from this city.

lege,

lege, who lodge in the town: but the Professors have good houses in the college. Young gentlemen of fortune have private tutors, who have an eye to their conduct; the rest live entirely at their own discretion.

The library is a very handsome room, with a gallery round it, supported by pillars. That beneficent nobleman the late Duke of *Chandos*, when he visited the college, gave 500l. towards building this apartment.

Messrs. *Robert* and *Andrew Foulis*, printers and booksellers to the university, have instituted an academy for painting and engraving; and like good citizens, zealous to promote the welfare and honor of their native place, have at vast expence formed a most numerous collection of paintings from abroad, in order to form the taste of their *eleves*.

The printing is a very considerable branch of business; and has long been celebrated for the beauty of the types and the correctness of the editions. Here are preserved in cases numbers of monumental and other stones*, taken out of the walls on the *Roman* stations in this part of the kingdom: some are well cut and ornamented: most of them were done to perpetuate the memory of the *vexillatio*, or party, who performed such or such works; others in memory of officers who died in the country.

Churches. The cathedral is a large pile, now divided into two churches: beneath, and deep under ground,

---

* Several have been engraven by the artists of the academy. The Provost of the University did me the honor of presenting me with a set.

is

is another, in which is also divine service, where the congregation may truely say, *clamavi e profundis:* the roof is fine, made of stone, and supported by pillars; but the beauty much hurt by the crowding of the pews. Near this is the ruin of the castle, or Bishop's palace.

The new church is a very handsome building, with a large elegant porch; but the outside is much disfigured by a slender square tower with a pepper-box top: and in general, the steeples of *Glasgow* are in a remarkable bad taste, being, in fact, no favorite part of architecture with the church of *Scotland*. The inside of that just spoken of is most neatly finished, supported by pillars, and very prettily stuccoed: it is one of the very few exceptions to the slovenly and indecent manner in which Presbitery keeps the houses of GOD: reformation in matters of religion seldom observes mediocrity: here it was outrageous; for a place of worship commonly neat was deemed to favor of popery: but, to avoid the imputation of that extreme, they run into another; for in many parts of *Scotland* our LORD seems still to be worshipped in a stable, and often in a very wretched one. Many of the churches are thatched with heath, and in some places are in such bad repair as to be half open at top; so that the people appear to worship, as the *Druids* did of old, in open temples.

SEPT. 10.
Went to see *Hamilton* House, twelve miles from *Glasgow:* rode through a rich and beautifull corn country, adorned with small woods, gentlemen's seats, and well watered. Hereabout I saw the first muddy stream since I had left *Edinburgh*; for the Highland

Highland rivers running generally through a bed of rock, or pure gravel, receive no other teint, in the greateſt floods, than the brown cryſtalline tinge of the moors, out of which they riſe.

Bothwell Bridge. See on the weſt, at a little diſtance from the road, the ruins of *Bothwell* caſtle, and the bridge, remarkable for the Duke of *Monmouth*'s victory over the Rebels in 1679. The church was collegiate, founded by *Archibald* Earl of *Douglas*, 1398, and is, as I heard, * oddly incruſted with a thin coat of ſtone.

Hamilton. *Hamilton* Houſe, or Palace, as it is called here, is ſeated at the end of a ſmall town; is a large diſagreeable pile of building, with two deep wings at right angles with the centre. The gallery is of great extent, and furniſhed (as well as ſome other rooms) with moſt excellent paintings: that of *Daniel* in the Lion's den, by *Rubens*, is a great performance: the fear and devotion of the prophet is finely expreſſed by his uplifted face and eyes, his claſped hands, his ſwelling muſcles, and the violent extenſion of one foot: a Lion looks fiercely at him with open mouth, and ſeems only reſtrained by the almighty power from making him fall a victim to his hunger; and the ſignal deliverance of *Daniel* is more fully marked by the number of human bones ſcattered over the floor, as if to ſhew the inſtant fate of others, in whoſe favor the Deity did not interfere.

The marriage-feaſt, by *Paul Veroneſe*, is a fine piece, and the obſtinacy and reſiſtance of the in-

---

* Biſhop *Pocock's manuſcript Journal*.

truder,

truder, who came without the wedding garment, is strongly expressed.

The treaty of peace between *England* and *Spain*, in the reign of *James* I. by *Juan de Pantoxa*, is a good historical picture. There are six Envoys on the part of the *Spaniards*, and five on that of the *English*, with their names inscribed over each: the *English* are the Earls of *Dorset*, *Nottingham*, *Devonshire*, *Northampton*, and *Robert Cecil*.

Earls of *Lauderdale* and *Lanerk* settling the covenant, both in black, with faces full of puritanical solemnity.

Several of the Dukes of *Hamilton*. *James* Duke of *Hamilton*, with a blue ribband and white rod. His son, beheaded in 1649. His brother, killed at the battle of *Worcester*. The Duke who fell in the duel with Lord *Mohun*.

Fielding, Earl of *Denbigh* *; his hair grey, a gun in his hand, and attended by an *Indian* boy. The finest I ever saw of *Vandyk*'s portraits: it seems perfectly to start from the canvas, and the action of his countenance looking up has matchless spirit. His daughter, and her husband the Marquiss of *Hamilton*.

Old Duke of *Chatelherault*, in black, with an order about his neck.

Two half-lengths in black; one with a fiddle in his hand, the other in a grotesque attitude; both with the same countenances; good, but swarthy;

---

* The person who shewed the house called him governor of *Jamaica*; but that must be a mistake. If any errors appear in my account of any of the pictures, I flatter myself it may be excused; for sometimes they were shewn by servants; sometimes the owners of the house were so obliging as to attend me, whom I could not trouble with a number of questions.

mistakenly

miftakenly called *David Rizzo's*; but I could not learn that there was any portraits of that unfortunate man.

Maria Dei Gratia Scotorum Regina, 1586. *Æt.* 43. a half-length; a ftiff figure, in a great ruff, auburne hair, oval but pretty full face, of much larger and plainer features than that at Caftle *Braan*, a natural alteration from the increafe of her cruel ufage, and of her ill health; yet ftill with a refemblance to that portrait. It was told me here, that fhe fent this picture, together with a ring, to the Duke of *Hamilton*, a little before her execution.

A head, faid to be *Anna Bullen*, very handfome, dreffed in a ruff and kerchief edged with ermine, and in a purple gown; over her face a veil, fo tranfparent as not to conceal

> The bloom of young defire and purple light of love.

Earl *Morton*, Regent of *Scotland*.

The rough reformer *John Knox*.

Lord *Belhaven*, author of the famous fpeech againft the union.

Philip II. at full length, with a ftrange figure of Fame bowing at his feet with a label and this motto, *Pro merente adfto.*

Chatelherault. About a mile from the houfe, on an eminence above a deep wooded glen, with the *Avon* at its bottom, is *Chatelherault*; fo called from the eftate the family once poffeffed in *France:* is an elegant banqueting houfe, with a dog-kennel, gardens, &c. and commands a fine view of the country. The park is now much inclofed: but I am told that *Wild cattle.* there are ftill in it a few of the breed of the wild cattle,

cattle, which *Boethius** says were peculiar to the *Caledonian* forest, were of a snowy whiteness, and had manes like lions: they were at this time in a distant part of the park, and I lost the sight of them.

I regret also the not being able to visit the falls of the *Clyde* near *Lanerk*, which I was informed were very romantic, consisting of a series of cataracts of different heights from ten to fifteen feet, some falling in sheets of water, others broken, and their sides bounded by magnificent rocks covered with trees.

Returned to *Glasgow*.

Crossed the country towards *Sterling*. Passed through the village of *Kylsithe*, noted for a victory gained by *Montrose* over the Covenanters. Thro' a bog, where numbers of the fugitives perished, is now cutting part of the canal that is to join the Firths of *Forth* and *Clyde*. Saw the spot where the battle of *Bannockbourne* was fought, in which the *English* under *Edward* II. had a shamefull defeat. *Edward* was so assured of conquest that he brought with him *William Baston* a *Carmelite*, and famous poet, to celebrate his victory; but the monarch was defeated, and the poor bard taken and forced by the conqueror, *invitâ minervâ*, to sing his success, which he did in such lines as these:

SEPT. 11.
Kylsithe.

---

* *Gignere solet ea sylva boves candidissimos in formam Leonis jubam habentes, cætera mansuetis simillimos verò adeo feros,* &c. Descr. Regni Scotiæ, fol. xi. I was also informed that the same kind is found in the Duke of *Queensbury*'s Park at *Drumlanrig*: but at present, in no part of *North Britain* in an unconfined state. I imagine these to have been the same with the *jubatos Bisontes* of *Pliny*, which were found in his time in *Germany*, and might be common both to our island and the continent.

Hic

Hic capit, hic rapit, hic terit, hic ferit, ecce dolores;
Vox tonat; æs sonat; hic ruit; hic luit; arcto modo
  res.
Hic secat; hic necat; hic docet; hic nocet; iste fugatur:
Hic latet, hic patet; hic premit, hic gemit; hic superatur.

St. Ninian.   Went through the small town of St. *Ninian* *, a mile south of *Sterling*. The church had been the powder-magazine of the Rebels, who, on their retreat, blew it up in such haste, as to destroy some of their own people and about fifteen innocent spectators.

Sterling.   *Sterling* and its castle, in respect of situation, is a miniature of *Edinburgh*; is placed on a ridged hill, or rock, rising out of a plain, having the castle at the upper end on a high precipitous rock. Within its walls was the palace of several of the *Scotch* Kings, a square building, ornamented on three sides with pillars resting on grotesque figures projecting from the wall, and on the top of each pillar is a statue, seemingly the work of fancy. Near it is the old parlement-house, a vast room 120 feet long, very high, with a timbered roof, and formerly had a gallery running round the inside. Below the castle are the ruins of the palace belonging to the Earls of *Mar*, whose family had once the keeping of this fortress. There are still the *Erskine* arms and much ornamental carving on parts of it. The town of *Stirling* is inclosed with a wall; the

---

* Apostle of the *Picts*, son of a prince of the *Cumbrian Britains*, converting the *Picts* as far as the *Grampian* hills. Died 432.

ftreets are irregular and narrow, except that which leads to the caftle. Here, and at the village of *Bannockbourne*, is a confiderable manufacture of coarfe carpets.

From the top of the caftle is by far the fineft view in *Scotland*. To the eaft is a vaft plain rich in corn, adorned with woods, and watered with the river *Forth*, whofe meanders are, before it reaches the fea, fo frequent and fo large, as to form a multitude of moft beautifull peninfulas; for in many parts the windings approximate fo clofe as to leave only a little ifthmus of a few yards. In this plain is an old abby, a view of *Alloa*, *Clackmanna*, *Falkirk*, the Firth of *Forth*, and the country as far as *Edinburgh*. On the north, the *Ochil* hills, and the moor where the battle of *Dumblain* was fought. To the weft, the ftraith of *Menteith*, as fertile as the eaftern plain, and terminated by the Highland mountains, among which the fummit of *Ben-Lomond* is very confpicuous.

The *Sylva Caledonia*, or *Caledonian* Foreft, begun a little north of *Sterling*, and paffing through *Menteith* and *Straithern*, extended, according to *Boethius*, as far as *Athol* on one fide, and *Lochaber* on the other. It is very flightly mentioned by the antients *; but the fuppofed extent is given by the *Scottifh* hiftorian.

Lie at *Falkirk*, a large ill-built town, fupported *Falkirk.* by the great fairs for black cattle from the Highlands, it being computed that 24,000 head are annually fold here. There is alfo a great deal of

* By *Pliny*, lib. iv. c. 16. and *Eumenius*, in his Panegyric on *Conftantius*, c. 7.

money got here by the carriage of goods, landed at *Carron* wharf, to *Glasgow*. Such is the increase of trade in this country, that about twenty years ago not three carts could be found in the town, and at present there are above a hundred that are supported by their intercourse with *Glasgow*.

In the church-yard, on a plain stone, is the following epitaph on *John de Graham*, styled the right hand of the gallant *Wallace*, killed at the battle of *Falkirk* in 1298 *:

> Here lies Sir *John* the *Grame* both wight and wise,
> Ane of the chief reskewit *Scotland* thrise.
> Ane better knight not to the world was lent,
> Nor was gude *Grame* of trueth, and of hardiment.
> Mente manuque potens, et VALLÆ fidus Achates
> Conditur hic Gramus bello interfectus ab Anglis.
> 22, Julii. 1298.

Near this is another epitaph, occasioned by a second battle of *Falkirk*, as disgracefull to the *English* as the other was fatal to the *Scots*: the first was a well disputed combat; the last, a pannic on both sides, for part of each army flew, the one west, the other east, each carrying the news of their several defeats, while the total destruction of our forces was prevented by the gallant behaviour of a brigadier, who with two regiments faced such of the rebels as kept the field, and prevented any further advantages. The epitaph I allude to is in memory

---

* Fought between *Falkirk* and *Carron* works, at a place called to this day *Graham*'s Moor.

of Sir *Robert Monro* *, the worthy chieftain of that loyal clan, a family which loſt three brothers the ſame year in ſupport of the royal cauſe. Sir *Robert* being greatly wounded in the battle was murthered in cool blood, by the Rebels, with his brother Dr. *Monro,* who with fraternal piety was at that time dreſſing his wounds: the third was aſſaſſinated by miſtake for one who well deſerved his death for ſpontaneous barbarities on Highlanders approaching according to proclamation to ſurrender their arms.

I have very often mentioned fields of battles in this part of the kingdom; ſcarce a ſpot has eſcaped unſtained with gore; for had they no publick enemy to contend with, the *Scots,* like the *Welſh* of old, turned their arms againſt each other.

* Conditur heic quod poterit mori
Roberti Monro *de Foulis*, Eq. Bar.
Gentis ſui Principis
Militum Tribuni:
Vita in caſtris curiaque *Britannica*
Honeſtè producta
Pro Libertate religione Patriæ
In acie honeſtiſſimè defuncta
Prope Falkirk *Jan.* xviii. 1746. Æt. 62.
Virtutis conſiliique fama
In *Montanorum* cohortis Præfectura
Quamdiu prœlium Fontonæum memorabitur
Perduratura;
Ob amicitiam et fidem amicis
Humanitatem clementiamque adverſariis
Benevolentiam bonitatemque omnibus,
Trucidantibus etiam,
In perpetuum deſideranda.
Duncanus Monro *de Obſtale*, M.D. Æt. 59.
Frater Fratrem linquere fugiens,
Saucium curans, ictus inermis
Commoriens cohoneſtat Urnam.

Carron

Iron founderies.

Carron iron-works lie about a mile from *Falkirk*, and are the greatest of the kind in *Europe*: they were founded about eight years ago, before which there was not a single house, and the country a meer moor. At present, the buildings of all sorts are of vast extent, and above twelve hundred men are employed. The iron is smelted from the stone, then cast into cannon, pots, and all sorts of utensils made in founderies. This work has been of great service to the country, by teaching the people industry and a method of setting about any sort of labor, which before the common people had scarce any notion of.

Carron wharf lies on the *Forth*, and is not only usefull to the works, but of great service even to *Glasgow*, as considerable quantities of goods destined for that city are landed there. The canal likewise begins in this neighborhood, which, when effected, will prove another benefit to these works.

Arthur's Oven.

At a small distance from the founderies, on a little rising above the river *Carron*, stood that celebrated antiquity called *Arthur*'s Oven, which the ingenious Mr. *Gordon** supposes to have been a *sacellum*, or little chapel, a repository for the *Roman Insignia*, or standards: but, to the mortification of every curious traveller, this matchless edifice is now no more; its barbarous owner, a *gothic* knight, caused it to be demolished, in order to make a mill-dam with the materials, within less than a year, the *Naiades*, in resentment of the sacrilege, came down in a flood and entirely swept it away.

---

* *Itin. Septentr. p.* 24. *tab.* iv. as the book is very scarce, I have taken the liberty of having that plate copied into this work.

Saw

ARTHUR'S OVEN

TWO LOCHABER AXES

SEPT. 12.
Graham's Dyke.

Saw near *Callendar*-Houſe ſome part of *Antoninus*'s Wall, or, as it is called here, *Graham*'s Dyke.* The *vallum* and the ditch are here very evident, and both are of a great ſize, the laſt being forty feet broad and thirteen deep; it extended from the Firth of *Forth* to that of *Clyde*, and was defended at proper diſtances by forts and watch-towers, the work of the *Roman* legions under the command of *Lollius Urbicus*, in the reign of *Antoninus Pius*. According to Mr. *Gordon*, it began at old *Kirk Patrick* on the Firth of *Clyde*, and ended two miles weſt of *Abercorn*, on the Firth of Forth, being in length 36 miles, 887 paces.

Paſſed thro' *Burrowſtoneſs*, a town on the Firth, inveloped in ſmoke from the great ſalt-pans and vaſt collieries near it. The town-houſe is built in form of a caſtle. There is a good quay, much frequented by ſhipping; for conſiderable quantities of coal are ſent from hence to *London*; and there are beſides ſome *Greenland* ſhips † belonging to the town.

The whole country from *Falkirk* for ſome diſtance from the Firth is very low, and in many places protected from the ſea by banks. I obſerved in certain places far from the water, vaſt

---

* So called from *Graham*, who is ſaid to have firſt made a breach in this wall ſoon after the retreat of the *Romans* out of *Britain*. Vide *Boethius*, cxxxi.

† This year the whale-fiſhery began to revive; which for a few years paſt had been ſo unſucceſsfull, that ſeveral of the adventurers had thoughts of diſpoſing of their ſhips. Perhaps the whales had till this year deſerted thoſe ſeas; for *Marten*, p. 185, of his voyage to *Spitzbergen*, remarks, "That theſe animals, either "weary of their place, or ſenſible of their own danger, do often "change their harbours."

beds

Hopeton-House.

beds of oister-shells; a mark of it having once been possest by that element.

Reach *Hopeton*-House, the seat of the Earl of *Hopeton*; a house began by Sir *William Bruce*, and finished by Mr. *Adams:* is the handsomest I saw in *North Britain:* the front is enriched with pilasters; the wings at some distance joined to it by a beautifull colonade: one wing is the stables, the other the library.

The great improvements round the house are very extensive; but the gardens are still in the old taste: trees and shrubs succeed here greatly; among others were two *Portugal* laurels thirty feet high. Nothing can equal the grandeur of the approach to the house, or the prospect from it. The situation is bold, on an eminence, commanding a view of the Firth of *Forth*, bounded on the north by the county of *Fife*; the middle is chequered with islands, such as *Garvey*, *Inch Keith* *, and others; and to the south-east is a vast command of *East-Lothian*, and the terminating object the great conic hill of *North Berwick*.

The whole ride from *Sterling* to *Queen's-Ferry* (near *Hopeton*-House) is not to be paralleled for the elegance and variety of its prospects: the whole is a composition of all that is great and beautifull:

---

* This isle is opposite *Leith*. By order of council, in 1497, all venereal patients in the neighborhood were transported there, *Ne quid detrimenti res publica caperet.* It is remarkable, that this disorder, which was thought to have appeared in *Europe* only four years before, should make so quick a progress. The horror of a disease, for which there was then supposed to be no cure, must have occasioned this attention to stop the contagion; for even half a century after, one of the first monarchs of *Europe*, *Francis* I. fell a victim to it.

towns, villages, feats, and antient towers, decorate each bank of that fine expanse of water the *Firth*; while the busy scenes of commerce and rural œconomy are no small addition to the still life. The lofty mountains of the Highlands form a distant but august boundary towards the northwest; and the eastern view is enlivened with ships perpetually appearing or vanishing amidst the numerous isles.

Pass by *Queen's-Ferry*; fall into the *Edinburgh* road, and finish, this evening, in that capital, a most agreeable and prosperous Tour. It was impossible not to recall the idea of what I had seen; to imagine the former condition of this part of the kingdom, and to compare it with the present state, and by a sort of second-sight make a probable conjecture of the happy appearance it will assume in a very few years. Nor could I forbear repeating the prophetic lines * of *Aaron Hill*, who seemed seized with a like *rêverie:*

> Once more! O North, I view thy winding shores,
> Climb thy bleak hills, and cross thy dusky moors.
> Impartial view thee with an heedfull eye,
> Yet still by nature, not by censure try.
> *England* thy sister is a gay coquet,
> Whom art enlivens, and temptations whet:
> Rich, proud, and wanton, she her beauty knows,
> And in a conscious warmth of beauty glows:
> *Scotland* comes after like an unripe fair,
> Who sighs with anguish at her sister's air;
> Unconscious, that she'll quickly have her day,
> And be the toast when *Albion*'s charms decay.

After a few days experience of the same hospitality in *Edinburgh* that I had met with in the Highlands, SEPT. 18.

* Written on a window in *North Britain*.

lands, I continued my journey south, through a rich corn country, leaving the *Pentland* hills to the west, whose sides were covered with a fine turf. Before I reached *Crook*, a small village, the country grew worse: after this it assumed a Highland appearance, the hills were high, the vales narrow, and there was besides a great scarcity of trees, and hardly any corn; instead, was abundance of good pasturage for sheep, there being great numbers in these parts, which supply the north of *England*. The roads are bad, narrow, and often on the edges of precipices, impending over the river *Tweed*, here an inconsiderable stream. Reach

MOFFAT. *Moffat*, a small neat town, famous for its spaws; one said to be usefull in scrophulous cases, the other a chalybeate, which makes this place much resorted to in summer. Doctor *Walker*, minister of the place, shewed me in manuscript his natural history of the *western isles*, which will do him much credit whenever he favors the world with it.

SEPT. 19. The country between *Moffat* and *Lockerby* is very good, a mixture of downs and corn-land, with a few small woods: the country grows quite flat and very unpleasant. Cross a small river called the *Sark*, which divides the two kingdoms, and enter CUMBERLAND.

About three miles farther cross the *Esk* over a handsome stone-bridge, and lie at the small village of *Longtown*. The country is very rich in corn, but quite bare of trees, and very flat. Near this village, at *Netherby*, are the ruins of a *Roman* station,

tion, where statues, weapons and coins are often dug up.

Cross the *Eden* to *Carlisle*, a pleasant city, surrounded with walls, like *Chester*, but they are very dirty, and kept in very bad repair. The castle is antient, but makes a good appearance at a distance: the view from it is fine, of rich meadows, at this time covered with thousands of cattle, it being fair-day. The *Eden* here forms two branches, and insulates the ground; over one is a bridge of four, over the other one of nine arches. There is besides a prospect of a rich country, and a distant view of *Coldfells*, *Cross-fells*, *Skiddaw*, and other mountains.

Sept. 20. Carlisle.

The cathedral * is very imperfect, *Cromwell* having pulled down part to build barracks with the materials. There remains some portion that was built in the *Saxon* times, with very massy pillars and round arches. The rest is more modern, said to have been built in the reign of *Edward* III. who had in one part an apartment to lodge in. The arches in this latter building are sharp-pointed: the east window remarkably fine.

The manufactures of *Carlisle* are chiefly of printed linnens, for which near 3000 l. *per ann.* is paid in duties. It is also noted for a great manufacture of whips, which employs numbers of children.

Salmons appear in the *Eden* in numbers so early as the months of *December* and *January*; and the *London*, and even *Newcastle* markets, are supplied with early fish from this river: but it is remarkable,

---

* Begun by *Walter*, deputy of these parts, under *William Rufus*; but the new choir was not founded till about 1354.

that

that they do not visit the *Esk* in any quantity till *April*, notwithstanding the mouths of both these waters are at a small distance from each other. I omitted in its proper place an account of the *Newcastle* fishery, therefore insert here the little I could collect relating to it: the fish seldom appear in the *Tyne* till *February*: there are about 24 fisheries on the river, besides a very considerable were, and the whole annual capture amounts to about 36,000 fish. I was informed that once the fish were brought from *Berwick* and cured at *Newcastle*; but at present, notwithstanding all goes under the name of *Newcastle* Salmon, very little is taken there, in comparison of what is caught in the *Tweed*.

The country near *Carlisle* consists of small enclosures; but a little farther on, towards *Penrith*, changes into coarse downs. On the east, at a distance, are ridges of high hills running parallel to the road, with a good inclosed country in the intervening space. Above *Penrith* is a rich inclosed tract, mixed with hedge-row trees and woods. On the south-west, a prospect of high and craggy mountains. After I left *Lockerby*, Nature, as if exhausted with her labors in the lofty hills of *Scotland*, seemed to have lain down and reposed herself for a considerable space; but here began to rise again with all the sublimity of *alpine* majesty.

PENRITH. PENRITH is an antient town, seated at the foot of a hill: is a great thoroughfare for travellers; but has little other trade, except a small one of checks. The church is very neat, the gallery supported by large columns, each formed of a single stone. In the church-yard is a monument of great antiquity,

antiquity, confisting of two stone pillars eleven feet six inches high, and five in circumference in the lower part, which is rounded; the upper is square, and tapers to a point: in the square part is some fret-work, and the relievo of a cross. Both these stones are mortised at their lower part into a round one: they are about fifteen feet asunder; the space between them is inclosed on each side with two very large but thin semicircular stones; so that there is left a walk between pillar and pillar of two feet in breadth. Two of these lesser stones are plain, the other two have certain figures at present scarce intelligible.

Cross the *Emot*, a small river, and soon after the *Lowther*, over *Yeoman*'s Bridge, near which I enter WESTMORLAND. About four miles farther cross *Clifton* Moor, where the Rebels made a short stand in 1745, and sacrificed a few men to save the rest of their army. Pass over *Shap* Fells, more black, dreary, and melancholy, than any of the Highland hills, being not only very barren but destitute of every picturesque beauty. This barren scene continued till within a small distance of

SEPT. 21.

KENDAL, a large town on the river *Kent*, in a rich and beautifull vale, well cultivated, and prettily wooded. Here is a very great trade in knit worsted-stockings, some linsies, and a coarse sort of cloth, called cottons, for the *Guinea* trade.

Kendal.

Near *Burton* enter LANCASHIRE. Reach its capital, *Lancaster*, a large and well-built town, seated on the *Lune*, a river navigable for ships of 250 tuns as high as the bridge. The custom-house is a small but most elegant building, with a portico

Lancaster.

supported

supported by four ionic pillars, on a beautifull plain pediment. There is a double flight of steps, a rustic surbase and coins; a work that does much credit to Mr. *Giller*, the architect, an inhabitant of this town.

The church is seated on an eminence, and commands an extensive but not a pleasing view. The castle is entire, the courts of justice are held in it; and it is also the county jail. The front is very handsome, consists of two large angular towers, with a handsome gateway between.

SEPT. 22. Hastened through *Preston*, *Wiggan*, *Warrington*, and *Chester*, and finished my journey with a rapture of which no fond parent can be ignorant, that of being again restored to two innocent prattlers after an absence equally regretted by all parties.

APPENDIX.

APPENDIX.

NUMBER I.

Concerning the Constitution of the Church of *Scotland*.

PResbyterian government in *Scotland* took place after the reformation of popery, as being the form of ecclesiastical government most agreeable to the genius and inclinations of the people of *Scotland*. When *James* VI. succeeded to the crown of *England*, it is well known, that during his reign and that of his successors of the family of *Stewart*, designs were formed of altering the constitution of our civil government and rendering our kings more absolute. The establishment of episcopacy in *Scot-*

land was thought to be one point proper in order to facilitate the execution of these designs. Episcopacy was accordingly established at length, and continued to be the government of the church till the revolution, when such designs subsisting no longer, presbyterian government was restored to *Scotland.* It was established by act of parliament in 1690, and was afterwards secured by an express article in the treaty of union between the two kingdoms of *England* and *Scotland.* Among the ministers of *Scotland*, there subsists a perfect equality; that is, no minister, considered as an individual, has an authoratative jurisdiction over another. Jurisdiction is competent for them only when they act in a collective body, or as a court of judicature: and then there is a subordination of

one

APPENDIX.

one court to another, or inferiour and superiour courts.

The courts established by law are the four following, *viz.* Church Sessions, Presbyteries, Provincial Synods, and above all a National or General Assembly.

A Church Session is composed of the Minister of the parish and certain discreet Laymen, who are chosen and ordained for the exercise of discipline, and are called Elders. The number of these Elders varies according to the extent of the parish. Two of them, together with the Minister, are necessary, in order to their holding a legal meeting. The Minister always presides in these meetings, and is called Moderator; but has no other authority but what belongs to the *Præses* of any other court. The Church

Church Seffion is appointed for inspecting the morals of the parishioners, and managing the funds that are appropriated for the maintainance of the poor within their bounds. When a person is convicted of any instance of immoral conduct, or of what is inconsistent with his christian profession, the Church Seffion inflicts some ecclesiastical censure, such as giving him an admonition or rebuke: or if the crime be of a gross and publick nature, they appoint him to profess his repentance in face of the whole congregation, in order to make satisfaction for the publick offence. The highest church censure is excommunication, which is seldom inflicted but for contumacy, or for some very atrocious crime obstinately persisted in. In former times there were certain civil pains and penalties which followed upon a sentence of excommunication,

APPENDIX.

munication, but by a *British* statute these are happily abolished. The church of *Scotland* addresses its censures only to the consciences of men; and if they cannot by the methods of persuasion reclaim offenders, they think it inconsistent with the spirit of true religion, to have recourse to compulsive methods, such as temporal pains and penalties.

If the person thinks himself aggrieved by the Church Session, it is competent for him to seek redress, by entering an appeal to the Presbytery, which is the next superiour court. In like manner he may appeal from the Presbytery to the Provincial Synod, and from the Synod to the Assembly, whose sentence is final in all ecclesiastical matters.

A Pres-

A Presbytery consists of the Ministers within a certain district, and also of one ruling Elder from each Church Session within the district. In settling the boundaries of a Presbytery, a regard was paid to the situation of the country. Where the country is populous and champaign, there are instances of thirty Ministers and as many Elders being joined in one Presbytery. In mountainous countries where travelling is more difficult, there are only seven or eight Ministers, in some places fewer, in a Presbytery. The number of Presbyteries is computed to be about seventy. Presbyteries review the procedure of Church Sessions, and judge in references and appeals that are brought before them. They take trials of candidates for the ministry: and if upon such trial they find them duly qualified, they licence them

them to preach, but not to dispense the sacraments. Such licentiates are called Probationers. It is not common for the church of *Scotland* to ordain or confer holy orders on such licentiates till they be presented to some vacant kirk, and thereby acquire a right to a benefice.

It is the privilege of Presbyteries to judge their own members, at least in the first instance. They may be judged for heresy, that is, for preaching or publishing doctrines that are contrary to the publick standard imposed by Act of Parliament and Assembly; or for any instance of immoral conduct, prosecutions for heresy were formerly more frequent than they are at present; but happily a more liberal spirit has gained ground among the Clergy of *Scotland*. They think more freely than they did of old,

old, and confequently a fpirit of inquiry and moderation feems to be on the growing hand; fo that profecutions for herefy are become more rare, and are generally looked upon as invidious. Some fenfible men among the clergy of *Scotland* look upon fubfcriptions to certain articles and creeds of human compofition as a grievance, from which they would willingly be delivered.

Prefbyteries are more fevere in their cenfures upon their own members for any inftance of immoral conduct. If the perfon be convicted, they fufpend him from the exercife of his minifterial office for a limited time: but if the crime be of a heinous nature, they depofe or deprive him of his clerical character; fo that he is no longer a minifter of the church of *Scotland*, but forfeits his title to his benefice,

APPENDIX.

fice, and other privileges of the established church. However, if the person thinks himself injured by the sentence of the Presbytery, it is lawful for him to appeal to the Provincial Synod, within whose bounds his Presbytery lies: and from the Synod he may appeal to the National Assembly. Presbyteries hold their meetings generally every month, except in remote countries, and have a power of adjourning themselves to whatever time or place within their district they shall think proper. They chuse their own *Præses* or Moderator, who must be a Minister of their own Presbytery. The ruling Elders who sit in Presbyteries must be changed every half-year, or else chosen again by their respective Church Sessions.

Provincial Synods are the next superiour courts to Presbyteries, and are composed

APPENDIX.

composed of the several Presbyteries within the province and of a ruling Elder from each Church Session. The ancient dioceses of the Bishops are for the most part the boundaries of a Synod. Most of the Synods in *Scotland* meet twice every year, in the months of *April* and *October*, and at every meeting they chuse their *Præses* or Moderator, who must be a clergyman of their own number. They review the procedure of Presbyteries, and judge in appeals, references and complaints, that are brought before them from the inferiour courts. And if a Presbytery shall be found negligent in executing the ecclesiastical laws against any of their members, or any other person within their jurisdiction, the Synod can call them to account, and censure them as they shall see cause.

The

APPENDIX.

The General Assembly is the supreme court in ecclesiastical matters, and from which there lies no appeal. As they have a power of making laws and canons, concerning the discipline and government of the church, and the publick service of religion, the King sends always a commissioner to represent his royal person, that nothing may be enacted inconsistent with the laws of the state. The person who represents the King is generally some *Scots* nobleman, whom his Majesty nominates annually some time before the meeting of the assembly, and is allowed a suitable salary for defraying the expence of this honourable office. He is present at all the meetings of the assembly, and at all their debates and deliberations. After the assembly is constituted, he presents his commission and delivers a speech;

and

and when they have finished their business, which they commonly do in twelve days, he adjourns the assembly, and appoints the time and place of their next annual meeting, which is generally at *Edinburgh* in the month of *May*.[1]

The Assembly is composed of Ministers and ruling Elders chosen annually from each Presbytery in *Scotland*. As the number of Ministers and Elders in a Presbytery varies, so the number of their representatives must hold a proportion to the number of Ministers and Elders that are in the Presbytery. The proportion is fixed by laws and regulations for that purpose. Each Royal Burgh and University in *Scotland* has likewise the privilege of chusing a ruling Elder to the Assembly. All elections must at least be made forty days before the meeting

APPENDIX.

meeting of the Affembly. Their jurifdiction is either conftitutive or judicial. By the firft they have authority to make laws in ecclefiaftical matters: by the other they judge in references and appeals brought before them from the fubordinate courts, and their fentences are decifive and final. One point which greatly employs their attention is the fettlement of vacant parifhes. The common people of *Scotland* are greatly prejudiced againft the law of patronage. Hence when a patron prefents a candidate to a vacant parifh, the parifhioners frequently make great oppofition to the fettlement of the prefentee, and appeal from the inferiour courts to the Affembly. The Affembly now-a-days are not difpofed to indulge the parifhioners in unreafonable oppofition to prefentees. On the other hand, they are unwilling to fettle settle the presentee in opposition to the whole people, who refuse to submit to his ministry, because in this case his ministrations among them must be useless and without effect. The Assembly therefore for the most part delay giving sentence in such cases, till once they have used their endeavours to reconcile the parishioners to the presentee. But if their attempts this way prove unsuccessful, they proceed to settle the presentee in obedience to the act of parliament concerning patronages. Upon the whole it appears that in the indicatories of the church of *Scotland*, there is an equal representation of the Laity as of the Clergy, which is a great security to the Laity against the usurpations of the Clergy.

The business of every Minister in a parish is to perform religious worship, and

APPENDIX.

and to preach in the language of the country to his congregation every *Sunday*, and likewise on other extraordinary occasions appointed by the laws and regulations of the church. The tendency of their preaching is to instruct their hearers in the essential doctrines of natural and revealed religion, and improve these instructions in order to promote the practice of piety and social virtue. Of old, it was customary to preach upon controverted and mysterious points of divinity, but it is now hoped that the generality of the Clergy confine the subject of their preaching to what has a tendency to promote virtue and good morals, and to make the people peaceable and useful members of society.

Ministers likewise examine their parishioners annually. They go to the

the different towns and * villages of the parish; and in an easy and familiar manner converse with them upon the essential doctrines of religion. They make trial of their knowledge by putting questions to them on these heads. The adult as well as children are catechised. They likewise visit their parishes and inquire into the behaviour of their several parishioners, and admonish them for whatever they find blameable in their conduct. At

---

* I must observe, that Bishop *Burnet* (by birth a *Scotchman*) adopted in his diocese the zeal of the church of his native country, and its attention to the morals and good conduct of the clergy and their flocks. Not content with the usual triennial visitations, he every summer, during six weeks, made a progress through some district of his diocese, preaching and confirming from church to church, so that before the return of the triennial visitation he became well acquainted with the behaviour of every incumbent. He preached every Sunday in some church of the city of *Salisbury*; catechised, and instructed its youth for confirmation; was most vigilant, and strict in his examination of candidates for holy orders; was an invincible enemy to pluralities, and of course to non-residents; filled his office with worth and dignity, and by his espiscopal merits, it is to be hoped, may have atoned for the acknowledged blemishes in his biographical character.

these

APPENDIX.

these visitations the Minister inculcates the practice of the relative and social duties, and insists upon the necessity of the practice of them. And if there happen to be any quarrels among neighbours, the Minister endeavours by the power of persuasion to bring about a reconciliation. But in this part of their conduct, much depends upon the temper, prudence, and discretion of Ministers, who are cloathed with the same passions, prejudices and infirmities, that other men are:

To this sensible account of the Church of *North Britain*, I beg leave to add another, which may be considered as a sort of supplement, and may serve to fling light on some points untouched in the preceding: it is the extract from an answer to some queries I sent a worthy correspondent in the

the Highlands, to whom I am indebted for many senfible communications:

"To apprehend well the prefent
"ftate of *our* church patronage and
"mode of fettlement, we muft
"briefly view this matter from the
"Reformation. At *that* remarkable
"period the whole temporalities of the
"church were refumed by the Crown
"and Parliament; and foon after a
"new maintenance was fettled for
"minifters in about 960 parifhes.
"The patrons of the old, fplendid
"Popifh livings, ftill claimed a pa-
"tronage in the new-modelled poor
"ftipends for parifh minifters. The
"Lords, or Gentlemen, who got from
"the Crown, grants of the fuperiorities
"and lands of old *abbies*, claimed alfo
"the patronage of all the churches
"which were in the gift of thofe
            "*abbies*

APPENDIX.

" *abbies* during popery. The *King*
" too claimed the old patronage of
" the *Crown*, and thofe of any ec-
" clefiaftic corporations not granted
" away.

" Lay-patronages were reckoned
" always a great grievance by the
" Church of *Scotland*, and accord-
" ingly from the beginning of the
" reformation the Church declared
" againſt lay-patronage and prefen-
" tations. The ecclefiaftic laws, or
" acts of affembly, confirmed at laſt
" by parliament, required, in order
" to the fettlement of a miniſter,
" fome concurrence of the congre-
" gation, of the gentlemen who had
" property within the cure, and of
" the elders of the parifh.

" The Elders, or *Kirk*-Seffion, are
" a number of perſons, who, for their
" wifdom,

APPENDIX.

" wisdom, piety and knowledge, are
" elected from the body of the people
" in every parish, and continue for
" life, *sese bene gerentibus*, to assist
" the parish minister in suppressing
" immoralities and regulating the af-
" fairs of the parish. Three of these
" men and a minister make a quo-
" rum, and form the lowest of our
" church courts.

" Thus matters continued to the
" year 1649, when by act of parlia-
" ment patronages were *abolished* en-
" tirely, and the election or nomina-
" tion of ministers was committed to
" the *Kirk*-Session or Elders; who,
" in those days of universal sobriety
" and outward appearance at least of
" religion among the Presbyterians,
" were generally the gentlemen of
" best condition in the parish who
" were in communion with the
" church.

APPENDIX.

" church. After the *restoration* of
" King *Charles* II. along with epis-
" copacy patronages returned, yet
" under the old laws; and all de-
" bates were finally determinable by
" the *General Assembly*, which even
" under episcopacy in *Scotland* was
" the supreme ecclesiastic court.
" Thus they continued till the Re-
" volution, when the presbyterian
" model was restored by act of par-
" liament.

" The people chose their own mi-
" nisters, and matters continued in
" this form till the year 1711, when
" Queen *Anne*'s ministry intending to
" defeat the *Hanover* succession, took
" all methods to harass such as were
" firmly attached to it, which the
" Presbyterian Gentry and Clergy ever
" were, both from principle and inte-
" rest. An act therefore was obtained,
" and

"and which is still in force, restoring
"patrons to their power of electing
"ministers.

"By this act the King is now in
"possession of the patronage of above
"500 churches out of 950, having
"not only the old rights of the
"crown, but many patronages ac-
"quired at the reformation not yet
"alienated; all the patronages of
"the 14 *Scots* Bishops, and all the
"patronages of the Lords and Gen-
"tlemen forfeited in the years 1715
"and 1745. Lords, gentlemen and
"magistrates of burroughs, are the
"patrons of the remaining churches.
"A patron must present a qualified
"person to a charge within six
"months of the last incumbent's re-
"moval or death, otherwise his right
"falls to the Presbytery.

"A Pref-

APPENDIX.

"A Presbytery consists of several Ministers and Elders. All parishes are annexed to some Presbytery. The Presbytery is the second church court, and they revise the the acts of the *Kirk*-Session, which is the lowest. Above the Presbytery is the Synod, which is a court consisting of several Presbyteries. And from all these there lies an appeal to the General Assembly, which is the supreme church court in *Scotland*. This supreme court consists of the King represented by his Commissioner, Ministers from the different Presbyteries, and ruling Elders. They meet annually at *Edinburgh*, enact laws for the good of the church, finally determine all controverted elections of ministers. They can prevent a clergyman's transportation from one
"charge

"charge to another. They can find
"a presentee qualified or unqualified,
"and consequently oblige the patron
"to present another. They can de-
"pose from the ministry, and every
"intrant into holy orders becomes
"bound to submit to the decisions
"of this court; which, from the days
"our reformer *John Knox*, has ap-
"propriated to itself the titles of The
"VERY VENERABLE and VERY REVE-
"REND ASSEMBLY of the Church of
"*Scotland*.

"All the clergymen of our com-
"munion are upon a par as to autho-
"rity. We can enjoy no pluralities.
"Non-residence is not known. We
"are bound to a regular discharge of
"the several duties of our office. The
"different cures are frequently visited
"by the Presbytery of the bounds;
"and at these visitations strict en-
                                    "quiry

"quiry is made into the life, doc-
"trine and diligence of the incum-
"bent. And for default in any of
"these, he may be suspended from
"preaching: or if any gross immo-
"rality is proved against him, he can
"be immediately deposed and ren-
"dered incapable of officiating as a
"minister of the gospel. Appeal
"indeed lies, as I said before, from
"the decision of the inferior to the
"supreme court.

"Great care is taken in preparing
"young men for the ministry. After
"going through a course of philo-
"sophy in one of our four Universi-
"ties, they must attend at least for
"four years the Divinity-Hall, where
"they hear the prelections of the
"professors, and perform the dif-
"ferent exercises prescribed them:
"they must attend the Greek, the
"Hebrew,

"Hebrew, and Rhetoric claſſes; and
"before ever they are admitted to
"tryals for the miniſtry before a Preſ-
"bytery, they muſt lay teſtimonials
"from the different profeſſors of their
"morals, their attendance, their pro-
"greſs, before them: and if upon
"tryal they are found unqualified,
"they are either ſet aſide as unfit for
"the office, or enjoined to apply to
"their ſtudies a year or two more.

"Our livings are in general from
"60 to 120 l. ſterling. Some few
"livings are richer, and a few poorer.
"Every miniſter beſides is entitled to
"a manſion-houſe, barn and ſtable;
"to four acres of arable and three of
"paſturage land. Our livings are
"exempted from all public duties;
"as are alſo our perſons from all
"public ſtatute-works. As ſchools
"are erected in all our pariſhes, and
"that

"that education is cheap, our young
"generation is beginning to imbibe
"some degree of taste and liberal
"sentiment unknown to their illite-
"rate rude forefathers. The English
"language is cultivated even here
"amongst *these* bleak and dreary
"mountains. *Your* Divines, *your*
"Philosophers, *your* Historians, *your*
"Poets, have found their way to our
"sequestred vales, and are perused
"with pleasure even by our lowly
"swains; and the names of *Tillotson*,
"of *Atterbury*, of *Clerk*, of *Secker*,
"of *Newton*, of *Locke*, of *Bacon*, of
"*Lyttelton*, of *Dryden*, of *Pope*, of
"*Gay*, and of *Gray*, are not unknown
"in our distant land."

APPENDIX.

NUMBER II.

Account of the fasting Woman of *Rossshire*.

Dunrobin, Aug. 24, 1769.

The Information of Mr. *Rainy*, Missionary - Minister in *Kincardine*, anent *Katharine M'Leod*.

*K*Atharine *M'Leod*, daughter to *Donald M'Leod*, farmer in *Croig*, in the parish of *Kincardine*, *Rossshire*, an unmarried woman, aged about thirty-five years, sixteen years ago contracted a fever, after which she became blind. Her father carried her to several physicians and surgeons to cure her blindness. Their prescriptions proved of no effect. He carried her also to a lady skilled in physic, in the neighborhood,

borhood, who, doubtfull whether her blindness was occasioned by the weakness of her eye-lids, or a defect in her eyes, found by the use of some medicines that the blindness was occasioned by a weakness in her eye-lids, which being strengthened she recovered her sight in some measure, and discharged as usual every kind of work about her father's farm; but tyed a garter tight round her forehead to keep up her eye-lids. In this condition she continued for four or five years, enjoying a good state of health, and working as usual. She contracted another lingering fever, of which she never recovered perfectly.

Some time after her fever her jaws fell, her eye-lids closed, and she lost her appetite. Her parents declare that for the space of a year and three-quarters they could not say that any meat or liquid went down her throat.

throat. Being interrogated on this point, they own'd they very frequently put something into her mouth. But they concluded that nothing went down her throat, because she had no evacuation; and when they forced open her jaws at one time, and kept them open for some time by putting in a stick between her teeth, and pulled forward her tongue, and forced something down her throat, she coughed and strained, as if in danger to be choaked. One thing during the time she eat and drank nothing is remarkable, that her jaws were unlocked, and she recovered her speech, and retained it for several days, without any apparent cause for the same; she was quite sensible, repeated several questions of the shorter catechisms; told them that it was to no purpose to put any thing into her mouth, for that nothing went down her

APPENDIX.

her throat; as also that sometimes she understood them when they spoke to her. By degrees her jaws thereafter fell, and she lost her speech.

Some time before I saw her she received some sustenance, whey, water-gruel, &c. but threw it up, at least for the most part, immediately. When they put the stick between her teeth, mentioned above, two or three of her teeth were broken. It was at this breach they put in any thing into her mouth. I caused them to bring her out of bed, and give her something to drink. They gave her whey. Her neck was contracted, her chin fixed on her breast, nor could by any force be pulled back: she put her chin and mouth into the dish with the whey, and I perceived she sucked it at the above-mentioned breach as a child would suck the breast, and immediately

diately threw it up again, as her parents told me she used to do, and she endeavoured with her hand to dry her mouth and chin. Her forehead was contracted and wrinkled; her cheeks full, red, and blooming. Her parents told me that she slept a great deal and soundly, perspired sometimes, and now and then emitted pretty large quantities of blood at her mouth.

For about two years past they have been wont to carry her to the door once every day, and she would shew signs of uneasiness when they neglected it at the usual time. Last sum-summer, after giving her to drink of the water of the well of *Strathconnen*, she crawled to the door on her hands and feet without any help. She is at present in a very languid way, and still throws up what she drinks.

APPENDIX.

NUMBER III.

Parallel Roads in *Glen-Roy*.

ALL the description that can be given of the Parallel Roads, or Terrasses, is, that the Glen of itself is extremely narrow, and the hills on each side very high, and generally not rocky. In the face of these hills, both sides of the glen, there are three roads at small distances from each other, and directly opposite on each side. These roads have been measured in the compleatest parts of them, and found to be 26 paces of a man five feet ten inches high. The two highest are pretty near each other, about 50 yards, and the lowest double that distance from the nearest to it. They are carried along the sides of the glen with the utmost regularity, nearly as exact as drawn with a line of rule and compass.

Where deep burns or gullies of water cross these roads, they avoid both the descent and ascent in a very curious manner; so that on the side where the road enters those hollows, they rather ascend along the slope, and descend the opposite side until they come to the level, without the traveller being sensible of ascent or descent. There are other smaller glens falling into this *Glen-Roy*. The parallel roads surround all these smaller ones; but where *Glen-Roy* ends in the open country there are not the smallest vestiges of them to be seen. The length of these roads in *Glen-Roy* are about seven miles. There are other two glens in that neighbourhood where these roads are equally visible, called *Glen-Gluy* and *Glen-Spean*,

APPENDIX.

Spean, the former running north-west and the latter south from *Glen-Roy*. Both these roads are much about the same length as *Glen-Roy*.

It is to be observed that these roads are not causeway, but levelled out of the earth. There are some small rocks, though few, in the course of these roads. People have examined in what manner they made this passage through the rocks, and find no vestige of roads in the rock; but they begin on each side, and keep the regular line as formerly. So far I am indebted to Mr. *Trapaud*, Governor of *Fort Augustus*.

I cannot learn to what nation the inhabitants of the country attribute these roads: I was informed that they were inaccessible at the east end, open at the west, or that nearest to the sea, and that there were no traces of buildings, or *druidical* remains, in any part, that could lead us to suspect that they were designed for œconomical or religious purposes. The country people think they were designed for the chace, and that these terrasses were made after the spots were cleared in lines from wood, in order to tempt the animals into the open paths after they were rouzed, in order that they might come within reach of the bowmen, who might conceal themselves in the woods above and below. Ridings for the sportsmen are still common in all great forests in *France*, and other countries on the continent, either that they might pursue the game without interruption of trees, or shoot at it in its passage.

Mr. *Gordon*, p. 114, of his Itinerary, mentions such terrasses, to the number

number of seventeen or eighteen, raised one above the other in the most regular manner, for the space of a mile, on the side of a hill, in the county of *Tweedale*, near a village called *Romana*, and also near two small *Roman* camps. They are from fifteen to twenty feet broad, and appear at four or five miles distance not unlike a great amphitheatre. The same gentleman also has observed similar terrasses near other camps of the same nation, from whence he suspects them to be works of the *Romans*, and to have been thrown up by their armies for itinerary encampments. Such may have been their use in those places: but what could have been the object of the contrivers of the terrasses of *Glen-Roy*, where it is more than probable those conquerors never came, remains a mystery, except the conjecture above given should prove satisfactory.

APPENDIX.

NUMBER IV.
GALIC PROVERBS.

1. *L*EAGHAIDH *a Chòir am bèul an Anmhuinn.*

    Juſtice itſelf melts away in the mouth of the feeble.

2. *'S làidir a thèid, 's anmhunn a thig.*

    The ſtrong ſhall fall, and oft the weak eſcape unhurt.

3. *'S fàda Làmh an Fhèumanaich.*

    Long is the hand of the needy.

4. *'S làidir an t' Anmhunn ann Uchd Treòir.*

    Strong is the feeble in the boſom of might.

5. *'S maith an Sgàthan Sùil Càrraid.*

    The eye of a friend is an unerring mirror.

6. *Cha bhi 'm Bochd ſògh-ar Saibhir.*

    The luxurious poor ſhall ne'er be rich.

7. Far

APPENDIX.

7. *Far an tàin' an Abhuin, 's ànn as mùgha a fùaim.*

    Moſt ſhallow——moſt noiſy.

8. *Cha neil Clèith air an Olc, ach gun a dhèanamh.*

    There is no concealment of evil, but not to commit it.

9. *Gìbht na Cloinne-bìge, bhi 'ga tòirt 's ga gràd-iarraidh.*

    The gift of a child, oft granted---oft recalled.

10. *Cha neil Saoi gun a choi-meas.*

    None ſo brave without his equal.

11. *'S mìnic a thainig Comhairle ghlic a Bèul Amadain.*

    Oft has the wiſeſt advice proceeded from the mouth of Folly.

12. *Tuiſhlichidh an t' Each ceithir-chaſach.*

    The four-footed horſe doth often ſtumble; ſo may the ſtrong and mighty fall.

13. *Mar*

13. *Mar a chaimheas Duin' a Bheatha, bheir e Brèith air a Chòimhearſnach.*

As *is* a man's own life, ſo is his judgment of the lives of others.

14. *Fànaidh Duine ſòna' re Sìth, 's bheir Duine dòna duì-leum.*

The fortunate man *awaits*, and he ſhall arrive in peace: the unlucky *haſtens*, and evil ſhall be his fate.

15. *Cha do chùir a Ghuala ris, nach do chuir Tuar haris.*

Succeſs muſt attend the man who bravely ſtruggles.

16. *Cha Ghlòir a dhearabhas ach Gnìomh.*

Triumph never gain'd the ſounding words of boaſt.

17. *'S tric a dh' fhàs am Fuigheal-fochaid, 's a mbeith am Fuigheal-faramaid.*

Oft has the object of cauſeleſs ſcorn arriv'd at honour, and the once mighty ſcorner fallen down to contempt.

18. *Cha*

18. *Cha do delobair* FEANN *Rìgh nan Làoch riamh Fear a làimhe-deife.*

The friend of his right-hand was never deserted by FINGAL the king of heroes.

19. *Thig Dia re h' Airc, 's cha 'n Airc nar thig.*

GOD cometh in the time of diftrefs, and it is no longer diftrefs when he comes.

EPITAPH.
By BEN JOHNSON.

UNderneath this marble hearfe
   Lies the fubject of all verfe;
Sidney's fifter, *Pembroke*'s mother:
Death, ere thou haft kill'd another,
Fair and learn'd, and good as fhe,
Time fhall throw a dart at thee.

Tranflated into *Galic*.

AN fho na luighe fo Lic-lìghe
   Ha adh-bheann nan uille-bhuadh,
Mathair *Phembroke*, Piuthar *Philip*:
   Ans gach Daan bith' orra luadh.
A Bhais man gearr thu fios a coi-meas,
   Beann a dreach, fa h' Juil, fa Fiach,
Briftidh do Bhogh, gun Fhave do fhaighid:
   Bithi'---mar nach bith' tu riamh.

Y   A Sailor's

APPENDIX.

A Sailor's Epitaph in the Church-yard of Great *Yarmouth, Norfolk.*

THO' *Boreas*' blow and *Neptune*'s waves
    Have toft me to and fro,
By God's decree, you plainly fee,
    I'm harbour'd here below:
Where I muft at anchor lye
    With many of our fleet;
But once again we muft fet fail,
    Our Admiral CHRIST to meet.

Tranflated into *Galic.*

LE Uddal-cuain, 's le fheide Gaoidh
    'S lionmhor Amhra thuair mi riamh;
Gam luafga a nùl agus a nàl,
    Gu tric gun Fhois, gun Deoch, gun Bhiadh.
Ach thanig mi gu Calla taimh,
    'S leg mi m' Achdair ans an Uir,
Far an caidil mi mo Phramh,
    Gus arifd an tog na Sùill.
Le Guth na Troimp' as airde fùaim
    Dus gidh mì, 's na bheil am choir
Coinnich' fhin ARD-ADMHIRAL a Chuain
    Bhon faith fhin Fois, is Duais, is Lònn.

SAPPHO's

APPENDIX. 263

SAPPHO's ODE.

BLEST as the immortal Gods is he,
The youth who fondly fits by thee, &c.

Tranflated into *Galic*.

1. 'A Dhmhur mar Dhia neo bhafmhor 'ta
  'N t' Oglach gu caidreach a fhuis re d' fqa:
  Sa chluin, fa chìth re faad na hùin
  Do Bhriara droigheal, 's do fhrea gradh cùin.

2. Och! 's turr a d' fhogair thu mo Chlofs
  'Sa dhuifg thu 'm Chroidh' gach Buaireas bochd;
  'N tra dhearc mi ort, 's mi goint le 't Aadh
  Bhuail reachd am uchd, ghrad mheath mo Chail!

3. Theogh 'm Aigne arìs, is fhruth gu dian
  Teafghradh air feadh gach Baal am Bhiann:
  Ghrad chaoch mo fhuil le Ceodhan Uain
  'S tac aoidh mo Chluas le bothar-fhuaim.

4. Chuer Fallas 'tlàth mo Bhuil gun Lùth
  Rith Eal-ghris chuin tre m' fhuil gu dlu,
  Ghrad thug am Plofg a bheannachd leom
  Is fhnìomh mi fheach gun' Diog am Chòmm.

Y 2　　　　EPITAPH

APPENDIX.

EPITAPH on a Lady, in the Parish-Church of *Glenorchay*, in *North-Britain*.

1. AN ſho na luigh ta ſan Innis
   Bean bu duilich leom bhi ann
Beul a cheuil, is Lamh a Ghrinnis,
   Ha iad 'nioſhe ſho nan tamh.

2. Tuill' cha toir am Bochd dhuit beannachd:
   An lom-nochd cha chluthaich thu nis mo'
Cha tiormaich Dèur bho ſhùil na h'Ainnis:
   Co tuill' O Lagg! a bheir dhuit treoir?

3. Chan fhaic ſhin tuille thu ſa choinni:
   Cha ſuidh ſhin tuille air do Bhòrd:
D'fhàlabh uain ſuairceas, ſeirc is mòdhan
   Ha Bròn 's bì-mhulad air teachd oiru.

In *Engliſh*.

1. LOW ſhe lies here in the duſt, and her memory fills me with grief: ſilent is the tongue of melody, and the hand of elegance is now at reſt.

2. No more ſhall the poor give thee his bleſſing: nor ſhall the naked be warmed with' the fleece of thy flock. The tear ſhalt thou not wipe away from the eye of the wretched. Where, now O Feeble, is thy wonted help!

3. No

3. No more, my fair, shall we meet thee in the social hall: no more shall we sit at thy hospitable board. Gone for ever is the sound of mirth: the kind, the candid, the meek is now no more. Who can express our grief! Flow ye tears of *Woe!*

A young LADY's Lamentation on the Death of her LOVER.

Translated from the *Galic*.

GLoomy indeed is the night and dark, and heavy also is my troubled soul: around me all is silent and still; but sleep has forsaken my eyes, and my bosom knoweth not the balm of peace. I mourn for the loss of the dead---the *young*, the *beauteous*, the *brave*, alas! lies low.---Lovely was thy form, O youth! lovely and fair was thy open soul---Why did I know thy worth---Oh! why must I now that worth deplore?

Length of years seemed to be the lot of my Love, yet few and fleeting were his days of joy---Strong he stood as the tree of the vale, but untimely he fell into the silent house. The morning Sun saw thee flourish as the lovely rose---before the noon-tide heat low thou droop'st as the withered plant.

What *then* availed thy bloom of youth, and what thy arm of strength? Ghastly is the face of Love---dim and dark the soul-expressing eye---The mighty fell to arise no more!

Whom now shall I call *my* friend? or from whom can I hear the sound of joy? In *thee* the friend has fallen---in thy grave my joy is laid.---We lived---we grew together. O why *together* did we not also fall!

Death---thou cruel spoiler! how oft hast thou caused the tear to flow! many are the miserable thou hast made, and who can escape thy dart of woe?

Kind Fate, come lay me low, and bring me to my house of rest. In yonder grave, beneath the leafy plane, my Love and I shall dwell in peace. Sacred be the place of our repose.

O seek not to disturb the ashes of the dead!

APPENDIX.

NUMBER V.

Of the Columns in *Penrith* Church-Yard.

SINCE the printing of p. 218, I have been favored with two beautifull drawings of the pillars * in *Penrith* Church-Yard. One was communicated to me by the Rev. Mr. *Farish* of *Carlisle*, and represents them in their present state; the other by the Rev. Mr. *Monkhouse*, Fellow of *Queen's College, Oxford*, which is a view of them before they were mutilated. The first is certainly a most authentic representation of them; the last varies in many particulars from the form they now appear in: in that

---

* The lesser pillar engraven with these is by tradition of the country thought to belong to these; but Mr. *Farish* thinks it is at too great a distance from them to admit of that supposition: its height is six feet.

the

APPENDIX.

the columns are drawn entirely square from top to bottom, whereas the lower part of the pillars now extant are rounded. There is no fret-work on the old drawing of these columns, but instead are two small rude figures of human heads. The thin semicircular stones are deeply and regularly indented on their edges, which appear of an equal thickness throughout; whereas the others are very sharp, or ridged at one extremity, and dilate gradually till they arrive at a considerable thickness at the other. The figures in the old sketch are of a boar, and perhaps a bear. The upper ends of these pillars seem faithfully to supply what has been destroyed, a cross and a capital.

How this great variation in the drawings of the same columns happened, is not easy to say; for it does not

not appear that there ever were any others in the place. Time has obliterated the figures of the animals; but whether any workman had chizzled the whole fhafts of the pillars to their prefent form, is, I think, fcarcely to be conjectured; they bear all the appearance of antiquity. The old drawings are done with much elegance, and are copied from fome collections in the cuftody of Mr. *Monkhoufe*, formed by *Hugh Todd*, D. D. Prebendary of *Carlifle* and Vicar of *Penrith*, as materials for the antiquities of the diocefe he belonged to. Notwithftanding my doubts about the entire fidelity of the old drawing, (which was done about the year 1690) I caufe it to be engraven as a companion to the other, in hopes that fome antiquarian of the country will oblige the Publick by clearing up the point.

APPENDIX.

By Mr. *Monkhouse*'s permission I annex Doctor *Todd*'s account of these antiquities:

"At the north door of the church are erected two large stone pillars of a pyramidical form, cruciated towards the top, each of them fifteen feet high, and plac'd at the distance of seventeen feet from each other. The space between them is surrounded with the rude figures of four boars, or wild hogs. What this monument denotes, and for what reason it was first erected, may be somewhat uncertain. The common vulgar report is, That one *Ewen* or *Owen Cæsarius*, a very extraordinary person, famous in these parts for hunting and fighting, about 1400 years ago, whom no hand but the hand of Death could overcome,

APPENDIX.

"overcome, lyes buried in this place.
"His stature, as the story says, was
"prodigious, beyond that of the
"*Patagons* in *South America*, viz.
"fifteen feet. That the two pillars
"denote his height, and the four
"rough unpolish'd stones betwixt re-
"present so many wild boars which
"had the honour to be kill'd by this
"wonderful giant. That there might
"be, in remote times, in these re-
"gions, men of large gigantick fi-
"gures, as there are now near the
"*Magellanic* Streights, and that they
"might affect *Roman* sirnames and
"distinctions as the *Americans* about
"*Darien* do *Spanish*, needs not either
"be discussed or denied. But those
"persons give the best account of the
"original, nature, and design of these
"stones, who look upon them as of
"a much later date, and for a very
"different intention. That they were
"erected

"erected long after the introduction of chriſtianity at the north (or Death's) door of the church in the form of a croſs, in order to reſt the bodies of the dead upon them, and to pray for their ſouls (as the manner was): And that the four figures of Boars are the cognizance * of the Earls of *Warwick*, ſome of whom held the ſeigniory of *Penrith* and lived in the caſtle, and might be at the expence of the work."

* The Bear and ragged-ſtaff was; but I do not recollect that the Boars had any thing to do with the Earls of *Warwick:* But as Boars and Bears are repreſented on the ſtones, it ſeems as if this Mr. *Cæſarius* was a knight-errant, who cleared the country of monſters; ſo in memorial of his exploits theſe figures were engraven. The heads too might have been cut on the columns in memory of ſome petty tyrants of the neighborhood whom he had demoliſhed; for ſuch bloody trophies were in former days very common: witneſs, among the *Welſh*, the *Tri pen Sais*, or three Engliſhmen's heads, borne in the arms of many of our families, as a token of the prowess of their anceſtors.

PILLARS IN PENRITH CHURCH YARD

APPENDIX.

A Recapitulation of the ANIMALS mentioned in the TOUR, with some additional Remarks in Natural History.

Wild Cattle. THE offspring of them now domesticated are said to be found in *Hamilton* Park. *Vide* p. 206.

Roebuck. Inhabits the forests on the south of *Lough-Raynach*, those in the neighborhood of *Invercauld*, the woods near *Tarnaway* and *Calder* castles, and about *Lough-Moy* and *Lough-Ness*; and its most northerly haunts are the woods of *Langwall*, at the entrance into *Cathness*.

A full-grown Roe weighs 60lb. the hair in summer is short, smooth, and glossy, red at the tips, cinereous beneath. At approach of winter the hair grows very long and hoary, and proves an excellent defence against the rigor of the highland air. The rump and underside of the tail white. The tail very short. Below the first joint of the outside of the hind leg is a long tuft of hair, such as is found on the legs of certain Antelopes. The horns

horns of a Roebuck of the second year are strait, slender, and without any branch: in the third become bifurcated: in the fourth, trifurcated, and grow more scabrous and stronger, in proportion to their longevity. It feeds during summer on grass, and is remarkably fond of the *Rubus Saxatilis*, called in the Highlands on that account the Roebuck Berry. When the ground is covered with snow it feeds on the extreme branches of the pine and juniper. It brings two young at a time. The Fawns are elegantly spotted with white. It is extremely difficult to rear them; commonly eight out of ten dying in the attempt. The flesh of the Roe is by some accounted a delicacy: to me it seemed very dry. They keep in small families of five or six.

Stag.

Notwithstanding it is not quite peculiar to *Scotland* in a wild state, yet is mentioned here on account of some singularities relating to its natural history, which I collected in my journey. Stags abound all over the Highlands and in the Isle of *Skie*. In the last are so numerous as to oblige the farmer to watch his corn: are very fond

I. Roebuck. II. White Hare.

fond of crowsfoot, and, like the *Rein*, will eat lichens. I have been assured that they are greatly delighted with the sound of musick, and that they will be tempted to remain in the deepest attention: that they are frequently shot, allured to their destruction by the melody of the pipe. Fallow Deer are very scarce in *North-Britain*, and wholly confined in parks.

Highland Grebound. Is the kind which *Boethius* takes notice of, and says is one of the three that are not to be found any where else. He calls it, *Genus venaticum cum celerrimum tum audacissimum : nec modo in feras sed in hostes etiam Latronesque ; præsertim si dominum ductoremve injuriam affici cernat aut in eos concitetur.*

This sort of dog is become very rare. *Vide* p. 127.

Wolfish breed. I saw at *Gordon* castle a dog the offspring of a Wolf and *Pomeranian* bitch. It had much the appearance of the first, was very good-natured and sportive; but being slipped at a weak Deer it instantly brought the animal down and tore out its throat. This dog was bred by Mr. *Brook*,

animal-

animal-merchant, in *London*, who told me that the congress between the wolf and the bitch was immediate, and the produce at the litter was ten.

White Hare. Peculiar to the summits of the highest mountains of the Highlands: is less than the common Hare; its limbs more slender; its flesh more delicate: it never descends into the vallies, or mixes with the common kind: is very agile and full of frolick when kept tame: is fond of honey and carraway comfits, and prognosticates a storm by eating its own dung: in a wild state, does not run an end, but seeks shelter under stones as soon as possible.

During summer its predominant color is grey: about *September* it begins to assume a snowy whiteness; the alteration of color appearing about the neck and rump, and becomes entirely white, except the edges and tips of the ears: in *April* it again resumes its grey coat.

Lavellan. A small animal, mentioned by Sir *Robert Sibbald*, as being common in *Cathness*, living in the water, and whose breath is noxious to cattle. I suspect

APPENDIX.

suspect from the description that I had given me, that it is the same with the Water Shrewmouse, *Br. Zool. illustr.* p. 83.

I could get no account of Sir *Robert*'s mouse with a black back, which he says kills moles.

Seals. The Seals on the coasts of *North-Britain* are the common and the great. *Syn. Quad.* N^{ris}. 265. 266. But I could not learn that the *Walrus* was ever seen in any of the SCOTTISH Seas; notwithstanding it was found about the *Orkney* Isles in the days of *Boethius*. Vide *Desc. Regn. Scotiæ.* xvi.

BIRDS.

Eagles. The Sea Eagle breeds in ruined towers, and leaves its summer haunts before winter. The Ring-tail Eagle, *Br. Zool.* breeds in rocks, and continues in *North-Britain* the whole year.

Falcons. The Peregrine and the Gentil Falcons breed in *Glenmore*, and other lofty rocks of the Highlands. The Gyr-Falcon has been shot in *Aberdeenshire*. A large white Hawk, I suppose an unspotted

spotted bird of the last species, has bred for these last twelve years at *Hilleigh-Green*, near *Hackness*, four miles from *Scarborough*.

Goshawks. — Breed in trees in the highland part of *Aberdeenshire*.

Owl. — The great-horned or Eagle Owl has been shot in the shire of *Fife*.

Crow. — The common species is very rare in the Highlands, there being scarce any other sort found there than the *Royston* or Hooded Crow, which resides there the whole year. Whence those that visit us annually during winter migrate from is uncertain.

Chatterer. — Visits the neighborhood of *Edinburgh* annually, appearing in flocks during winter, and feeds on the berries of the mountain ash.

Chough. — Is found in the farthest parts of *Glenlion*, and near *Achmore*.

Cock of the Wood. — This bird is found in a few woods north of *Lough-Ness*; perhaps in those near *Castle-Grant?* Formerly, was common throughout the Highlands, and was called *Capercalze*, and *Auercalze*;

Cock of the Wood.

I. Ptarmigan. II. Hen of the Wood.

APPENDIX.

Auercalze; and in the old law-books, *Capercally*. The variety of the black game, mentioned by M. *Brisson* under the name of *Coq de Bruyere piqueté*, was a mixed breed between these two birds; but I could not hear that any at present were to be found in *North Britain*. *Linnæus* has met with them in *Sweden*, and describes them under the title of *Tetrao cauda bifurca subtus albo punctata*.

Ptarmigan. Another of the grous kind, common on the summits of the highest highland hills. *Vide* p. 79. and *Br. Zool. illustr.* p. 21. If I mistake not, I have heard that a few are still found on the *Cumberland* mountains.

Bustard. Now extinct in *Scotland*. *Boethius* says that in his days it was found in *Merch*.

Ring-dove Stare. I found in the Journal of Mr. *James Robertson* an ingenious *eleve* of Doctor *Hope*, that these two birds are found in great abundance during summer in the Isle of *Arran*. Ring-Ouzels are very common in the Highlands.

Nightingale. Not found in *North-Britain*.

A a 2   *Stone-Chatter.* This

APPENDIX.

Stone-Chatter. This bird is seen near *Edinburgh* during winter; so does not migrate.

Pine-Bulfinch. Br. Zool. illustr. p. 59. Found during summer in the pine-forests of *Aberdeenshire*, and probably breeds there.

Snow-flake. I have had lately an opportunity of comparing this bird with the greater Brambling, and find them to be different, and not as I once thought, varieties of the same kind. The size of this is less, and the claw of the hind toe much shorter. A few of these birds breed with the *Ptarmigans* on the summits of the highest mountains; but the greatest numbers migrate from the most distant north, even from *Greenland* and *Spitzbergen*. Vide Br. Zool. illustr. p. 17.

WATER FOWL.

Whimbrel. Breeds in the hills about *Invercauld*.

Red Godwit. Breeds in *Lincolnshire*. For the list of other fen birds, vide p. 9, 10.

Auks. The black-billed Auk and lesser Guillemot appear during winter in flocks innumerable

APPENDIX.

innumerable in the Firth of *Forth*, and are called there *Marrots*. Their fummer retreat is not yet traced. The little *Auk* is fometimes fhot near *Aberdeen*.

Arctic Gull. Is called in *North Britain* the *Dirty Aulin*. I faw one flying over the Firth of *Forth* near the *Queen*'s Ferry.

Goofander. Doctor *Walker* of *Moffat* fhewed me one killed during fummer in the weftern ifles; alfo fome other birds which were fuppofed to have migrated out of *Great-Britain*. He alfo difcovered in the Ifle of *Tirey* the *Tringa interpres*.

REPTILES.

Snake. A new *British* Snake was difcovered in *Aberdeenshire* by the late Doctor *David Skene*, a gentleman whofe lofs will be deplored by every lover of natural hiftory; for to great knowlege was added the moft liberal and communicative difpofition. The account he favored me with of this reptile was this: Its length was fifteen inches: it had no *scuta abdom.* or *caudalia*, but was entirely covered with fmall fcales, which on the upper part

part of the head were larger than the rest: the tongue was broad and forked: the nostrils small and round, and placed near the tip of the nose: the eyes lodged in oblong fissures above the angle of the mouth: the belly was of a bluish lead-color with small white spots irregularly dispersed: the rest of the body of a greyish brown with three longitudinal blackish brown lines, one extending from the back of the head to the point of the tail, the two others were broader and extended the whole length of the sides. Doctor *Skene* informed me that it was the same with the *Anguis Eryx* of *Linnæus*, p. 392.

FISH.

Basking Shark. This species frequents the Firth of *Clyde* and the seas of the western isles: the Trustees for the forfeited estates encourage the fishery, and furnish the adventurers with money to purchase the proper materials.

Picked Dog. Swarms on the eastern coast of *Scotland*, and is taken and cured for the use of the common people. Mr. *James Robertson* observed near the
Isle

Isle of *Skie* a species called there the *Blind-hive,* which is reckoned a great restorative.

Draco major seu araneus Salvian. 70.

This species was taken near *Scarborough,* and communicated to me by Mr. *Travis.*

Its length eleven inches; greatest depth one inch and three-quarters: head flat: eyes large: edges of the jaws rough with minute teeth; the lower jaw the longest, and slopes less than that of the common species: the head covered with minute tubercles; cheeks and gills covered with small scales; on the last is a sharp spine.

First dorsal fin is black, and consists of five spines; the second reaches within a small distance of the tail: the pectoral has thirteen branched rays; the ventral six; the anal extends as far as the second dorsal: tail large, triangular, and even at the end.

The scales run in oblique lines from the back to the belly, with a division between each row.

Codfish. One

Codfish. One was taken at *Scarborough* in 1755, which measured five feet eight inches, and its girth round the shoulders five feet: its weight 78 lb. and was sold for a shilling.

Saury. *Saurus* Rondel. 232.

After a violent storm from the N.E. in *November* last, a great number of these fish were flung on shore in the Firth of *Forth* on the sands of *Leith*. An account and an accurate figure of one of them was communicated to me by Mr. *George Paton* of *Edinburgh*, a gentleman who is a zealous promoter of natural knowlege.

Its length is eleven inches: the nose slender: the jaws produced like those of the Sea Needle, but of equal lengths, and the upper mandible slightly recurvated; their length one inch: eyes large: body slender and anguilliform, but towards the tail grows suddenly smaller, and tapers to a very inconsiderable girth: on the lower part of the back is a small fin, with six spurious between that and the tail, like those of the Mackrel: correspondent to these are the anal and

APPENDIX.

and six spurious: the pectoral and ventral fins very small: the tail much forked: the back when fresh was of a dark color, the belly bright and silvery.

Rondeletius describes this fish among those of the *Mediterranean*; but speaks of it as very rare even there.

CRUSTACEA.

Thorney Crab. *Cancer spinosus, maximus, orientalis* Seb. Mus. 56. tab. xxii. fig. 1. *Cancer spinosus amboinensis*---44. tab. xviii. fig. 10.

C. *Horridus* Lin. syst. 1047.

C. *spinosus, thorace cordato, mucronato: pedibus tantum tribus cursoriis: chelis inæq. ped. minoribus,* Gronov. Zooph. No. 976.

Body of a heart-shape: length from the snout to the end of the back five inches one-tenth: snout projecting and bifurcated: the upper crust covered with thick spines; those on the margins very long, sharp and strong: the claws covered on all sides with great spines; the right claw twice as large as the left: the fangs beset with small tufts of hair: on each side only three legs echinated like the claws, and nine inches long. No *British* crustaceous animal is so well guarded as this.

I have seen this species almost wholly incrusted with the *Lepas balanus*, and *Anomia squammula*. Doctor *Skene* favored me with a fine specimen, it being taken on the coast of *Aberdeen*.

INSECTS.

Oniscus.	Oestrum,	Sea on the *Yorkshire* coast.
	Psora,	*ibid.*
	Marinus,	*ibid.*
	Oceanicus,	*ibid.*
	Trifurcatus novus,	*ibid.*
	Quadratus novus,	*ibid.*
Phalangium.	Grossipes,	Sea near *Aberdeen*. Dr. *Skene*.
	Balænarum,	*ibid.*

QUERIES,

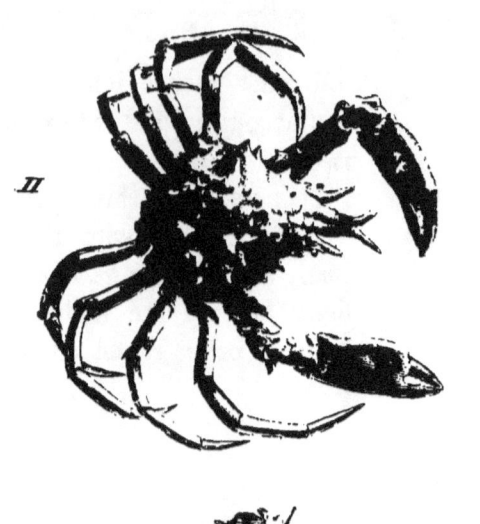

I. Thorney Crab. II. Cordated Crab.

APPENDIX.

QUERIES,

Addressed to the Gentlemen and Clergy of *North-Britain*, respecting the Antiquities and Natural History of their respective Parishes*, with a View of exciting them to favor the World with a fuller and more satisfactory Account of their Country, than it is in the Power of a Stranger and transient Visitant to give.

I. WHAT is the ancient and modern name of the parish, and its etymology?

II. What number of hamlets or villages are in it, their names and situation?

III. What are the number of its houses and inhabitants?

IV. What number of people have been married, christened and buried, for the space of 20 years last

---

* Many of the parishes in *North Britain* are of such extent as to supply ample materials for a history of each alone; so it is to be hoped some parochial *Geniuses* will arise and favor the Publick with what is much wanted, LOCAL HISTORIES.

past,

past, compared with the first 20 years of the register? When did the register begin? If there are any curious remarks made therein, please to give an account thereof.

V. Are there any vaults or burial places peculiar to any ancient or other families? What are they, and to whom do they belong?

VI. Are there any ancient or modern remarkable monuments or grave-stones in the church or chancel, &c. Please to give the inscriptions and arms, if any, on the same, if worthy notice, especially if before the 16th century.

VII. Are there any remarkable ones in the church-yard? Please to give an account what they are. Are there any paintings in the windows either of figures or arms? Add a copy or description.

VIII. Are there any tables of benefactions or other inscriptions which are worthy notice, on any of the walls of the church, either within or without? Please to insert them at full length.

IX. Are there any particular customs or privileges or remarkable tenures in any of the manors in the parish?

X. What ancient manor or mansion-house, seats or villas, are in the parish?

XI. Are

APPENDIX.

XI. Are there any annual or other proceſſions, perambulations, or any hoſpital, alms or ſchool-houſe; by whom and when founded, and who has the right of putting people into them?

XII. Have you any wake, whitſon ale, or other cuſtoms of that ſort uſed in the pariſh?

XIII. Is there any great road leading thro' the pariſh, and from what noted places?

XIV. Are there any croſſes or obeliſks or any things of that nature erected in the pariſh?

XV. Are there any remains or ruins of monaſteries or religious houſes? Give the beſt account thereof you can.

XVI. Are there any *Roman*, *Pictiſh*, or *Daniſh* caſtles, camps, altars, roads, forts, or other pieces of antiquity remaining in your pariſh; what are they, and what traditions are there, or hiſtorical accounts of them?

XVII. Have there been any medals, coins, or other pieces of antiquity dug up in your pariſh; when and by whom, and in whoſe cuſtody are they?

XVIII. Have

APPENDIX.

XVIII. Have there been any remarkable battles fought, on what spot, by whom, when, and what traditions are there relating thereto?

XIX. Has the parish given either birth or burial to any man eminent for learning or other remarkable or valuable qualifications?

XX. Are there any parks or warrens, the number of deer, and extent of the park, &c. any heronries, decoys, or fisheries?

XXI. Do any rivers rise in or run thro' the parish, which are they; if navigable, what sort of boats are used on them, and what is the price of carriage *per* hundred or ton, to your parish?

XXII. Are there any, and what bridges, how are they supported, by private or public cost, of what materials, what number of piers or arches, the length and breadth of the bridge and width of the arches?

XXIII. Are there any barrows or tumuli, and have any been opened, and what has been found therein?

XXIV. Are there any manufactures carried on in the parish, and what number of hands are employed?

XXV. What

APPENDIX.

XXV. What markets or fairs are kept in the parish, what commodities are chiefly brought for sale; if any of the manufactures or produce of the country, live cattle, or other things, that toll is paid and to whom, and where are they kept?

XXVI. Is there any statute fair for hiring of servants, and how long has it been established; what are the usual wages for men and maids, &c. for each branch of husbandry?

XXVII. Are there in any of the gentlemen's houses, or on their estates, any pictures which give insight into any historical facts, or any portraits of men eminent for any art, science, or literature; any statues, busto's, or other memorial which will give any light to past transactions?

QUERIES

APPENDIX.

QUERIES

Relating to the Natural History of the Parish.

I. WHAT is the appearance of the country in the parish; is it flat or hilly, rocky or mountainous?

II. Do the lands consist of woods, arable, pasture, meadow, heath, or what?

III. Are they fenny or moorish, boggy or firm?

IV. Is there sand, clay, chalk, stone, gravel, loam, or what is the nature of the soil?

V. Are there any lakes, meers or waters, what are they, their depth, where do they rise, and whither do they run?

VI. Are there any subterraneous rivers, which appear in one place, then sink into the earth, and rise again?

VII. Are there any mineral springs, frequented for the drinking the waters; what are they; at what seasons of the year reckoned best, and what distempers are they frequented for?

VIII. Are

APPENDIX.

VIII. Are there any periodical springs, which rise and fall, ebb and flow, at what seasons, give the best account you can?

IX. Are there any mills on the rivers, to what uses are they employed?

X. Are there any and what mines; what are they; to whom do they belong; what do they produce?

XI. Have you any marble, moorstone, or other stone of any sort, how is it got out, and how worked?

XII. What sorts of manure or amendment do they chiefly use for their land, and what is the price of it on the spot?

XIII. What are the chief produce of the lands, wheat, rye, oats, barley, peas, beans, or what?

XIV. What sorts of fish do the rivers produce, what quantities, and what prices on the spot, and in what seasons are they best?

*XIV. What quadrupeds and birds are there in your parish? What migratory birds, and at what times do they appear and disappear?

XV. Are

APPENDIX.

XV. Are there any remarkable caves, or grottoes, natural or artificial? give the beſt deſcription and account thereof you can.

XVI. Are there any and what quantities of ſaffron, woad, teazels, or other vegetables of that ſort, growing in the pariſh, and the prices they ſell for on the ſpot?

XVII. Is the pariſh remarkable for breeding any cattle of remarkable qualities, ſize, or value, and what?

XVIII. Are there any chalk-pits, ſand or gravel-pits, or other openings in the pariſh, and what?

XIX. On digging wells or other openings, what ſtrata's of ſoil do they meet with, and how thick is each?

XX. How low do the ſprings lye, and what ſort of water do you meet with in the ſeveral parts of the pariſh?

XXI. Is there any marl, Fuller's earth, potters earth, or loam, or any other remarkable ſoils, as ochre, &c.

XXII. Are there any bitumen, naptha, or other ſubſtances of that nature found in the earth?

XXIII. Does

APPENDIX.

XXIII. Does the parish produce any quantities of timber, of what sort, and what are the prices on the spot, *per* load or ton? Are there any very large trees, and their size?

XXIV. Are any quantities of sheep raised or fed in the parish, and on what do they chiefly feed?

XXV. Are the people of the country remarkable for strength, size, complexion, or any bodily or natural qualities?

XXVI. What are the diversions chiefly used by the gentry, as well as the country people, on particular occasions?

XXVII. What is the nature of the air; is it moist or dry, healthy or subject to agues and fevers, and at what time of the year is it reckoned most so? and, if you can, account for the causes.

XXVIII. Are there any petrifying springs or waters that incrust bodies, what are they?

XXIX. Any hot waters or wells for bathing, and for what distempers frequented?

XXX. Are there any figured stones, such as echinitæ, belemnitæ, &c. Any having the impression of plants or fishes on them, or any fossil marine

rine bodies, such as shells, corals, &c. or any petrified parts of animals: where are they found, and what are they?

XXXI. Is any part of the parish subject to inundations or land floods, give the best account, if any things of that nature have happened, and when?

XXXII. Hath there been any remarkable mischief done by thunder and lightning, storms or whirlwinds, when and what?

XXXIII. Are there any remarkable echoes, where and what are they?

XXXIV. Have any remarkable phænomena been observed in the air, and what?

If the Parish is on the SEA COAST,

XXXV. What sort of a shore, flat, sandy, high, or rocky?

XXXVI. What sorts of fish are caught there, in what quantity, at what prices sold, when most in season, how taken, and to what market sent?

XXXVII. What other Sea animals, plants, sponges, corals, shells, &c. are found on or near the coasts?

XXXVIII. Are

APPENDIX.

XXXVIII, Are there any remarkable Sea weeds uſed for manure of land, or curious on any other account?

XXXIX. What are the courſes of the tides on the ſhore, or off at Sea, the currents at a mile's diſtance, and other things worthy remark?

XL. What number of fiſhing veſſels, of what ſort, how navigated, and what number of hands are there in the pariſh?

XLI. How many ſhips and of what burthen belong to the pariſh?

XLII. Are there any and what light-houſes, beacons, or land-marks?

XLIII. What are the names of the creeks, bays, harbours, headlands, ſands, or iſlands near the coaſts?

XLIV. Have there been any remarkable battles or ſea-fights near the coaſts, and when did any remarkable wrecks or accidents happen, which can give light to any hiſtorical facts?

XLV. If you are in a city, give the beſt account you can procure of the hiſtory and antiquity of the place; if remarkable for its buildings, age, walls, ſieges,

sieges, charters, privileges, immunities, gates, streets, markets, fairs, the number of churches, wards and guilds, or companies, or fraternities, or clubs that are remarkable; how is it governed? if it sends members to parliament, in whom does the choice lye, and what number of voters may there have been at the last poll?

ITINERARY.

Miles	
	DOWNING,
21	Chester, *Deonna, Devana* PTOL. *Deva* ANTON. RAV. CHOROG. *Deva, colonia legio cretica vicessima valeria victrix* R. C.
18	Northwich, *Condate* R. C.
8	Knutsford,
12	Macclesfield,
10	Buxton,
13	Middelton,
11	Chesterfield,
16	Worksop,
12	Tuxford,
8	Dunham Ferry, on the Trent, *Trivona fl.* R. C.
10	Lincoln, *Lindum* PTOL. ANTON. RAV. CHOROG. R. C.
6	Washenbrough and back to Lincoln,
12	Spittle,
12	Glanford Bridge,
12	Barton,
	Humber River, *Abus* PTOL. R. C.
5	Hull,
8	Burton Constable,
22	Burlington Quay,
	Its bay, *Gabrantuicorum portuosus sinus* PTOL. *Portus fælix* R. C.
5	Flamborough Head, *Brigantum extrema* R. C.
10	Hunmanby,

10 Scar-

ITINERARY.

Miles.
- 10 Scarborough,
- 13½ Robin Hood's Bay,
- 6½ Whitby,
- 13 Skellin Dam,
- 9 Guisborough,
- 12 Stockton,
- , Tees River, *Tisis fl.* R. C. its mouth, *Dunum sinus* PTOL.
- 20 Durham,
- Were River, *Vedra fl.* R. C.
- 6 Chester le Street, *Epiacum* R. C.
- 9 Newcastle, *Pons Aelii* NOTIT. IMP.
- Tyne River, *Vedra fl.* TTOL. *Tina fl.* R. C.
- 14 Morpeth,
- 9 Felton,
- 10 Alnwick, *Alauna* RAV. CHOROG.
- 16 Belford,
- 16 Berwick, *Tuessis* RAV. CHOROG.
- Tweed River, *Alaunus* PTOL. *Tueda* R. C.

SCOTLAND.

- 16 Old Cambus,
- 10 Dunbar, *Ledone* RAV. CHOROG.
- 6 North Berwick,
- 14 Preston Pans,
- 8 EDINBURGH,
- 9 South Ferry,
- Firth of Forth, *Boderia* PTOL. *Bodotria* TACITI. R. C.

2 North

ITINERARY.

Miles.
- 2 North Ferry,
  Fife County, *Horestii* R.C. *Caledonia* TACITI.
- 15 Kinross,
- 20 Rumbling Brig, Castle Campbell, and back to Kinross.
- 13 Castle Duplin, *Duablisis* RAV. CHOROG.
- 8 Perth, *Orrea* R.C.
  Tay River and its mouth, *Taus* TACITI. *Tava Æst.* PTOL. R.C.
- 1 Scone,
- 1 Lunkerty,
- 13 Dunkeld,
- 20 Taymouth,
- 15 Carrie on Lough Raynach,
- 20 Blair,
- 35 Through Glen-Tilt to Invercauld,
- 18 Tulloch,
- 15 Kincairn,
- 9 Banchorie,
- 18 Aberdeen,
  Dee River, *Diva fl.* PTOL. R.C.
  Ythen River, *Ituna fl.* R.C.
- 25 Bowness,
- 27 Craigston Castle,
- 9 Bamff,
  Devron River, *Celnius fl.* R.C.
- 8 Cullen,
- 12 Castle Gordon,
  Spey River, *Celnius fl.* PTOL. *Tuessis* R.C.
- 8 Elgin, *Alitacenon* RAV. CHOROG.

D d   10 Forres,

ITINERARY.

Miles.
- 10 Forres,
- 17 Tarnaway Castle, Calder, Fort George.
  Firth of Murray, *Tuæ. Æst.* PTOL. *Varar Æst.* R. C.
- 12 Inverness, *Pteroton, castra alata.* R. C.
- 10 Castle Dunie,
- 18 Dingwall Foules.
  Firth of Cromartie, *Loxa fl.* R. C.
  Rossshire, *Creones* R. C. the same writer places at *Channery* in this county, *Aræ finium Imp. Rom.*
- 15 Ballinagouan,
- 6 Tain, *Castra alata* PTOL.
- 9 Dornoch. Its Firth, *Vara æst.* TTOL. *Abona fl.* R. C.
  Sutherland County, *Logi* R. C.
- 9 Dunrobin Castle,
- 18 Hemsdale,
  Ord of Cathness, *Ripa alta* PTOL.
  Cathness County, *Carnabii, Cattini.* R. C.
  Virubium promontorium R. C.
- 8 Langwall,
- 15 Clythe; Clytheness, *Vervedrum prom.* R. C.
- 8 Thrumster,
- 3 Wick,
  Wick River, *Ilea fl.* TTOL.
- 16 Duncan's or Dungby Bay, and John a Grout's house.
  Dungsby Head, *Berubium promontorium* PTOL. *Caledonia extrema* R. C.

Stroma

ITINERARY.

Miles.

	Stroma Isle, *Ocetis Insula* R. C.
2	Canesby, and back the same road to
137	Inverness,
	Inverness County, *Caledonii* R. C.
17	General's Hut,
15	Fort Augustus,
	Lough Lochy, *Longus fl.* R. C.
28	Fort William. R. C. places *Banatia* near it.
14	Kinloch-Leven,
9	King's House,
19	Tyendrum,
12	Dalmalie,
16	Inveraray,
22	Tarbut,
	Loch-Lomond, *Lincalidor Lacus* R. C.
8	Luss,
12	Dunbarton, *Theodosia* R. C.
	Firth of Clyde, *Glota* TACITI. *Clotta æst.* R. C.
15	Glasgow, *Clidum* RAV. CHOROG.
24	Hamilton, and back to Glasgow,
13	Kylsithe,
18	Sterling,
8	Falkirk,
	Calendar, *Celerion* RAV. CHOROG.
15	Hopeton House,
11	EDINBURGH,
18	Lenton,
18	Bild,
18	Moffat,
18	Lockerby.

ITINERARY.

ENGLAND.

Miles.
- 21 Longtown in Cumberland, Netherby, *Caſtra exploratorum* ANTON. *Aeſica* RAV. CHOROG.
- 9 Carliſle, *Lugavallium* ANTON.
- 18 Penrith, *Bereda* RAV. CHOROG.
- 11 Shap in Weſtmorland,
- 15 Kendal, *Concangium* NOTIT. IMP.
- 14 Burton in Lancaſhire, *Coccium* R. C.
- 11 Lancaſter, *Longovicus* NOTIT. IMP. Lune River, *Alanna fl.* R. C.
- 11 Garſtang,
- 11 Preſton,
- 18 Wiggan,
- 13 Warrington,
- 21 Cheſter,
- 21 Downing in Flintſhire.

The antient names of places marked R. C. are borrowed from the late Dr. *Stukeley*'s account of *Richard* of *Cirenceſter*, with his antient map of *Roman Brittain* and the Itinerary thereof, publiſhed in 1757. The reſt from Mr. *Horſly*'s remarks on *Ptolemy*, *Antonine's Itinerary*, *Notitia imperii*, and *Ravennatis Britanniæ Chorographia*.

INDEX.

INDEX.

A

	Page
ABERDEEN, New,	112
Old,	116
Alnwick Castle,	31
Alum works in Yorkshire,	21, 22
Amber,	13
Appenines of *England*,	26
Argentine, *Struan*'s favorite fountain,	96
Arthur's Oven,	212
Augustus, Fort,	171
Auldearne,	133
Avosetta,	10
Aw, Lough,	187

B

Bamborough Castle, well regulated charity there,	32, 33
Bamff,	122
Bass Isle,	44
Beggars, few in *Scotland*,	83
Bel-tein, a singular superstition,	90
Benevish, higher than *Snowdon*,	179
Berridale,	150
Berwick on *Tweed*, its salmon-fishery,	38, 39
North,	45
Birch tree, its great use,	109
Birds,	

INDEX.

	Page
Birds, of *Lincolnshire*,	9, 10, 11
Flamborough Head,	15
Farn Islands,	36
Birnam Wood,	74
Black-meal, a forced levy so called,	176
Blair House,	97
Bodotria of *Tacitus*,	41
Bollitir, Pass of,	111
Botanic garden at *Edinburgh*,	58
Bowness Castle, its strange situation,	118
Braan Castle,	141
Brae-mar,	103
Bran, fine cascade on the,	75
Brotche,	83
Bulfinch, greater,	109
Bullers of *Buchan*,	119
Burlington,	13
Burnet, Bp. amiable in his episcopal character,	236
Buxton, its salubrious waters,	3

C

	Page
Caldor, or *Cawdor* Castle,	133
Cambus, Old,	41
Campbell, Castle,	66
Carron Iron-works,	212
Cathness,	156
Cattle, wild,	206
Cawdron Glen, a cataract there,	65
Chain the, what,	178
Chatterer,	278

Chester,

INDEX.

	Page
Chester, its singular streets,	1
Cathedral,	ibid
Hypocaust,	ibid
Chesterfield,	5
Chester Le Street,	29
Church *Scotch*, its constitution,	221
Clan-Chattan, or *M'Intoshes*,	161
Clergy *Scotch*, commendable conduct of,	134
Coal of *Sutherland*, its miraculous quality,	147
Cobles, a small boat,	35
Cock of the Wood,	278
Coker, its romantic situation,	28
Coldingham Moor and Abbey,	41
Coranich, or howling at funerals,	92
Cottages, wretched in the Highlands,	109
Crab, the Thorney,	285
Craigston Castle,	122
Crane, now unknown in *England*,	12
Cromartie, Firth of,	141
Crows, Royston or Hooded,	80, 278
Cullen House and Town,	124, 125
singular rocks near,	125
Culloden House and Moor,	136
Customs, singular ones in the Highlands,	90, 159
Cuthbert's Ducks, Saint,	35

D

Days, long in *Cathness*,	158
Dalkeith, pictures there,	60
Dean of Guild, what,	138

Delamere

INDEX

	Page
Delamere Forest,	2
Dingwall Town,	141
Dogger Bank, great fishery near,	18
Dornoch,	145
Dunbar,	42
Dunbeth Castle,	151
Dungsby Bay,	153
Dunkeld,	75
Dunrobin Castle,	145
Dunsinane,	72
Duplin Castle, pictures there,	67
Durham,	26

E

Eagles,	277
Eider Ducks,	35
Edinburgh, its lofty situation,	46
inconveniences,	47
reservoir,	48
University,	51
Elgin, a good town,	128
its cathedral,	ibid
Erse language, where spoken,	158, 198

F

Fairies, belief in,	94
Falcons,	277
Falkirk, great cattle fairs there,	209
Battle,	210
Farn Islands,	34
Fasting	

INDEX.

	Page
Fasting woman, extraordinary case of,	248
Fen, East, its fish and birds,	9, 10
Fiery cross, what,	164
Finchal monastery,	28
Fine, Lough, its herring-fishery,	190
Flamborough-Head, its birds,	15
Flixton,	16
Forchabus,	128
Forfeited estates, how applied,	139
Forres, great column near,	130
Foss-dyke,	6
Fraoch-Elan, the *Hesperides* of the Highlands,	188
Freeburgh Hill, a large Tumulus,	24
Freswick Castle, horrid situation of,	152
Funeral customs,	91
Fyers, fall of,	170

G

Gannet,	45, 155, 159
Geese, how often plucked,	8
George, Fort, Old,	137
New,	136
Gisborough,	25
Glen-Co,	182
Glen-Roy, strange roads there,	179, 253
Glen-Tilt, a dangerous pass,	101
Glen-Urqhie,	186
Godric, Saint, his austerities,	28
Gordon Castle,	126
Gowrie conspiracy,	71
	Graham,

Graham, John De, his epitaph,	210
Graham's Dyke,	213
Granite Quarries at *N. Ferry*,	62
Aberdeen,	116
Gre-hound, the Highland,	127, 275
Grout's, John a, house,	153
Gull, Arctic,	62

H.

Halydon Hill, battle of	40
Hares, white,	79, 276
Heronry, a great,	11
Herring fishery,	190, 191
High-bridge,	175
Highlands, awefull entrances into,	74
Dress of the Highland Men,	162
Women,	165
Arms,	163
Character of the Highlanders,	165
Sports and amusements of,	167
Hopeton House,	214
Huntings, magnificent in old times,	99, 103

I

Jameson, the painter,	81
Fine picture of his at *Taymouth*,	ibid
Other pictures of his,	122, 123
Jet, where found,	22
Inoculation practised as far as *Shetland* Isles,	158
Insects,	286
Inveraray,	

INDEX.

	Page
Inveraray Town and Castle,	189
Invercauld, its magnificent situation,	106
Inverlochy Castle,	177
Inverness,	137
Fair,	162
Joug, what,	134
Itinerary,	299

K

Kilchurn Castle,	187
Killicrankie, Pass of,	98
Kinloch-Leven,	182
Kinloss Abbey,	130
Kinross,	55
Kittiwake, a sort of Gull,	120

L

Labor, its price in *Scotland*,	68, 110
Late wake, a strange funeral custom,	92
Lavellan, the Water Shrew-mouse,	150, 276
Leith,	57
Lincoln, its beautifull cathedral,	6
Lochaber,	175, 179
Lochiel, his seat,	176
Loch-Leven,	64
its fish and birds,	65
Loncarty, battle of,	73
Lossie River,	129
Lothian, East, its fertility,	42

INDEX.

M

	Page
Macclesfield,	3
Mackrel-sture,	192
Mac Nabbs, an antient family of smiths,	186
Marble, white,	148
Marriage customs, singular,	160
Moffat,	216
Monrief, Hill of; its fine view,	69
Monro, Sir *Robert*, his epitaph,	211
Morpeth,	30
Mountain, the black,	182
Mummies, natural,	153

N

	Page
Natural history, recapitulation of, &c.	273
Ness, Lough,	168, 171
agitations of, in 1755,	173
Newbottle, pictures there,	57
Newcastle on *Tyne*,	29
its salmon-fishery,	218
Nightingale, none in *Scotland*,	279

O

	Page
Ord of *Cathness*, a high promontory,	149
Orkney Isles,	153
Ouzels, Ring,	80

P

	Page
Pearls,	71
Penrith, the pillars at,	218, 267
Perth,	

INDEX.

	Page
Perth, a fine town,	69
its trade,	71
Pictish castles,	146
Pine forests,	107, 183
Pines, vast plantations of,	142, 143
Poetry, *Erse*,	261, &c.
Preston Pans,	46
Proverbs, *Erse*,	258, &c.
Provisions, prices of, at *Edinburgh*,	56
at *Aberdeen*,	115
at *Inverness*,	138
Ptarmigans,	79, 279

Q

Queries relating to the antiquities and natural history of *North Britain*,	287
Quern, a hand-mill,	182

R

Raynach, Lough, pine forest near,	87
Rents, how paid in the Highlands,	110
raising of, ill effects of,	180
Roads, parallel in *Glen-Roy*,	253
Roads, the military,	184
Robin-Hood's Bay,	22
Roe-bucks,	273
Royston Crows,	80, 278
Rumbling Brig near *Glen-devon*,	65
near *Dunkeld*,	76

Sacrament,

S

	Page
Sacrament, indecently received in *N. Britain*,	83
Sailors and Soldiers, an attempt to colonize,	95
Salmon fisheries, antient laws to preserve,	117
in *England*,	24, 26, 39
in *Scotland*, 70, 115, 120, 128, 157	
Salt-Pits at *Northwich*,	2
Sand, inundations of,	118, 131
Saury, a new *British* fish,	284
Scarborough,	16
its fisheries,	18
Scone,	72
Scotland, unpromising entrance into,	40
Seals,	149, 157, 277
Second sight,	154
Sheelins, or summer dairies,	102
Slain's Castle,	119
Snake, a new species,	281
Snowflake,	280
Soland Geese,	45, 155, 159
Spalding,	12
Spectre story,	89
Spey, a violent river,	127
Spinie Castle and Lake,	129
Stags,	274
Steuart, *Mary*, pictures of,	140
Stocking trade in *Aberdeen*,	112
Stockton,	25
Straithearn, a fertile tract,	67
Stroma Isle,	153

Struan,

INDEX.

	Page
Struan, *Robertson* of, a poet,	88
Swineshead Abbey,	12
Sybilla, Queen, where buried,	84

T

Tantallon Castle,	44
Tarnaway Castle,	133
Tay, Lough,	78
never frozen till this year,	ibid
Isle, and convent on it,	84
Tay-Bridge, inscription on it,	81
Tay-Mouth, its beauties,	77, &c.
Theft of cattle, once held not dishonorable,	176
Tordown Castle, its singular cement,	173
Tumel, the falls of,	96
Lake,	97
Tunny,	192
Turner, Dr. *William*, the naturalist,	30
Tweed,	38
Tyendrum, highest seated house in *Scotland*,	185

U

Urquhart Castle,	169

V

Venereal patients, where formerly confined,	214

W

Weever, Greater,	283
Were, its fish,	27

Whitby,

INDEX.

	Page
Whitby,	23
Wick,	152
William, Fort,	177
Witches, where burnt,	55, 145
Macbeth's,	131
of *Thurso*,	145
Wolves, how long existing in *Scotland*,	178
Women, the common, hardly treated in *North Britain*,	121, 157

Y

Yew tree, a great,	85
Ythen River,	118

FINIS.

SUPPLEMENT

TO THE

TOUR

IN

SCOTLAND.

CHESTER:
PRINTED BY JOHN MONK.
MDCCLXXII.

SUPPLEMENT

TO THE

TOUR

IN

SCOTLAND.

D----

Page

*** *** ***

SCOTLAND.

Page

SUPPLEMENT
TO THE
TOUR
IN
SCOTLAND.

Dedication, page v. irresistable, *read* irresistible.

Page 5, line 22, after *Holland*, add, the country which less than half a century past, supplied not only these kingdoms, but most part of *Europe* with that commodity.

Page 7, line 25,
Revesby abby was founded A. D. 1142, by *William de Romara*, earl of *Lincoln*, who at last turned monk, and was buried in the monastery. On the dissolution it was granted to *Charles* duke of *Suffolk*, A. 30 *Hen*. VIII. The monks were of the *Cistercian* order.

Page 9, line 19, *after* Eels.
It is observable that once in seven or eight years, immense shoals of *Sticklebacks* appear in the *Welland*

land below *Spalding*, and attempt coming up the river in form of a vast column. They are supposed to be the collected multitudes washed out of the fens by the floods of several years; and carried into some deep hole. When overcharged in numbers they are obliged to attempt a change of place. They move up the river in such quantities as to enable a man who was employed in taking them to gain for a considerable time, four shillings a day by selling them at a halfpenny per bushel. They were used to manure land, and attempts have been made to get oil from them.

Page 12, line 23, *after* fen, *add* by way of note *
* *Crowland* abby was founded by *Ethelbald*, king of *Mercia*, A. D. 716. As the spot was too marshy to support the weight of a stone building, he first ordered vast piles of oak to be driven into the ground; and after that caused more compact earth to be brought in boats along canals from places nine miles distant, which was placed on the piles, to form a solid foundation for the sacred edifice.

Page 32, line 27, *after* battlements, *add*
These flues seem designed as so many supernumerary chimnies, to give vent to the smoke that the immense fires of the old hospitable times filled the room with. Halls smoky but filled with good cheer, were in those days thought no inconvenience

ence: thus my brave countryman, *Howel ap Rys**, when his enemies had fired his houfe about his ears, tells his people to rife and defend themfelves like men, for fhame, *for he had knowne as greate a fmoake in that hall upon a Chriftmas Even.*

Page 44, after enterprize, in the note*, add,
She was eldeft daughter of Sir *Thomas Randal*, of *Stradown*, Earl of *Murray*, and Nephew to *Robert Bruce*: fhe was called *Black Agnes*, fays *Robert Lindefey*, by reafon fhe was black fkinned.

Page 49, line 27, *after* organ, add,
This is the more furprizing, as the *Dutch*, who have the fame eftablifhed religion, are extremely fond of that folemn inftrument; and even in the great church at *Geneva*, the pfalmody is accompanied with an organ.

Page 51, line 16, after *Scotland*, add,
Almoft all imaginary, done by fome wretched painter from *Flanders*.

Line 23, *add*, as a note to entire*.
* I have lately feen a print of the infide of this chapel, engraven by Mr. *Mazel*, in the manner it was fitted up by *James* VII. At the upper end was a flight of fteps, with lions on one fide, and unicorns on the other; at top a chair of ftate for the fovereign; and on each fide the choir ftalls for the knights companions of the

* *Hift. Cwedir Family*, 118.

thiftle:

thistle: each stall was bounded by two columns of the *Corinthian* order, and above were trophies, flags, &c. The floor was laid with marble; but in 1688, the whole was demolished by a barbarous mob.

Page 52, *James* II. read, *James* VI.

Page 53, line 8, *George Darnley*, read, *Henry Darnley*.

Page 64, *after* the lowest paragraph,

St. Serf's isle is noted for having been granted by *Brude*, last king of the *Picts*, to *St. Servan* and the *Culdees*, a kind of priests among the first christians of North *Britain*, who led a sort of monastic life in cells, and for a considerable time preserved a pure and uncorrupt religion; at length, in the reign of *David* I, were suppressed, in favor of the church of *Rome*. The Priory of *Portmoak* was in this isle, of which some small remains exist.

Page 83, line 4, *after* dominions,

The church is a remarkably neat plain building, with a very handsome tower steeple.

Page 85,

On the *Brotche* were the Names of the three kings of *Cologhe*, *Jaspar*, *Melchior*, *Baltazar*, with the word *Consummatim*: it was probably a consecrated brotche, and worn, not only for use, but as an amulet.

Page 87, * *after* Earl of *Hardwicke*,
Who may be truely said to have given to *North-Britain* its great charter of Liberty.

Page 89, a note to *Cornfield**,
* These tales of spectral transportation are far from being new: Mr. *Aubrey*, in his miscellanies, p. 13, gives two ridiculous relations of almost similar facts; one in *Devonshire*, the other in the shire of *Murray*.

Page 90, Witch act was not repealed 'till the year 1736.

Page 92, note to line 19, night*,
* This custom was derived from their northern ancestors; *longè securius moriendum esse quam vivendum; puerperia luctu, funeraque festivo cantu, ut in plurimum concelebrantes.* OLAUS MAGNUS, p. 116.

Page 95, *after* line 30,
These have been supposed to have been magical stones, or gems, used by the *Druids*, and to be inspected by a chart boy, who was to see in them an apparition, informing him of future events: this imposture, as we are told by Doctor *Woodward*, was revived in the last century by the famous Doctor *Dee*, who called it his *Shew-stone*, and *Holy-stone*, and pretended by it's means to foretell future events. I find in *Monfaucon**, that it was customary, in early times, to deposit balls of this kind in urns and sepulchres; thus twenty

* Les monumens de la monarchie, *Françoise* l. 15.

were found at *Rome*, in an alabaſtrine urn; and one was diſcovered in 1655, in the tomb of *Childeric*, at *Tournai*: he was king of *France*, and died A. D. 48.

Page 97, note to line 16, owner*,

* The motto to the arms of this noble family demands explanation: *Furth Fortune, and fil the fetters*. A chieftain of this houſe was ſent by his king to ſubdue *McDonald* of the iſles; and at parting received from the monarch this good wiſh, *Go forth, be fortunate, and fill the fetters*; i. e. Bring home many captives.

Page 126. *Caſtle-Gordon* was founded by *George*, ſecond Earl of *Huntly*, and originally called the bog of *Gight*.

Page 130, line 9, *after* corn,
And the upper parts of the country produce great numbers of cattle.

Page 131, *after*
    She look'd not like an inhabitant of the earth!

Boethius tells his ſtory admirably well, but entirely confines it to the predictions of the three fatal ſiſters, which *Shakeſpear* has ſo finely copied in the ivth ſcene of the firſt act. The poet, in conformity to the belief of the times, calls them witches; in fact they were the *Walkyriur**, the fates of the northern nations, *Gunna*, *Rota*, and *Skulda*, the handmaids of *Odin* the arctic *Mars*, and were

* *Vide* note p. 17.

ſtyled

styled the *Chusers of the slain*, it being their office in battle to mark those devoted to death.

> We the reins to slaughter give,
> Ours to kill, and ours to spare;
> Spite of danger he shall live.
> (Weave the crimson web of war)*.

Boethius, sensible of their office, calls them *Parcæ*; and *Shakespear* introduces them just going on their employ:

> When shall we three meet again,
> In thunder, lightening, or in rain?

> When the Hurly Burly's done,
> When the Battle's lost or won.

But all the fine incantations that succeed, are borrowed from the fancifull *diableries* of old times, but sublimed, and purged from all that is ridiculous, by the judicious and creative genius of the inimitable poet of whom *Dryden* thus justly speaks:

> But *Shakespear*'s magic could not copied be,
> Within that circle none durst walk but he.

We laugh at the magic of others, but *Shakespear*'s makes us tremble: the windy caps of king *Eric* ** and the vendible knots of wind † of the *finland magicians*

---

* *Gray.*
** His Majesty was a great conjurer, who by turning his cap, caused the wind to blow as he listed, according to *Olaus Magnus*.
† Solebant aliquando *Finni*, negotiatoribus in eorum littoribus contraria ventorum tempestate impeditis, ventum venalem exhibere, mercedeque oblata, tres nodos magicos non cassioticos loro constrictos

magicians are infinitely ridiculous, but when our poet dresses up the same idea, how horrible! is the the Storm he creates.

> Though you *untie* the winds, and let them fight
> Against the churches; though the yesty waves
> Confound and swallow navigation up;
> Though bladed corn be lodged and trees blown down;
> Though castles topple on their warders head;
> Though palaces and pyramids do slope
> Their heads to their foundations; though the treasure
> Of nature's germins tumble all together,
> Even till destruction sickens, answer me
> To what I ask.

Page 132, barren for, *read* burnt for.

P. 133. note to *Gluve* *

* for *Glaive* an old word for a sword.
> Then furth he drew his trusty *Glaive*,
>   Quhyle thousands all arround,
> Drawn frae their sheaths glanst in the sun
>   And loud the bougills sound.
>   *Hardyknute.*

Ibid. line 30. *after* land

Before the recent introduction of the improved method of Agriculture.

strictos eisdem reddere, eo servato moderamine ut ubi primum *dissoluerint*, ventos haberent placidos; ubi alterum vehementiores; ut ubi tertium *laxaverint*, ita sævos tempestates se passuros, &c. *Olaus Magnus*, 97.

Page 134. note to G. II.*

* An account of the government of the church of *Scotland* was communicated to me by the Rev. Mr. *Brodie*, the late worthy minister of *Calder*. Vide Appendix, No. I.

Page 135, line 14, *Tweed* *

* To the WORTHY.
But if in these Days such Apostates appear,
(And such I am told are found there and here)
O pardon, dear friends a well-meaning zeal,
Too unguardedly telling the scandal I feel.
It touches not you, let the galled jades winch;
Sound in morals and doctrine you never should
  flinch. &c. &c. &c.

Page 137, line 3, *after* 'execrate him' to the person who informed him that he was approaching as a fugitive, foreseeing his own ruin as the consequence. His Lordship was at that time expecting the event of the battle, when a person came in and acquainted him that he saw the prince riding full speed and alone.

The battle was fought contrary to the advice of some of the most sensible men in the army, who advised retiring into the fastnesses beyond the *Ness*, the breaking down the bridge of *Inverness*, and defending themselves amidst the mountains. They politically urged that *England* was then engaged in bloody wars foreign and domestic, that it could at that time ill spare its troops, and that the government might from that consideration be
                                                  induced

induced to grant to the insurgents their lives and fortunes on condition they laid down their arms. They were sensible that their cause was desperate, and that their ally was faithless; yet knew that it would be long before they could be extirpated, so drew hopes from the sad necessity of our affairs at that season. But this rational plan was superseded by an overuling faction in the army, to whose guidance the unfortunate adventurer had resigned himself.

Regard to impartiality obliges me to give the following account, very recently communicated to me by an eye-witness, relating to the station of the chief on this important day:

'The *Scotch* army was drawn up in a single line; behind, at about 500 paces distance, was a *Corps de Reserve*, with which was the adventurer, a place of seeming security. His usual dress was that of the highlands, but this day he appeared in a brown coat, a loose great coat over it, and an ordinary countryman's hat on his head. Remote as this place was from the trifling conflict, yet a servant of his was killed by an accidental shot.

It is well known how short the battle was; but the moment he saw his right wing give way, he fled with the utmost precipitation, and without a single attendant.

Page 151, note to *Dunbeth**,

* This castle was taken and garrison'd by the Marquiss of *Montrose*, in 1650, immediately preceding his final defeat.

Page

Page 153, note to *vadis*.†,

† Quoted by Mr. *Wallace*, from the *Iter Balthi-cum* of *Conradus Celtes*.

Addition to note ‡, relating to the long preservation of human bodies, without the assistance of art. In vol. XLVII. of the pilosophical transactions at large, is an account of a body found entire and imputrid at *Staverton*, in *Devonshire*, 80 years after interment.

Page 156, Rofs-head, *read* Nofs-head.

Page 160, line 6, *after* from,
And this species of rural sacrifice was originally styled *Clou-an Beltein*, or the split branch of the fire of the rock. Vide Mr. *Mc'Pherson's Introduction*, &c. p. 156.

Page 165, line 4, *add* this note*,
* This custom was common to the northern parts of *Europe*, with some slight variation, as appears from Olaus Magnus, who, p. 146, describes it thus: *Bacculus tripalmaris, agilioris juvenis curfu precipiti, ad illum vel illum pagum seu villam hujusmodi edicto deferendus committitur, vel 3, 4, vel 8 die unus. duo. vel tres, aut viritim omnes vel singuli ab anno trilustri, cum armis et expensis 10 vel 20 dierum sub pæna combustionis domorum (quo uso bacculo) vel suspensionis* Patroni, *aut omnium (quæ fune allegato signatur) in tali ripa, vel campo aut valle comparere tenentur subito, causam vocationis.*
atque

atque ordinem executionis Præfecti *provincialis, quid fieri debeat audituri.*

Ibid. line 22,
I have also observed, during divine service, that the women keep drawing their *tanac* or plaid forward in proportion as their devotion increases, insomuch as to conceal at last their whole face, as if it were to exclude every external object that might interrupt their devotion.

Page 175, line 4, *after* year,
And was a melancholy instance of a fine understanding, and well-intending heart, being overpowered and perverted by the unhappy prejudices of education.

Page 176, line 16, black meal, *read* black mail.

Page 178, line 2, by order of *Cromwel, read,* by order of General *Monk.*

Page 201, line 7, West-side, *read,* South-side.

Page 203, Presbitery, *read,* Presbytery.

Page 214, The order of council for the removal of venereal patients out of *Edinburgh,* into *Inch-Keith*:

22. Sept. 1497.
It is our Soverane Lords Will and the Command of the Lordis of his Counsale send to the Provest and Baillies within this burt that this Proclamation
followand

followand be put till execution for the efchewing of the greit appearand danger of the Infection of his Leiges fra this contagious ficknefs call it the *Grandgor* and the greit uther Skayth that may occur to his Leiges and Inhabitants within this burt that is to fay we charge ftraitley and commands be the Authority above writtin that all manner of Perfonis being within the freedom of this burt quilks are infectit or hes been infectit uncurit with this faid contagious plage callit the *Grandgor*, devoyd, red and pafs furt of this Town and compeir apon the fandis of *Leith* at ten hours before none and there fall thai have and fynd Bolis reddie in the havin ordanit to them be the Officeris of this burt reddely furnift with Victuals to have them to the *Inche* and thair to remane quhil God proviyd for thair Health: And that all uther perfonis the Quilks taks upon thame to hale the faid contagious infirmitie and taks the cure thairof that they devoyd and pafs with thame fua that name of thair perfonis quhilks taks fic cure upon them ufe the famyn cure within this burt in pas nor peirt any manner of way. And wha fa beis foundin infectit and not pafs and to the *Inche* as faid is be *Mononday* at the fone ganging to, and in lykways the faid perfonis that takis the fd cure of fanitie upon thame gif they will ufe the famyn thai and ilk ane of them falle be brynt on the cheik with the marking Irne that thai may be kennit in tym to cum and thairafter gif any of them remains that they fall be banift but favors.

Page

Page 216, line 26, *after* unpleasant,

But incessant rains throughout my journey from *Edinburgh*, rendered this part of my tour both unpleasant and unedifying.

Page 220, Mr. *Giller*, *read*, Mr. *Gillow*.

Page 220, line 11, a new paragraph *after* between,

Eleven miles farther is the village of *Garstang*, seated on a fertile plain, bounded on the East by the Fells, on the West by *Pelling* moss, which formerly made an eruption like that of *Solway*. The adjacent country is famous for producing the finest cattle in all the county: a gentleman in that neighbourhood has refused 30 guineas for a three-year-old heifer: calves of a month old have been sold for ten, and bulls from 70 to 100 guineas, which have afterwards been hired out for the season for 30: so notwithstanding his misfortune, well might honest *Barnaby* * celebrate the cattle of this place,

    Veni *Garstang* ubi nata
    Sunt armenta fronte lata.
    Veni *Garstang*, ubi malè
    Intrans forum bestiale,
    Forte vacillando vico
    Huc et illuc cum amico,
    In Juvencæ dorsum rui,
    Cujus cornu læsus fui.

A little to the east is a ruined tower, the re-

* Better known by the name of Drunken *Barnaby*, who lived in the beginning of the last century; and published his four Itineraries into the north in *latin* rhyme.

mains

mains of *Grenehaugh* castle, built, as *Cambden* says, by Sir *Thomas Stanley*, first earl of *Derby*, to protect himself from the outlawed nobility, whose estates had been granted him by *Henry* VII.

Page 221, line 17, note to absolute *,

* The writer must mean in *Scotland*, for in *England* the two first monarchs of the name seem only to have attempted to support the plenitude of power exerted by, and delivered down to them by their immediate predecessors, which the servile spirit of the preceding times endured.

Note to *Walkyriur**, p. 8, of these pages,

* From *Walur*, slaughter in battle, and *Kyria*, to obtain by choice, for their office, besides selecting out those who were to die in battle, was to conduct them to *Valhalla*, the paradise of the brave, the hall of *Odin*. Their numbers are different, some make them three, others twelve, others fourteen: are described as being very beautifull, covered with the feathers of swans, and armed with spear and helmet. *Vide* Bartholinus *de cauf. contempt. mortis.* 553, 554, notæ. vet. Stephanii in Sax. Gramm. 88, and *Torfæus*, 36.

Page 164, line 17, name of, add Εγχειριδιον, *pugio*, or little dagger.

Page 234, Indicatories, *read*, Judicatories.

Page 287, note to QUERIES,

These queries were originally composed and printed

printed by order of the Society of *Antiquarians*, and difperfed thro' feveral parts of *England*. As the fpirit of enquiry feems at prefent reviving, I took the liberty of reprinting them, in hopes of their meeting with better fuccefs than they did formerly; and that gentlemen may be induced, from them, either to form *local* hiftories, or to tranfmit to fo refpectable a fociety fuch matters relating to the hiftory of their country as will merit it's attention.

Thomas Pennant.

www.ingramcontent.com/pod-product-compliance
Lightning Source LLC
Chambersburg PA
CBHW030404230426
43664CB00007BB/734